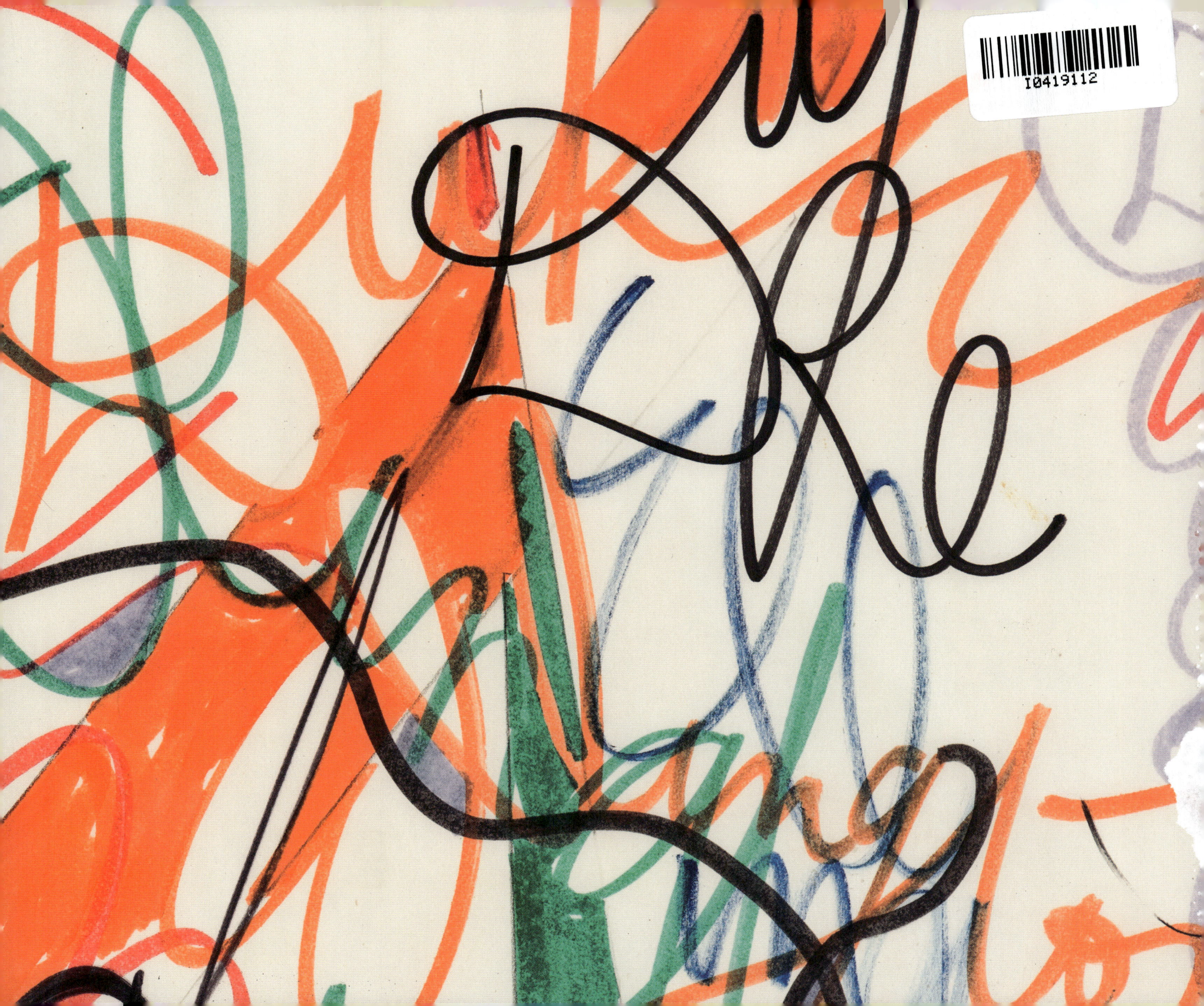

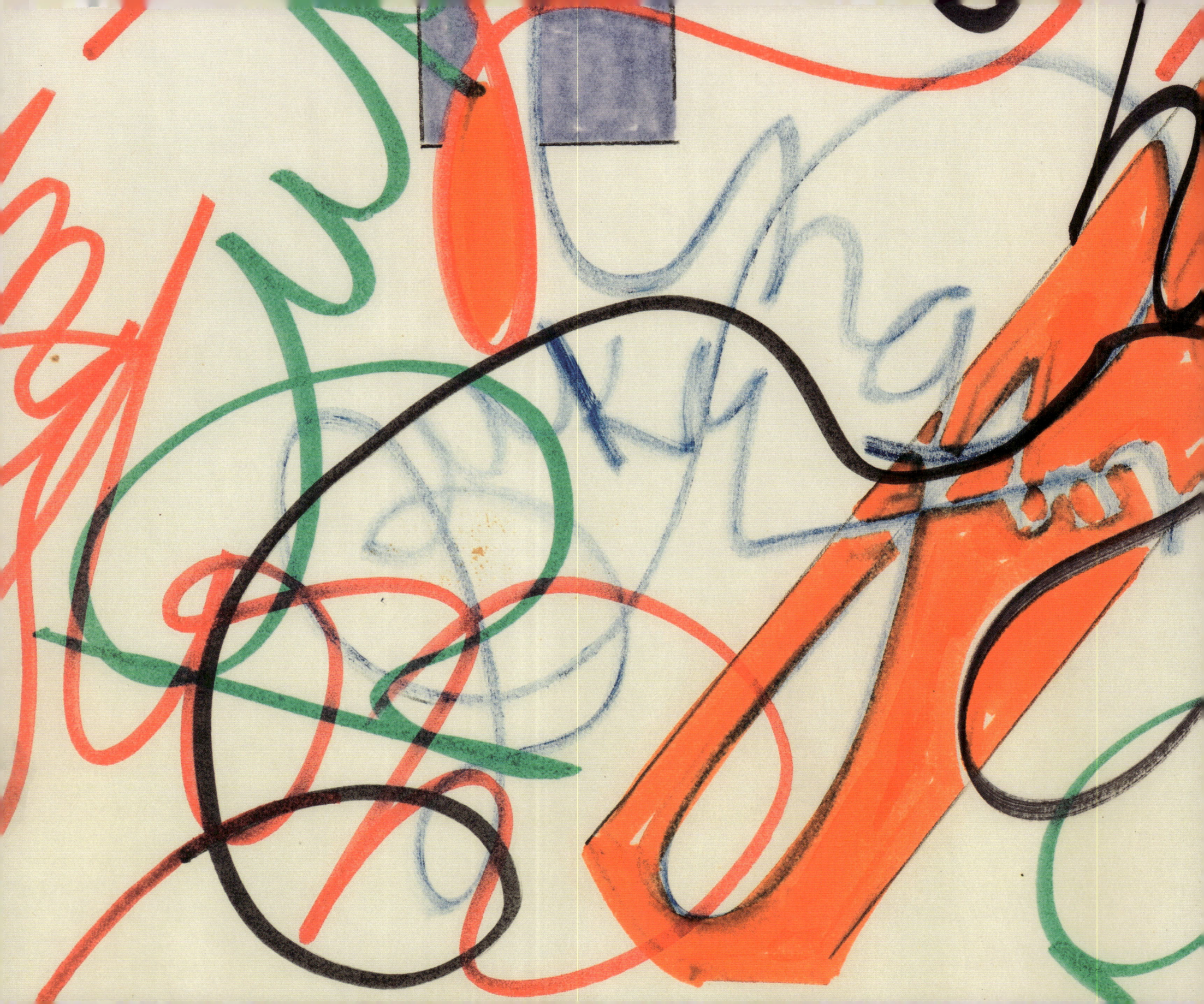

ROMARE BEARDEN   PARIS BLUES   PAINTING JAZZ

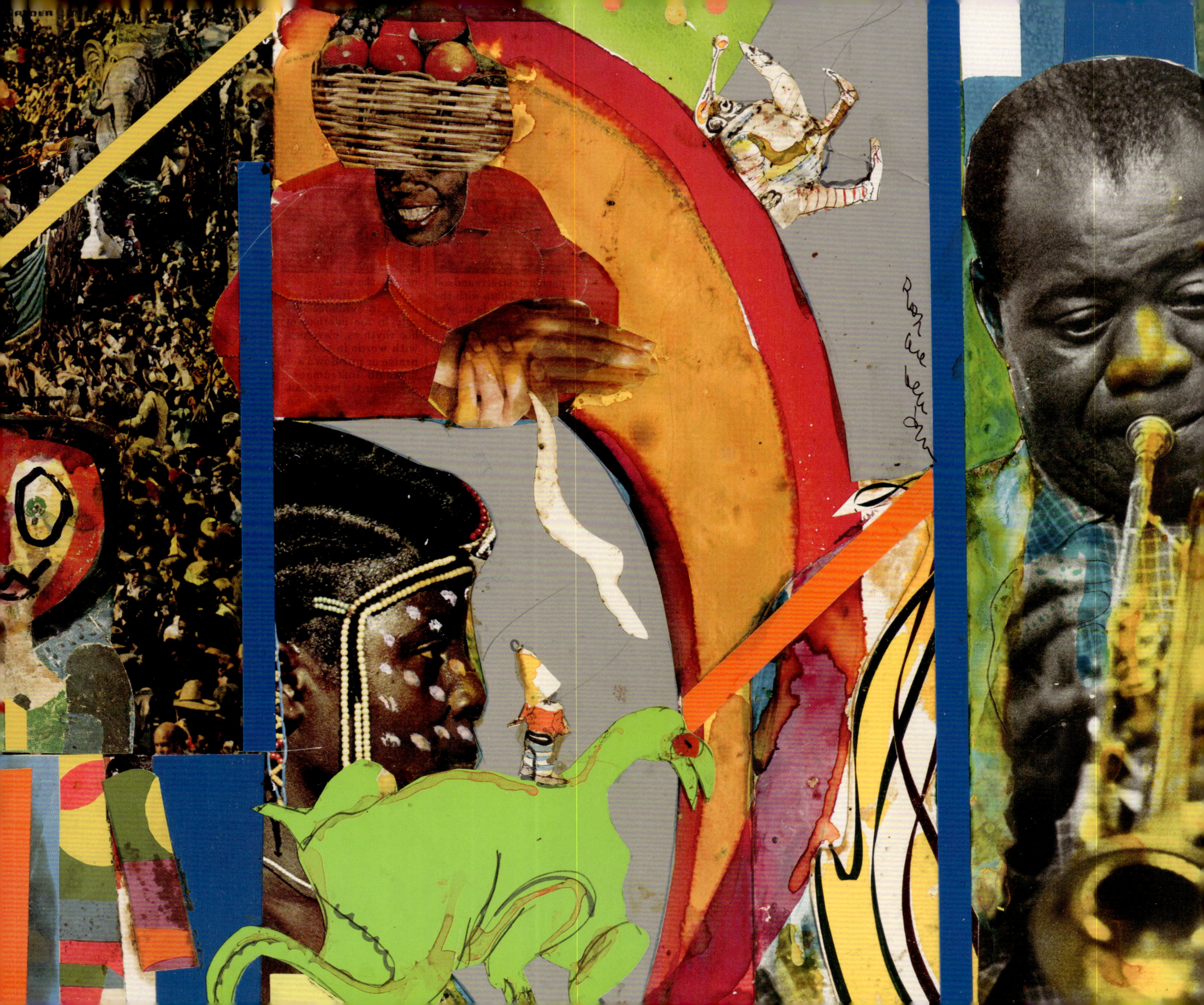

ROMARE BEARDEN
PARIS BLUES
PAINTING JAZZ

BY ROBERT G. O'MEALLY

PREFACE BY BRIDGET MOORE
REFLECTIONS BY MICKALENE THOMAS

RizzoliElecta

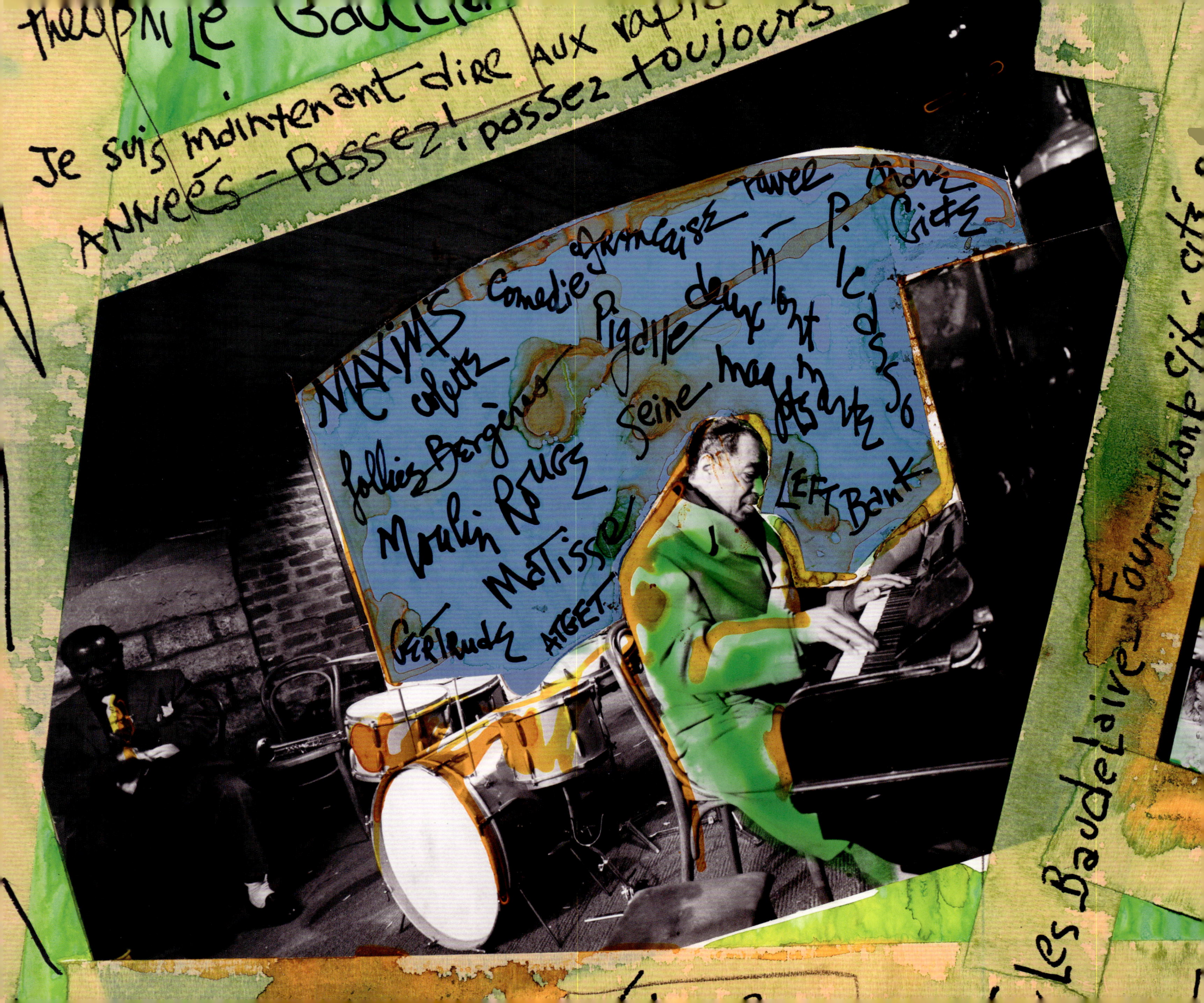

CONTENTS

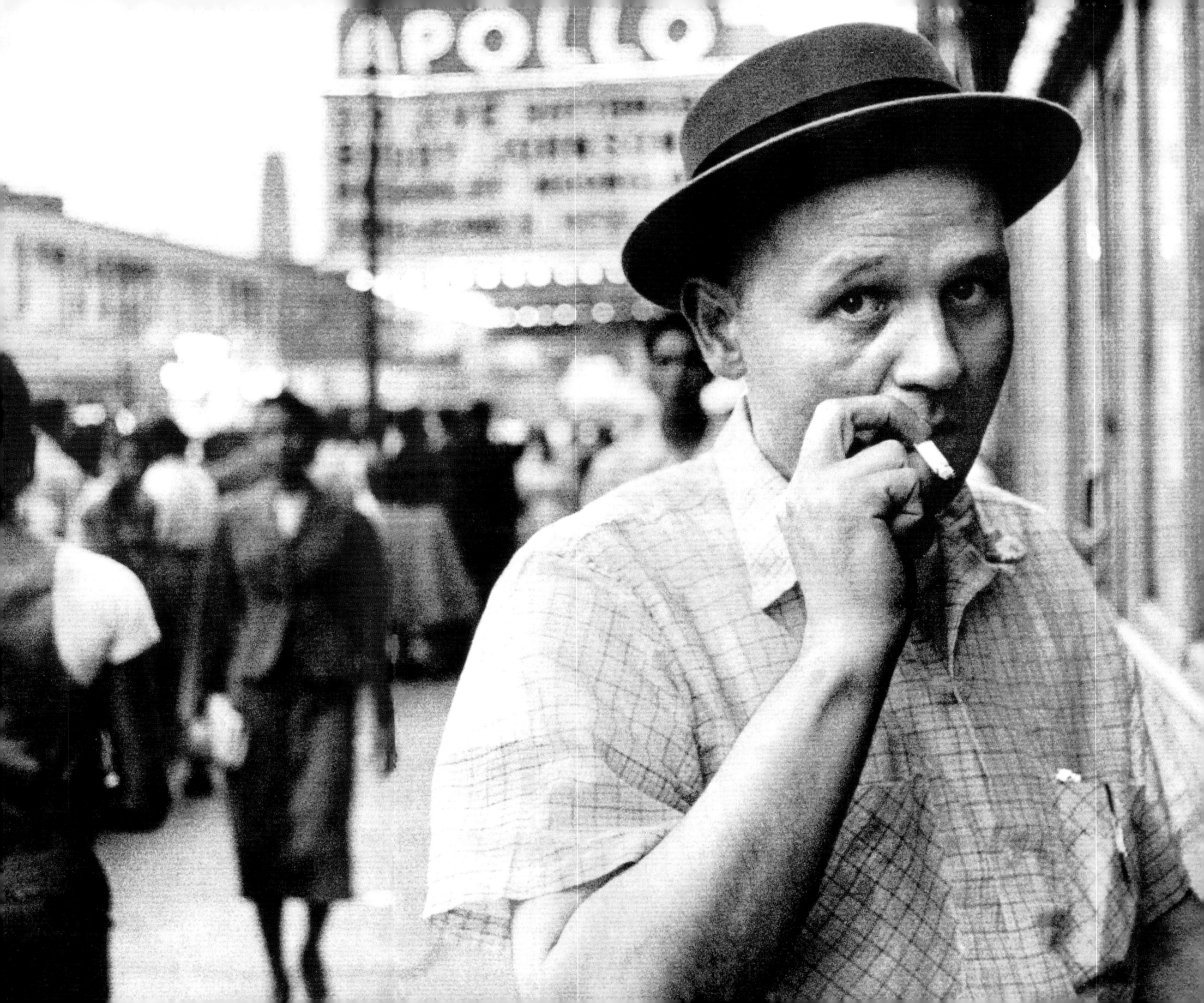

BRIDGET MOORE

PREFACE

In 1981, Romare Bearden was determined to tell a visual story of jazz through the lens of his time in Paris. Why Paris? Bearden had immersed himself in that city in 1950, traveling on the GI Bill. He took courses in philosophy, Buddhism, and the French language, walked endlessly through the Parisian streets, socialized with artists, writers, and musicians, and wholeheartedly took part in the intellectual life of the city. Paris was where he first met lifelong friends, including Albert Murray, Herbert Gentry, and James Baldwin. He found freedom in the city: to roam, to experience, and an unexpected respite from racial bias.

Bearden loved listening to jazz in Paris, in clubs that were not the Harlem, Midtown, or Village spots he knew so well in New York City. His parents had moved to Harlem from North Carolina in 1914, when he was three years old, and his formative years coincided with the height of the Harlem Renaissance. His mother, Bessye Bearden, was well known through her civic and journalistic career, and their house was an intellectual and artistic hub where Bearden met writers and musicians including Langston Hughes, Fats Waller, and Duke Ellington. Years later, Bearden drew a map of the Harlem streets showing the proximity of jazz clubs to his family home. But in Paris, there were jazz clubs with American and French musicians, music emanating freely into a city where the syncopation and rhythms adapted into a different world.

Maybe this is one of the reasons why when Bearden reluctantly returned to New York, with the hope to return to Paris as soon as he could, he diverted his artistic energy for several years endeavoring a career in writing jazz songs, which he did with a modicum of success. Perhaps by going away and re-experiencing the familiar in a new context, he became more aware of jazz's impact and continuing potential. This perspective remained in mind decades later, as he began his celebration of jazz, collaborating with his good friends Sam Shaw, the photographer and filmmaker, and Albert Murray, the critic and novelist. Shaw would provide photographs for source material, and Murray would write a text telling this larger story of jazz. Though this project did not come to full fruition, nineteen finished collages and drawings remain to show the intensity of this endeavor. The *Paris Blues/Jazz* series moves through Paris, New Orleans, and Harlem, mapping jazz onto city spaces. Depicting iconic jazz singers, musicians, and clubs, Bearden also looks to the city streets and infrastructure, as well as its inhabitants, that were vital sources of jazz music. These collages, which author Robert O'Meally calls "expressions of unruly Black cosmopolitanism," celebrate spaces where Black people and Black culture could assert artistic and political freedom.

There are many people to thank who share a deep commitment to widening the knowledge of Romare Bearden's art and legacy. The private and public collectors of Romare Bearden's work are owed a great debt of gratitude for being the stewards of artworks in their care.

Thank you to Sheila Rohan from the Nanette Bearden Trust who has always been an enthusiastic supporter of Bearden's work. Special appreciation goes to Nannette Maciejunes, Barry Frier, and Joseph Guglietti, whose wisdom and efforts helped greatly in the development of this project. We would like to acknowledge our friends at Rizzoli including Charles Miers, Ellen Cohen, Alyn Evans, and designer Robin Brunelle, whose energetic enthusiasm for Bearden is much appreciated. My colleagues Edward De Luca, Heidi Lange, Kate Larkin, Mark Valenti, and Dawson Batchelder have continued to work tirelessly to further awareness of Bearden, and on this project sincere thanks to Caroline Magavern for her steady involvement.

Foremost recognition should go to the ongoing work of the Romare Bearden Foundation. The Foundation was formed in 1990 following the wishes of Bearden who passed in 1988. Since that time the Foundation has worked to continue the scholarship, awareness, and visibility of this influential twentieth-century artist. Profound thanks to Diedra Harris Kelley, Johanne Bryant Reid, and Tallal El Boushi from the Romare Bearden Foundation and to Alva Greenberg whose involvement in the rediscovery of the *Paris Blues/Jazz* series has been invaluable.

We are honored that artist Mickalene Thomas has shared her personal engagement with Bearden's work in her introduction.

And for the great collaboration and friendship of Robert O'Meally, who first came to know Romare Bearden through his friendship with Albert Murray, we extend our heartfelt appreciation. O'Meally is uniquely suited to write about Bearden's *Paris Blues/Jazz* project given his extensive knowledge and passion for all things Bearden and his breadth of knowledge about jazz. We thank him for his in-depth exploration of Bearden's jazz project and his ongoing brilliance in bringing to light the many layers to understanding Romare Bearden.

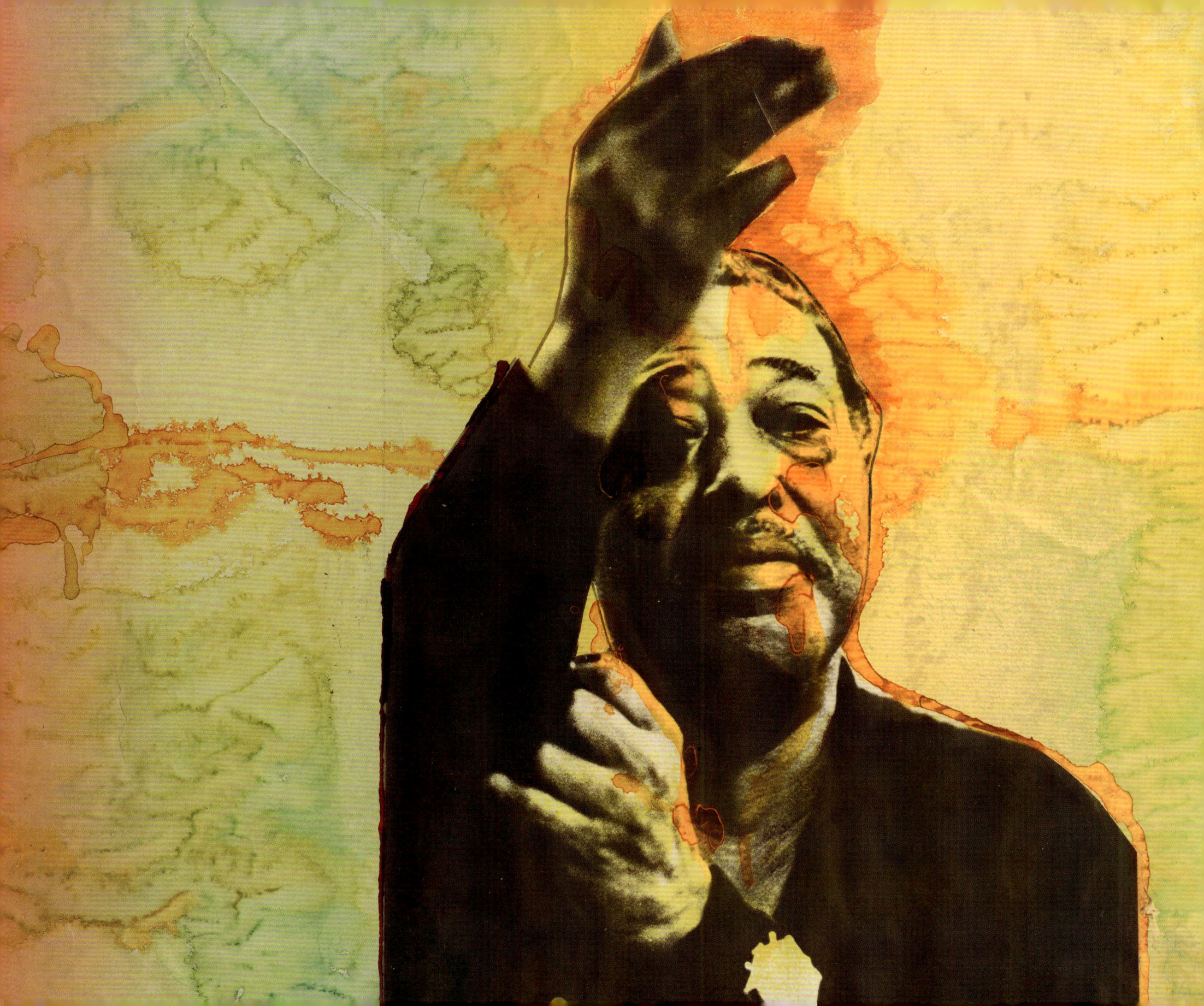

REFLECTIONS

I'm happy to speak here as an artist about my experience and inspiration through Bearden's work. His art is extraordinary. Looking at the images in this book, there are some I've never seen before—he was so prolific, right? He was just completely immersed in his craft and in the world around him. He used his creative process to tell stories, and that gave me hope as a young person. It was a kind of validation that I could become an artist too. In that way, through the example of his life and work, he became a mentor to me. I never met him— I never had the opportunity—but I met him through his work, through his images.

When I think about Bearden and try to remember one of the first pieces that really resonated with me, the one that comes to mind is *The Block*. And I know why. First of all, *The Block* was made in 1971—the year I was born. There's so much in that collage that speaks to Black life, to story, to narrative. Bearden was such a storyteller, not just through his imagery, but through his materials—metallic paper, pen, pencil—he created a whole environment, a sense of time and place. You can feel the energy of the neighborhood. You want to jump right into it. It reminds me of my home—even though my home wasn't Harlem. Bearden grew up in 1920s Harlem. What was that like? A young man surrounded by music, culture, sports—and his mother, a political activist, hosting people like Duke Ellington, Langston Hughes, W. E. B. Du Bois. Imagine that. As a young person, you're in a space filled with the great minds of Black thought and creativity. So it's no wonder he made such powerful images, or that he found his voice so clearly. Lately, I've been thinking about how I also use the world around me in my work—how my life extends into my art. I love that. And beyond *The Block*, I just love that I respond to so many of Bearden's images.

The first time I saw a Bearden, it was a reproduction. I was living in Portland, Oregon, at the time, and I discovered Bearden right around the moment I decided I wanted to be an artist. I had just been to the art supply store and picked up some oil pastels—this was only weeks after seeing Carrie Mae Weems's work at the Brooklyn Museum. Back then, I knew nothing about art—especially Black art or Black artists. But seeing Weems's Kitchen Table Series cracked something open in me. It created this sense of aspiration and discovery, like: Okay, who else is out there? So I went to Powell's Books—this massive bookstore in Portland with both new and used books—and found myself in the African American art section. I remember being in the stacks, pulling down books on Bill Traylor, William H. Johnson, Elizabeth Catlett . . . just flipping through page after page. And it was Romare Bearden's work, along with William H. Johnson's, that really spoke to me.

I think it probably did—because of the blocking, the cuts, and because, at the time, I didn't really know how I was going to make an image. I had no idea. And it just seemed like the easiest way forward—those flat planes of color, the geometric shapes that felt kind of childlike and playful and bright. It was

like, yeah, maybe I could do that. So I bought used copies of the books and took them home with my art supplies. I kept them open while I worked, mimicking the style as best I could—copying, looking at a shape and thinking, okay, do that shape. The work was awkward and chunky, but I was figuring it out as I went, and I loved that. Those became my first images. I used the Bearden and William H. Johnson books, postcards from the Carrie Mae Weems show—pulled them all together—and let them guide me. Bearden and Johnson helped me understand form and composition, and Weems gave me a sense of content and concept. I wasn't in art school at the time—so it felt like I was teaching myself how to do all of it. But I was lucky to be surrounded by artists who encouraged me. They'd say, keep going, keep making those things. And so I did. I made a lot. And then, slowly, the work started turning into my own stories—these little pieces of memory and childhood, showing up in the images without me even planning it.

Once I really delved into Bearden, I started to appreciate his trajectory, his practice, and where he was pulling from—his experiences, his histories. Whether it was European or African fiction, mythology, or storytelling, he was drawing from all of it. I always tell people: I discovered Manet and Matisse through Bearden. I wouldn't have known who they were if I hadn't been looking at his work first. And through him, I started learning about all these other artists.

I saw Bearden as a figure of discovery—someone rooted in narrative. And while I was exploring his work, I kept thinking about this quote from Nina Simone that I love: "It's an artist's duty to reflect the times in which we live."

Bearden was absolutely one of those artists—someone who always reflected the times.

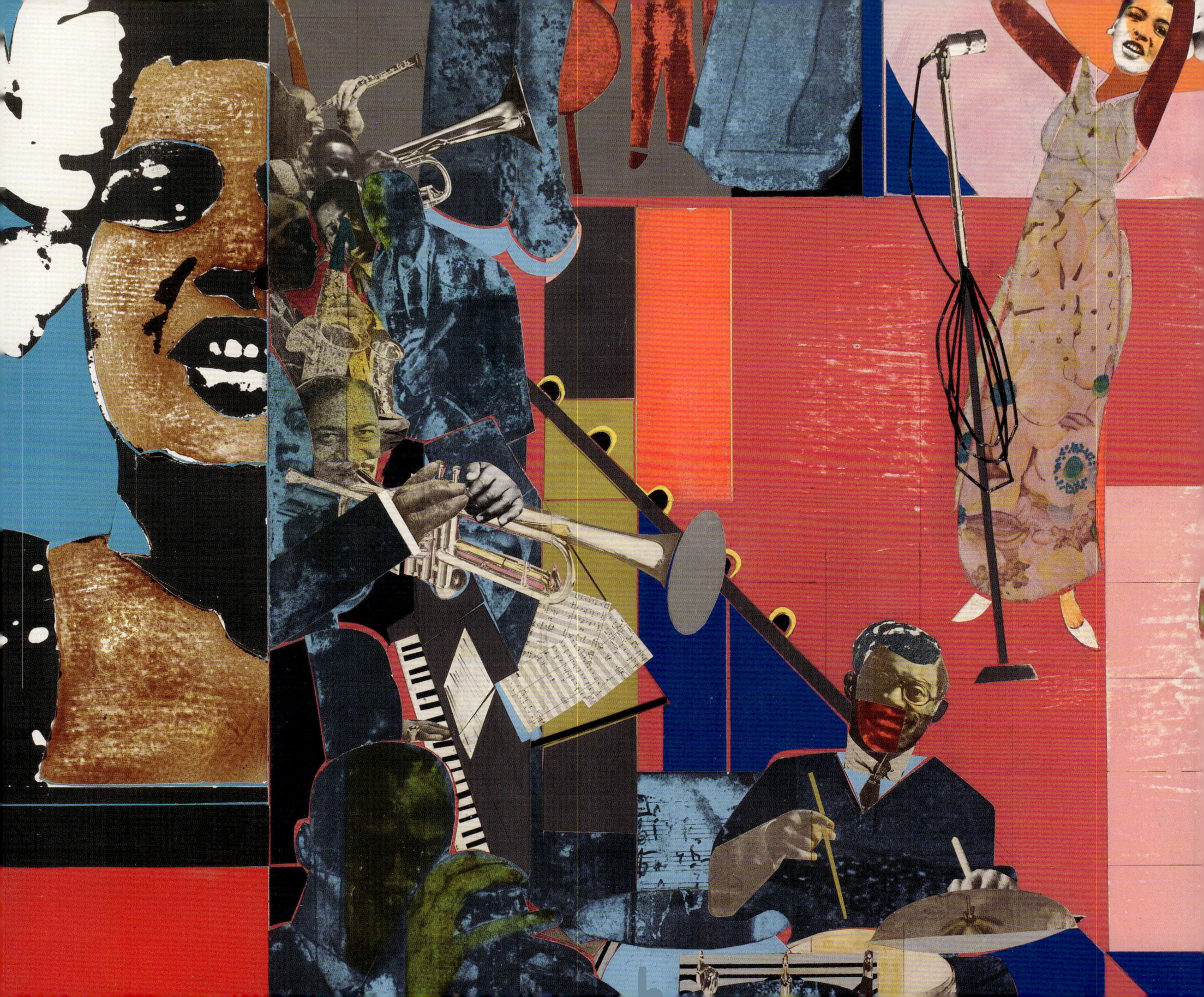

"MORE THAN ONESELF"

ROBERT G. O'MEALLY

BEARDEN'S JAZZ AND PARIS BLUES

For over a hundred years, this music has risen from churches, clubs, and the media to shape world culture—dance, fashion, philosophy, sports, art, theater, varieties of classical music, modes of social relations, politics, and creativity. Here is a model of great daring: of unleashed individual creativity within a collectively organized group that makes room for individuality & nurtured it. This is the robust product of a people of African descent whose taste and generosity allowed others in, like ambassadors or free-lance spirit healers. That's the half that's never been told forcibly enough.[1]

—John Szwed

You have to begin somewhere. So you put something down. Then you put something else with it. . . . Sometimes something just seems to fall into place, like the piano keys that every now and then just seem to be right where your fingers happen to come down.[2]

—Romare Bearden

Actually, what I'm doing here is making a keyboard.[3]

—Romare Bearden

OVERTURE

In the late 1970s, Romare Bearden's engagement with jazz music and culture reached a crescendo when he produced the *Paris Blues* or *Jazz* series, consisting of some twenty works, primarily in collage, made with two collaborators. Conceived as pages for an oversized book that would be a response to the Hollywood movie *Paris Blues* (1961)—although featuring Harlem and New Orleans along with Paris—the series has been little known until now, and the works rarely seen by the public. Brought to light, they afford a significant new opportunity to deepen our understanding of Bearden's life and work—a surprise package for Bearden enthusiasts created when he was at the zenith of his artistic powers.

Unveiled here as a complete set,[4] the *Paris Blues/Jazz* series presents a major statement by Bearden on jazz music's relationship with visual art and city spaces, where jazz has bloomed. Here the artist's project created vividly playful visual equivalents of the music that jazz players like to call *the music*—not merely painting about jazz but *painting jazz*.[5]

The series' launching point, *Paris Blues*, is a Hollywood-produced romantic drama of 1961, filmed in Paris and headlined by Paul Newman, Joanne Woodward, and Sidney Poitier, with Diahann Carroll in an early screen appearance. The film project began as the idea of the photographer Sam Shaw, Bearden's friend and sometimes Harlem studio mate since the late 1930s who was entranced by Bearden's accounts of his trip to Paris in 1950. Shaw was especially taken by Bearden's tales of the vibrancy of the Paris art and music scenes, of the vacation from U.S. racism and puritanical sexual mores, and of what seemed like the unending parties. Shaw soon went to work on storyboards and scripts and sought production partners, counting on his film-world connections to support the project.[6]

Rather quickly Shaw found doors closed to him, as it became clear that Hollywood was not prepared to make a movie featuring a Black artist (modeled on Bearden) living freely in the mid-century City of Light. Nor was the Sunset Strip of the '50s prepared for the other risky subjects explored in Shaw's early scripts (and in the 1957 novel *Paris Blues* by Harold Flender, a key source for the movie): "mixed race" and gay couples, adult sexuality in general, the treatment of Algerians in France, and the U.S. Black Freedom Movement; all were ultimately whitewashed or dropped altogether from the movie when it did find major-studio backing.[7] Shaw, however, hung on as the film's producer. Despite the white-out compromises, his presence meant that jazz (and thus artistic endeavor) remained central to the film. Through Shaw, Louis Armstrong, the reigning king of jazz, was brought in to appear in two important on-screen cameos, while master jazz composer/pianist/bandleader Duke Ellington and his frequent collaborator Billy Strayhorn, also a jazz royal, contributed the best thing about the movie: its score.

Equal to the finest extended works that Ellington or the Ellington-Strayhorn team had created since the 1930s—for two-sided 78 rpm shellac discs, for concert halls like Carnegie or popular stages like the Cotton Club, for festivals like Newport, and once before for a movie (*Anatomy of a Murder*, 1959)—*Paris Blues*, the score, is an intensely moving modern masterwork. Like other major composers' incidental music for specific sites and purposes, the music of *Paris Blues* could stand apart from the film as a full concert piece or, in sections, as goodtime party music or gems for contemplation. Like so much of their music, *Paris Blues* has what Ellington called a "terpsichorean urge," a drive to the dance floor or inspiration to modern choreographers like Alvin Ailey. I vote *yes* for *Paris Blues* as the soundtrack to any exhibition of the *Paris Blues/Jazz* collages by Bearden.

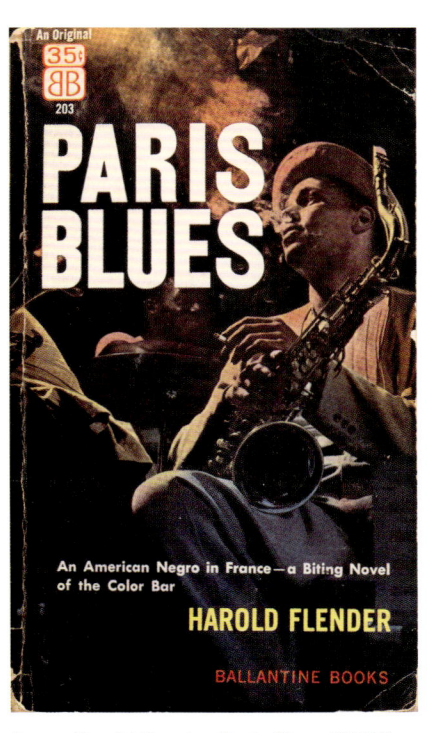

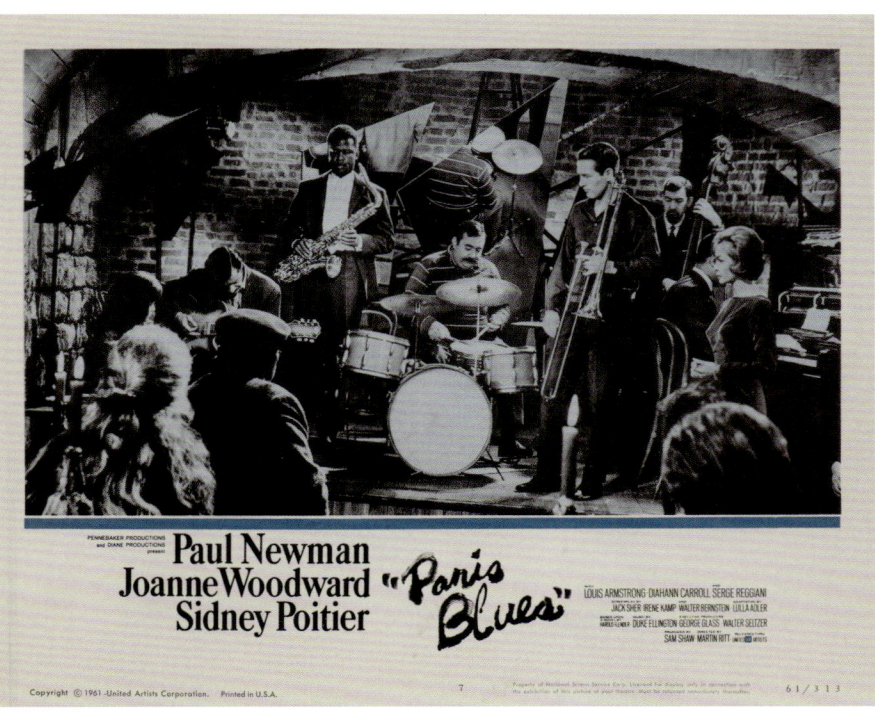

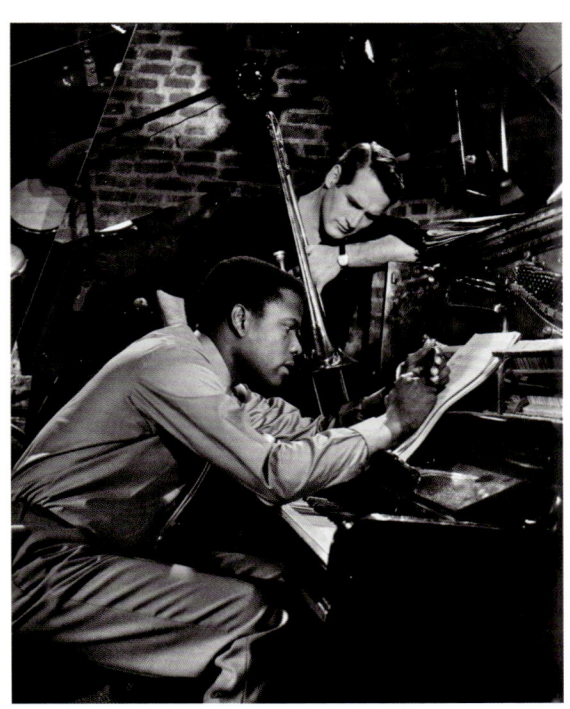

Cover, Harold Flender, *Paris Blues* (1957)

Promotional poster, *Paris Blues* (1961)

Sidney Poitier and Paul Newman in *Paris Blues* (Martin Ritt, 1961)

Ellington and Strayhorn were painters in music, never more than in *Paris Blues*. They were collage makers who used the orchestra's regular players and the instruments on which many doubled (sometimes with toilet plungers and other mutes), along with visitors in the studio who came to play, to create the musical textures, colors, and storylines. For the *Paris Blues* recording sessions, an oboist, Harry Smyles (one of the era's very few African Americans on that instrument), was a guest who provided that woodwind's distinctive tones and overtones. For certain sections of the score, Duke and Strays seated Smyles, Jimmy Hamilton (clarinet), and Leslie Spann (flute) together as a unit, in front of the veteran four-man sax section. These changing instrumental mixes invite us to think not only of collage but of the assertion, elaborated below, that jazz bands "flattened" the music—adding blue notes (sharps and flats) and sonic configurations that opposed Renaissance ideas of one-point perspective. For here every player was "up front," rhythm included. In fact, the *Paris Blues* band's drum roll included Sam Woodyard, Duke's regular, Philly Joe Jones, Jimmy Johnson, and Dave Jackson: an up-front battery (especially needed to create the film's "locomotive onomatopoeia") if ever there was one.[8]

Twenty years after the release of the movie, and clearly desiring to recoup what it had gotten wrong, Shaw and Bearden teamed up with the novelist and cultural critic Albert Murray to tell their version of the Black-artist-in-Paris story, this time in the form of a book of collages created by Bearden from Shaw's photographs, among other materials, with writing by Murray.[9] It seems likely that the idea for such a book was Shaw's. He had worked for years as a Hollywood photographer, creating formal and informal star portraits and set shots; and he had a deep archive of photos relating to life in Paris and, specifically, *Paris*

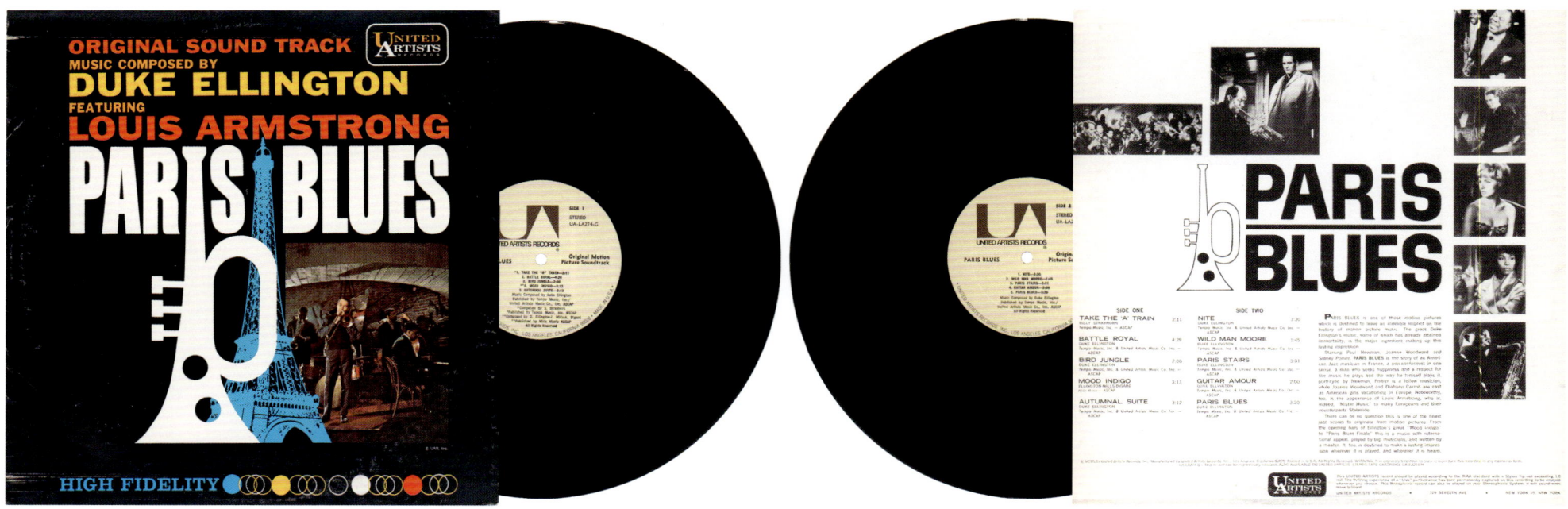

Album cover, original soundtrack, *Paris Blues* (1961)

Blues. He had released picture books connected to his film work before, including one for *The Seven Year Itch* (1955), the movie for which he carefully staged the billowing-skirt photograph of Marilyn Monroe: the shot seen 'round the world. In the case of *Paris Blues*, the collaborative trio would create a book big in size (fifteen by twenty-two inches, opened) and ambition. Bearden conceived the collages as akin to those Henri Matisse reproduced in his *Jazz* artist book (1947)—a volume Bearden greatly admired.

Recasting the movie's protagonists and sense of direction, the Bearden-Shaw-Murray team's stars would be the collages themselves, spotlighting top-flight masters of jazz—Armstrong and Ellington—alongside the sights and sounds of three vital stations on the map of jazz: New York, Paris, and New Orleans.

The cross-disciplinary venture was never completed. In addition to the finished collages presented here, there are fragments of the group's work that remain elsewhere, some repurposed for other projects, some still preserved in archival troves. The series' fragments and finished works alike stand as expressions of unruly cosmopolitanism, as lived in these three cities. Here is Bearden's own *Paris Blues* story—his freedom-in-the-world-of-jazz story—told this time by himself in collaboration with trusted friends, scored as a tale not of one city but of three.

As a central part of this project, Bearden, its lead visualizer, challenges us to contemplate the translatability of jazz: Do the ways and means of jazz music carry over onto the surfaces of visual art? Specifically, the say-amen-somebody patterns of call-and-response (which Bearden renamed "call-recall"), as well as the momentum and prevalence of polyrhythmic swing, improvisation, and the blues? What about their impact on other forms of art? Further, might jazzways apply practically to the realm of ethics and social interaction: the hard and fast world we all live in? In other words, can this music inspire not only visual and

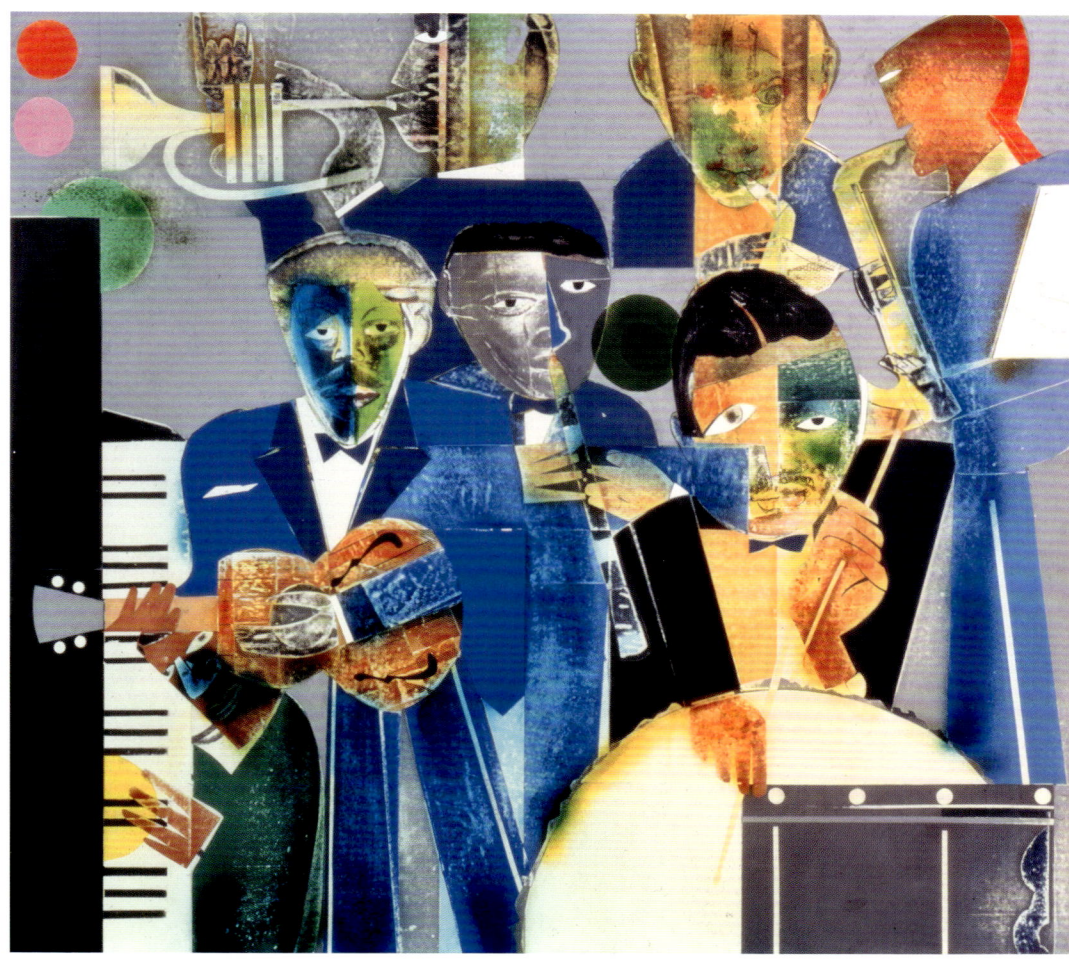

Of the Blues: One Night Stand, 1974. Collage with acrylic and lacquer on board. 49 × 50 in.

improvisatory artists but the rest of us, too, as citizens of the planet, with the unchanging responsibility to learn to call and recall together—to comp (as jazz artists shorten "accompany") as well as to solo; to really listen to one another; to witness and testify; to remember ourselves and our shared planet? Are these jazz collages, like the music itself, models for true democratic living? Are they the brightly colored, cut-and-pasted, swinging pictures of capital-letter, community-wide Love?

In these collages, Bearden also asks us to consider the role of cities: In what sense are they so necessary to jazz that, when asked to define the music, Thelonious Monk replied simply, "New York"?[10] What is it about the colors and textures, paces and rhythms, scales and shapes of this city, New Orleans, and Paris that has long made them such animating places for jazz musicians? And then for Bearden and other visual artists in search of the music's visual equivalences? What is it about these cities' skylines, landmarks, and grids, their old-town bridges, their goodtime clubs, and meandering path- and alleyways (Ellington would sometimes tell his band players to "get in the alley," meaning "make it funky," "make it sexy," "make it soulful")[11] that so strongly evokes this music? That's so suggestive of freedom (of civil rights, most profoundly defined) itself? Does this music—do the arts in general—play an indispensable part in our cities' infrastructure? There are answers-in-progress on the wondrously luminous surfaces of the *Paris Blues/Jazz* collages, where Bearden renders a quality in these cities uncharted by any maps or histories. As the novelist Ralph Ellison put it when memorializing the artist, Bearden's work records the "mystery which gets left out of history."[12] Do we see here some of the jazz-cityscape history-mysteries to which Monk and Ellison referred?

In blending jazz and cities, Bearden's *Paris Blues/Jazz* collages anticipate the vigorous contemporary conversation on "Black space": the prospects for creating territories where Blackness—Black people and Black culture—can assert the rowdy poetic freedom of a Louis Armstrong solo or a beyond-category Duke Ellington composition, complete with openings for soloists marked "ad lib" (to go for what you know)! As we will see, these Beardens celebrate unruly Black cosmopolitan people and Black spaces that were (and are) culturally and politically essential "open corners," places offering a "plenty good room, y'all come" refuge for Black Americans, and then for everyone, where freedom rings as freedom dreams.[13]

There's more: Bearden's *Paris Blues/Jazz* series asks what, most profoundly, this alluring music signifies about the human condition and about life beyond the human condition alone. And it answers with strategies for facing a world that is at present *so* unswinging—so evidently doomed by wanton me-firstism and violent hating on "the other"—but that ultimately, according to this music of hopefulness in the face of trouble ("the Danger Zone is everywhere," one blues song warns),[14] is bound for the glory of swinging again. "The demagogue," says Bearden, "sees chaos as his opportunity for power; the artist, on the other hand, sees it as a chance for redemption."[15]

How did Bearden—for whom *redemption* may have been the key word in his mission as an artist—become the Duke Ellington or Billie Holiday of painters? Before turning directly to Bearden's *Paris Blues/Jazz* works, let's take a step back to ask what led to this crescendo of a visual jazz project.

Where did *Paris Blues/Jazz* come from?

In what follows, I examine this question along two pathways: by looking more closely into the genesis of the *Paris Blues/Jazz* series and by exploring Bearden's deep-rooted connection to jazz music, which began early in his life and informed much of his artistic oeuvre.

I begin with Bearden, as I understand him to be the mastermind of *Paris Blues/Jazz*, and view it as a kind of culmination of his engagement with jazz—if never fully realized.

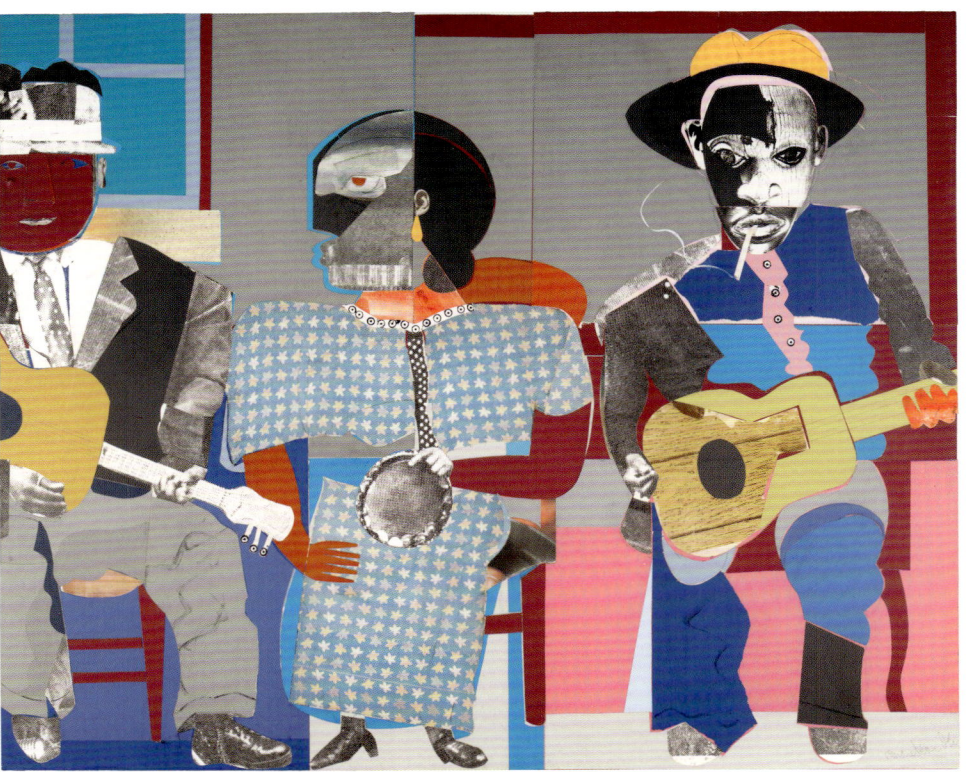

Soul Three, 1968. Collage of various papers and fabric on board. 44 × 55½ in. Dallas Museum of Art, General Acquisitions Fund and Roberta Coke Camp Fund, 2004.11

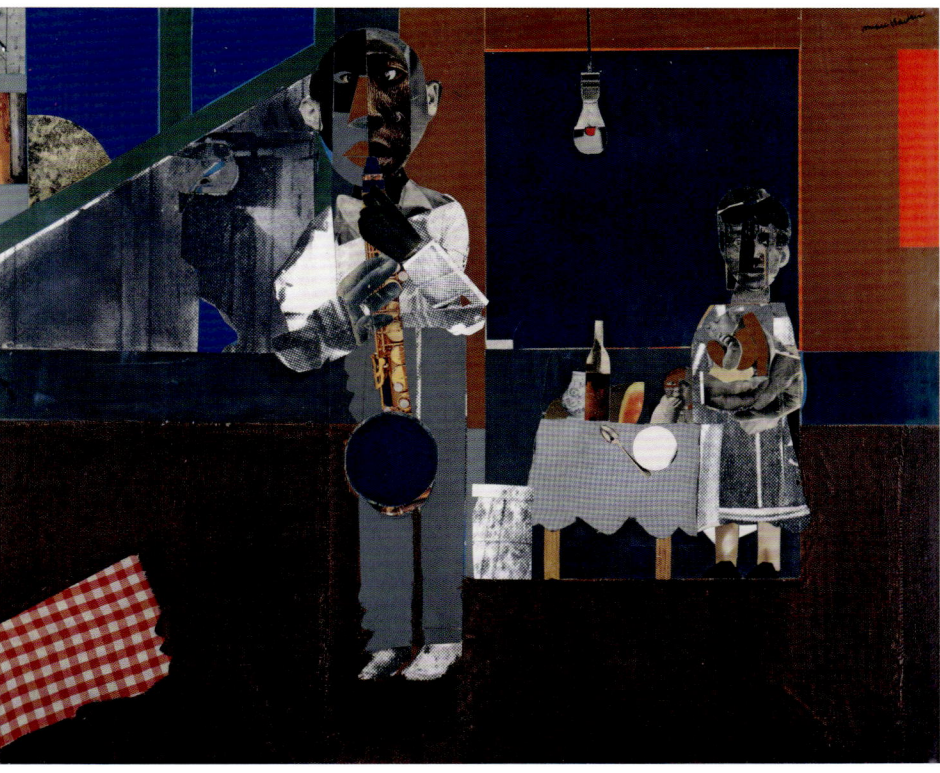

The Woodshed, 1969. Collage of various papers, fabric, graphite, and ink on fiberboard. 40½ × 50½ in. Metropolitan Museum of Art, NY, George A. Hearn Fund, 1970

BEARDEN AND THE JAZZ CENTURY

JAZZ CULTURE AND PHILOSOPHY

Jazz music has been so spectacularly impactful on the long twentieth century—stretching from the late nineteenth, with the music's first stirrings, into the twenty-first—that it's been rightly called the Jazz Century. And Romare Bearden is the dean of Jazz Century artists because his work offers the closest experience yet to witnessing the classic stances and instruments of these music makers and the places where they played. He is also the master of revealing the shapes and colors of the music itself. It is to marvel: to look at much of Bearden's art is to feel the music's power, *to see jazz!*

To point his viewers in this direction, Bearden frequently titled a work after a jazz composition: *Carolina Shout* (1974),

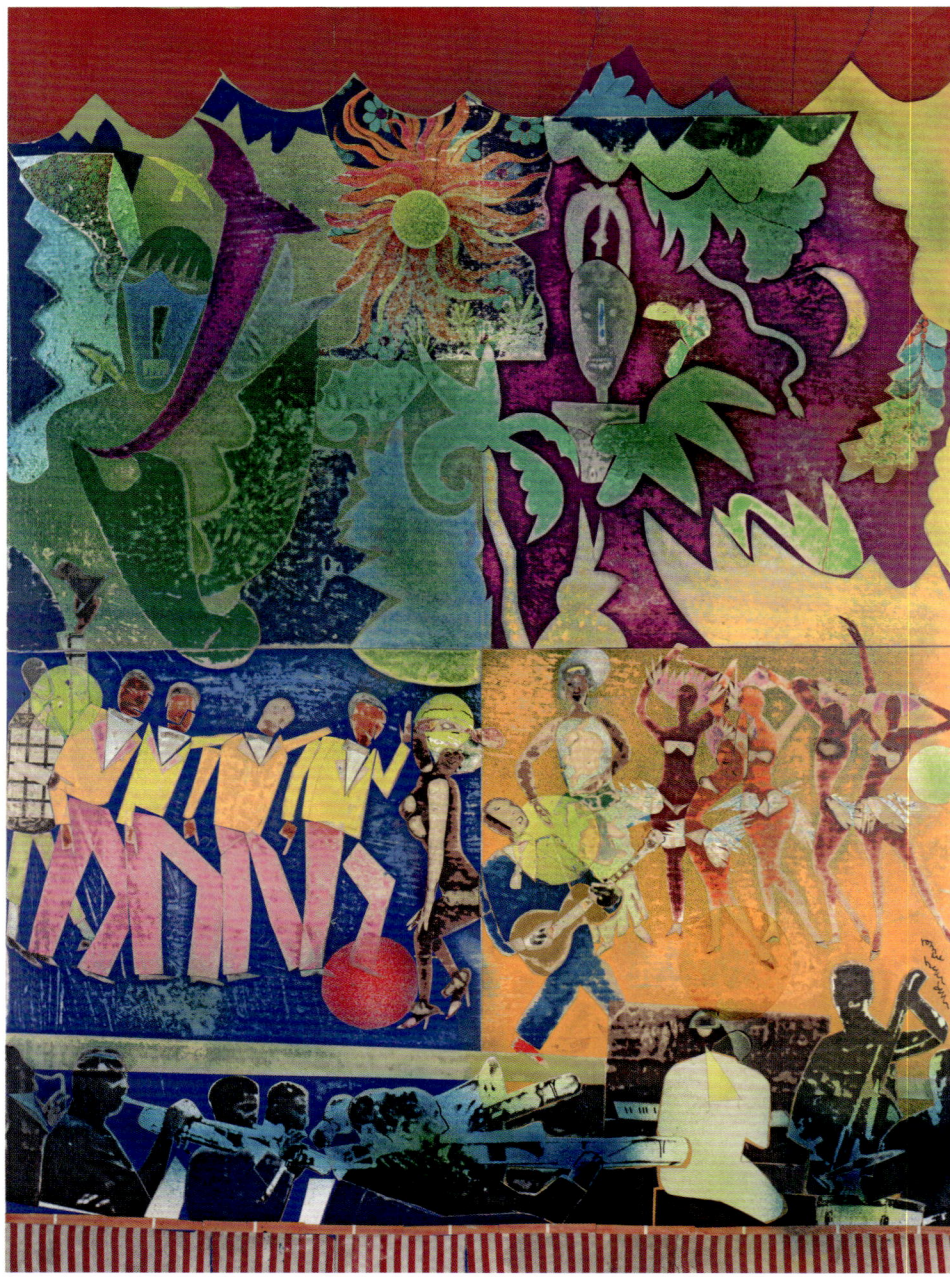

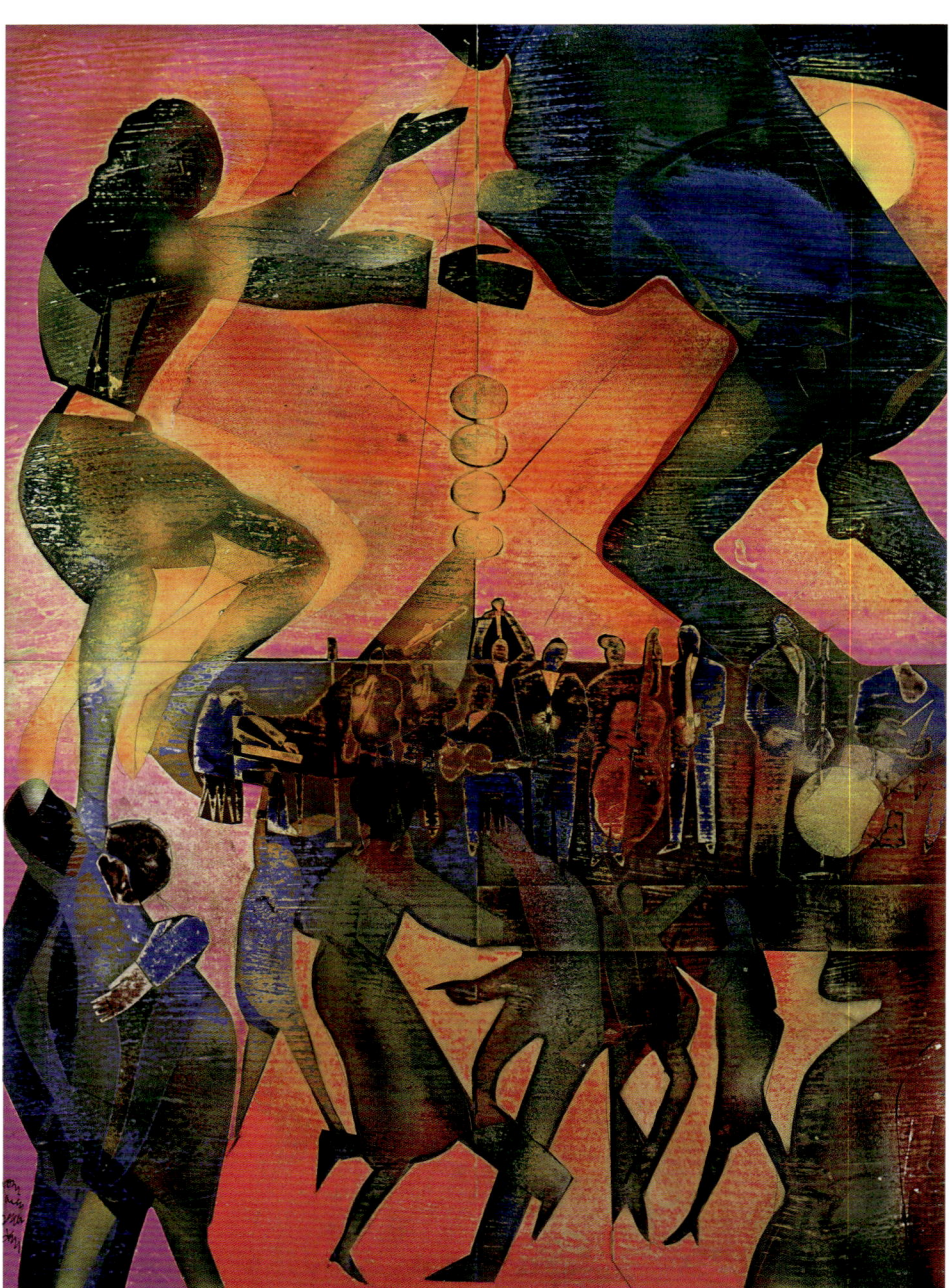

Of the Blues: Wrapping It Up at the Lafayette, 1974. Collage of various papers with fabric, paint, ink, and surface abrasion on fiberboard. 48 × 36 in. The Cleveland Museum of Art, OH, Mr. And Mrs. William H. Marlatt Fund 1985.41

Of the Blues: At the Savoy, 1974. Collage of various papers with paint, ink, and graphite on fiberboard. 48 × 36 in. Private Collection

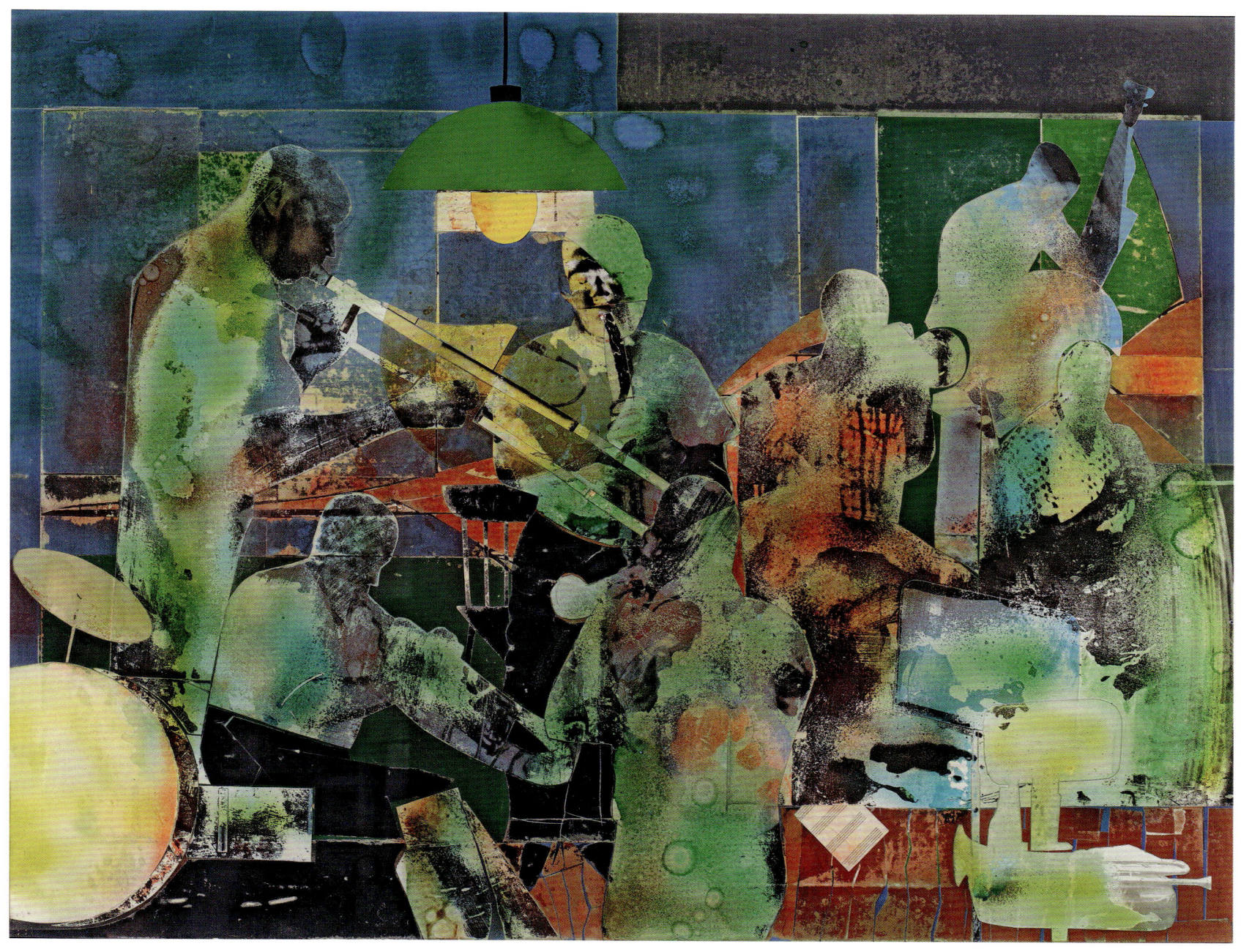

Of the Blues: After Hours, 1975. Collage of various papers, mixed media on paper. 35 ⅞ × 47 ⅞ in. Private Collection

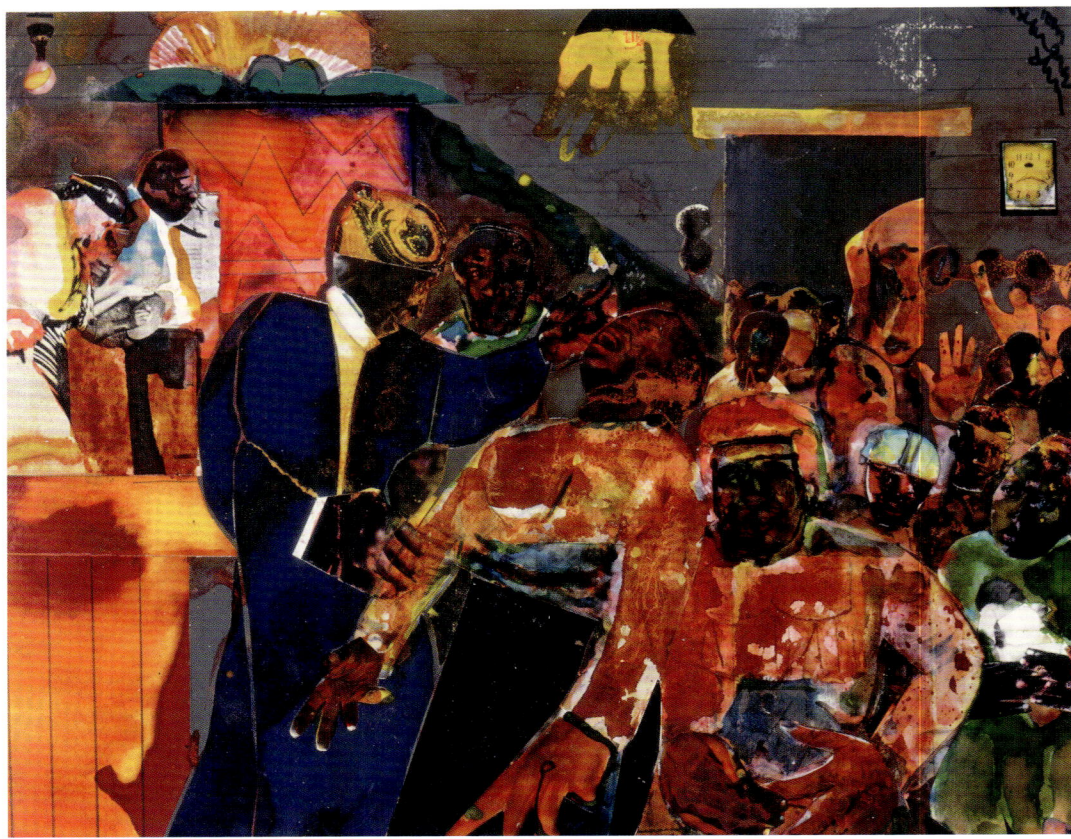

Profile/Part I, The Twenties: Mecklenburg County: Holiness Church Revival, 1978. Collage of various papers, mixed media on board. 12 × 15 in.

named for James P. Johnson's piano stride classic (as well as the painter's native state), may be the most famous example, although *Wrapping It Up at the Lafayette* (1974), named for a Fletcher Henderson composition (and shouting out to one of the music's most celebrated Harlem jazz theaters) is also significant. Bearden's collages taking titles from Duke Ellington compositions alone could fill an exhibition's walls: *Blue Light* (1973), *Daybreak Express* (1978), *I'm Slapping Seventh Avenue with the Sole of My Shoe* (1981), for starters. His 1981 collage *Rehearsal Hall* features photographs of Ellington scores—fresh arrangements of his songs "Solitude" and "It Don't Mean a Thing (If It Ain't Got That Swing)"—taken at an Ellington-Armstrong

recording session in 1970.[16] This collage is of particular interest because in 1979–80, both Duke and Louis played leading roles in Bearden's collaborative project with Sam Shaw and Albert Murray. And as we shall see, the *Paris Blues/Jazz* series—at the center of this book—is also a project that remained, in a sense, ever in rehearsal.[17]

In these and other Bearden works, we find jazz's definitive features: call-recall conversations, layered Afro-dance rhythms, improvisation, the blues. We find instances of what Bearden called "the prevalence of ritual": the music as part and parcel of community-wide gatherings serving to sustain participants as they seek to grow closer together (in courtship rites), to rid

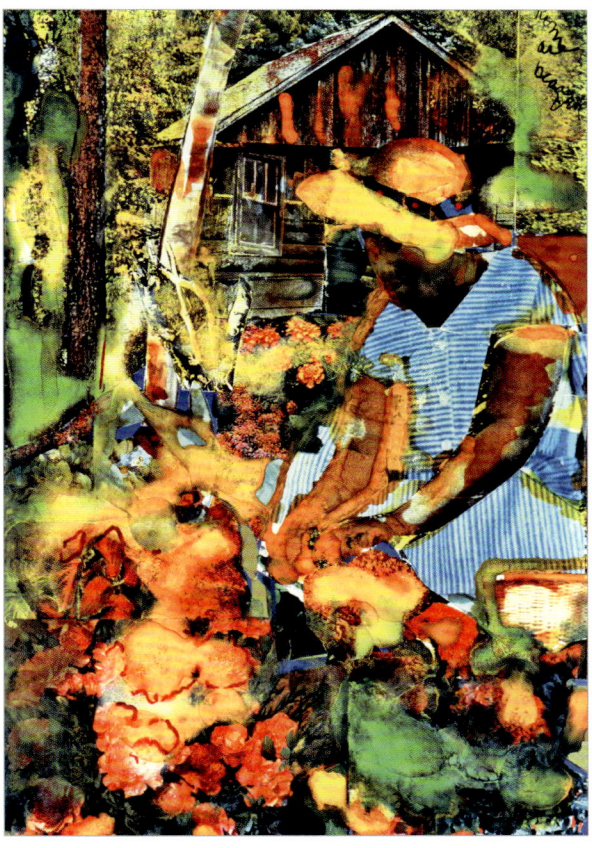

Profile/Part I, The Twenties: Mecklenburg County: Maudell Sleet's Magic Garden, ca. 1978. Collage of various papers, mixed media on board. 10 ⅛ × 7 in. Private Collection

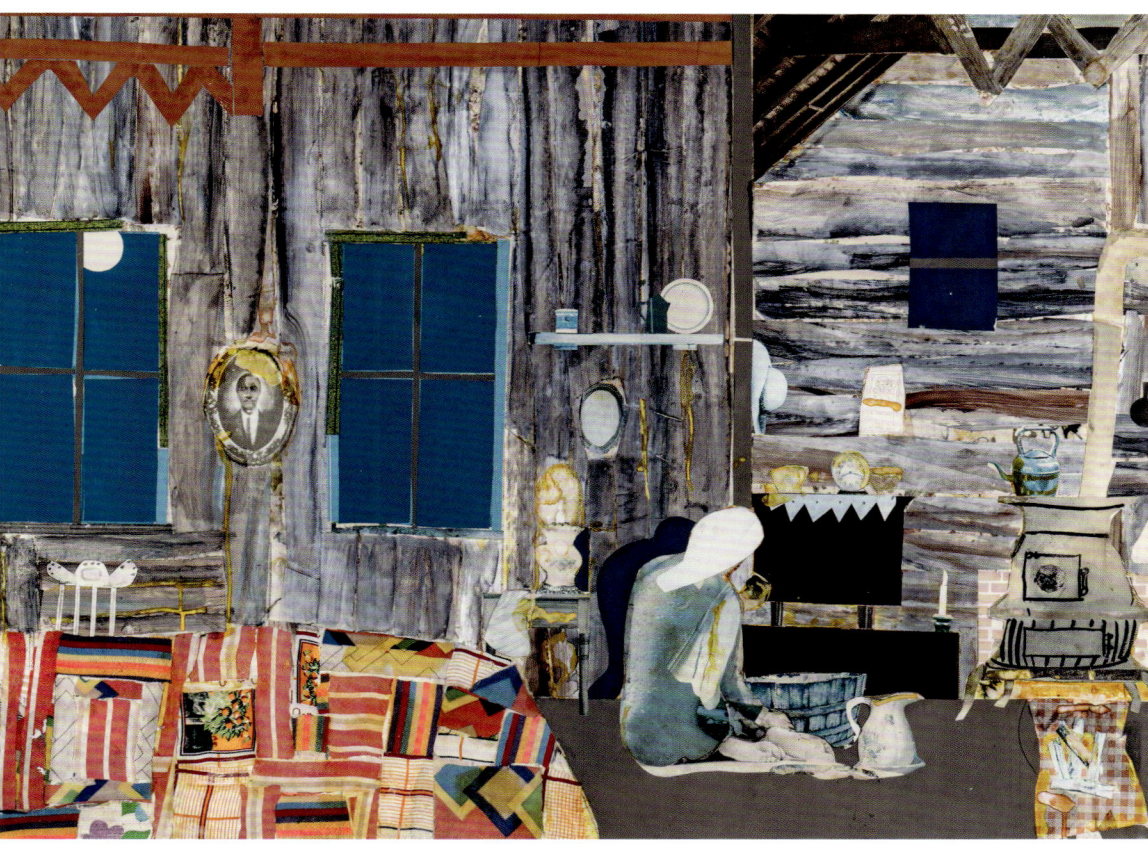

Profile/Part I, The Twenties: Mecklenburg County: Miss Mamie Singleton's Quilt, 1978. Collage of various papers, mixed media on board. 29 × 41 in. Private Collection

themselves of the blues (in rites of purification), if only for an evening, and, crucially, to proclaim that in spite of everything the sisters and the brothers are, as a Langston Hughes poem tersely proclaims, *still here*.[18] With such features in mind, we see Bearden's highly musical paintings as windows into the ecosystem of jazz as a *culture*. Here *influence*—of music on painting—is not quite the right word. For, as typically defined, influence draws a thin line of cause and effect, postulating starts and stops—one artist handing off to another. This does not account for a more kaleidoscopic understanding of influence, wherein an artist like Bearden is molded/inflected/modulated by jazz culture as an expression of give-and-take, call-recall, signification.

I refer now (switching metaphors) to the rhizoidal root system and tumbleweed wind-sand dances of an ongoing, ever-changing Black culture, a wide field of sensibilities and tastes from which many twentieth- and twenty-first-century forms have sprung—a concord of musical styles, most obviously, but also jazz dance (choreographed and vernacular), literature, and the visual arts, including jazz painting, jazz film, and jazz photography.[19] Some would even posit a jazz philosophy—the music's dissonant harmonies and echoes of blues lyrics intimating a tough-spirited existentialism (years before Europeans coined this term) and intervening in the debates within American pragmatism and chaos theory.[20] "In those days it was either live

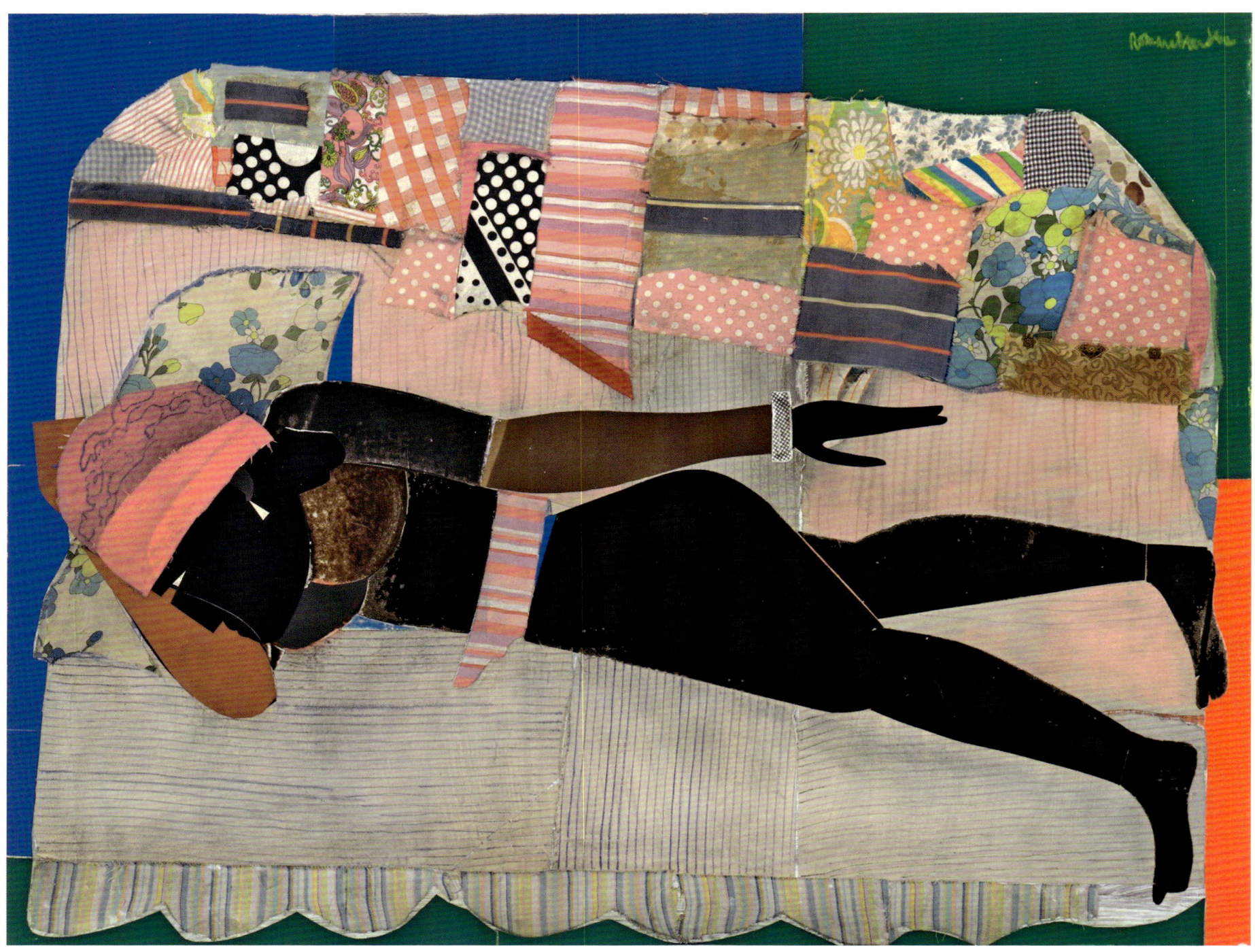

Patchwork Quilt, 1970. Collage of various papers, fabric, and gelatin silver print with acrylic on board. 35 ¾ × 47 ⅞ in. Museum of Modern Art, NY, Blanchette Hooker Rockefeller Fund

24

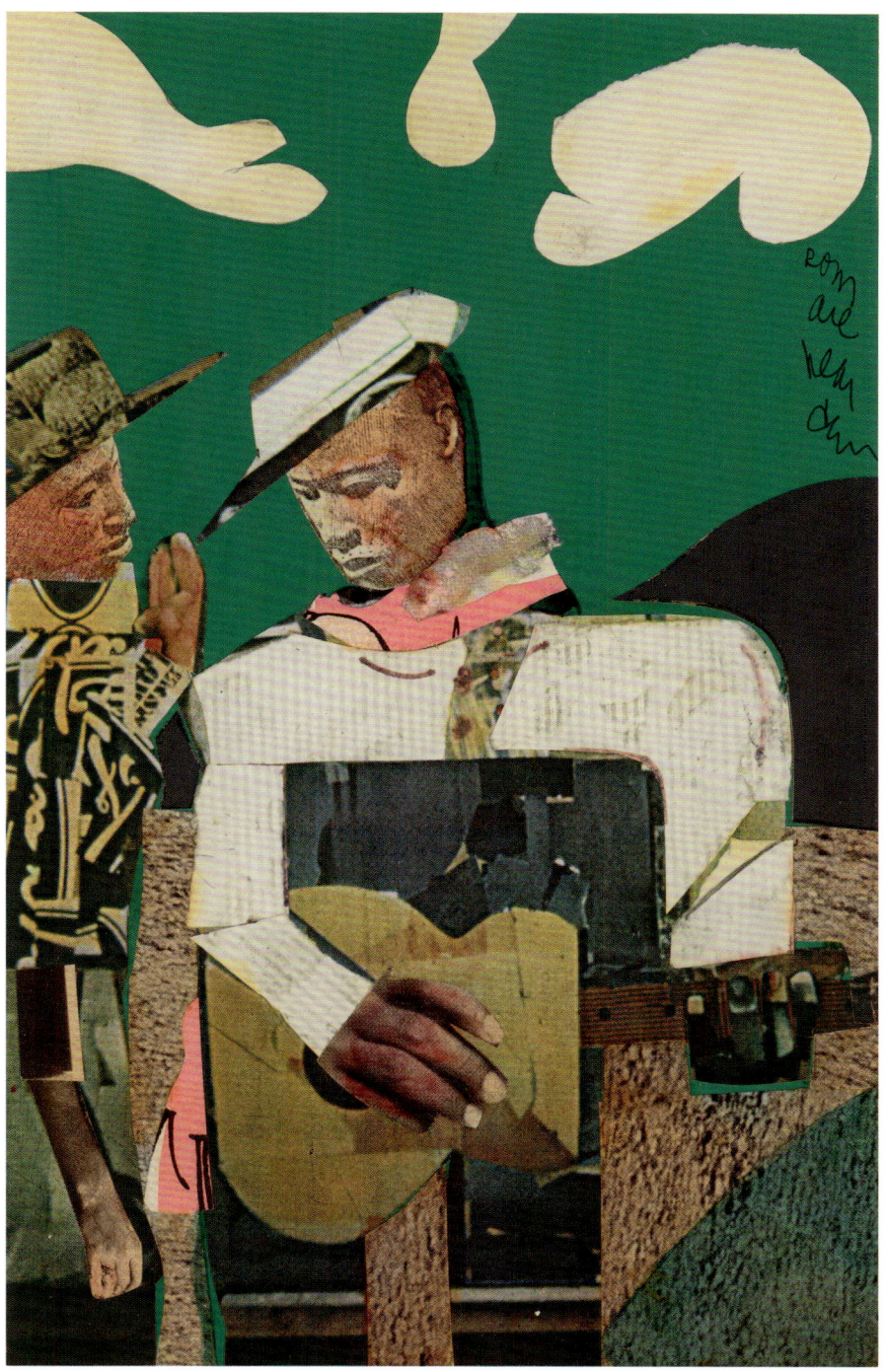

Guitar Executive, 1979. Collage of various papers, mixed media on board. 9 × 6 in.

with music or die with noise," wrote Bearden's friend Ralph Ellison, "and we chose rather desperately to live."[21]

As this book explores Bearden's *Paris Blues/Jazz* works, it also outlines Bearden's zigzag path toward mastery as a jazz artist. Along the way, we explore what visual jazz artistry entails, its playful but practice-practice-practice ways and means.

NORTH CAROLINA:
FIRST ENCOUNTERS WITH JAZZLIKE FORMS

Bearden's jazz story opens in Mecklenburg County, North Carolina, where he was born (9/2/1911) and spent his first years. Music and jazzlike art forms were all around him, perhaps most centrally in church. Sunday mornings, from church congregation benches, the young Bearden witnessed dramatic word artists—"God's Trombones," as the Harlem Renaissance (also called the New Negro Movement) writer James Weldon Johnson anointed them—some of the local preachers' sermons famous countywide.[22] And there were the Amen Corner regulars who could shake the church house when they shouted under the pressures of the Holy Ghost or broke out in upbeat shout-shoe dances. Of course, there were the singers and instrumentalists, including Bearden's father, who occasionally accompanied choirs from the piano. And the evening revival services whose pulses stirred the members: "You could hear the tambourines from a Holiness Church," wrote Bearden, "as far away as you could hear the dance bands."[23]

There also was secular music, musicians accompanying sports events and dances, as well as strolling players. It was on a visit to his Grandmother Cattie's home in Lutherville, Maryland (near Baltimore), that ten-year-old Bearden encountered Mr. E. C. Johnson, a blind strolling singer-guitarist known to forecast futures so accurately that many ran from the music man's dead-end news. Bearden remembered the sounds of Mr. E. C.'s guitar in poetic terms: "The music was strange to me and not like the church hymns, or the blues, or any of the popular songs that I knew. Finally, I asked Mr. Johnson what was the music he was playing. 'Oh, I don't know,' he said. 'I'm just wandering over the chords, just as if the wind was moving my fingers.'"[24] Bearden's later images of guitar players certainly recall Braque and Picasso, whose painted and cutout guitars, said jazz historian Barry Ulanov, "looked like music, a free expression, plastic in time."[25] But they also reflected Bearden's childhood experiences with Mr. E. C., and then with other U.S. string masters, North and South, through whom the artist found a sense of direction.

Aside from music itself, Mecklenburg presented other art forms to the young Bearden that were like jazz. Unless we start in the thick of the South Bearden knew, we might miss the look and touch of the patchwork quilts he lived with, on beds and settees. We could overlook his awareness of quilting as a Black woman's cooperative practice of repurposing swatches of cut and torn fabric to "make do": the making of something out of nothing that Bearden's friend, the poet Derek Walcott, described as *kind of a Black thing*.[26] Here was an improvisatory art of everyday use that exemplified certain "characteristics of Negro expression" (to quote Zora Neale Hurston): angularity, compelling insinuation, asymmetry, and the never-too-much-beauty rule that brilliant Zora called "the will to adorn."[27] "It was a beautiful sight," reminisced Bearden, standing in front of his collage *Miss Mamie Singleton's Quilt* (1978), "when Miss Mamie [one of his Carolina neighbors] would wash the quilts and hang them in her yard."[28] Prior to this work and another collaged homage to these quilt-circle ladies, *Quilting Time* (1979), Bearden had already borrowed some of the textures and compelling insinuations of quilting to create the early *Patchwork Quilt* (1970). These were among many Beardens not literally *about* jazz that nonetheless

capture some of its modes and flashes of spirit, the persistence of the will to freedom and beauty, *to jazz!*

With jazz as the connecting thread, I like to consider *Patchwork Quilt* alongside several of Bearden's other reclining nudes, which likewise suggest jazz culture. These would include one collage named after the Ellington composition "Daybreak Express" (1978), featuring a woman whose wry, half-smiling face resembles young Billie Holiday's (about whom more shortly). The train flying at the beautiful dreamer's window in this work suggests themes and sounds that are definitive of jazz. Ancient Ithaca is far from the Carolinas, but consider Bearden's collage called *Odysseus Leaves Circe* (1977), a Black and bluesy translation of a last-goodbye scene from Homer that the artist's friend, novelist Albert Murray, nicknamed "Blues for Lady Circe" or "Circe's Empty Bed Blues," this latter title echoing a blues hit by Bessie Smith. Along with Billie Holiday, Duke Ellington, and Louis Armstrong, Sister Smith keeps showing up in the world according to Bearden. She shares star status with Ellington and Armstrong in the *Paris Blues/Jazz* series. Like them, she was a touchstone of bodacious artistic experimentation and excellence: jazz at its best, personified.

Mecklenburg had other artists, too, although like the quilters they would not have claimed such a moniker for themselves. These were the hard-working gardeners Bearden frequently depicted—skilled-hand growers of beautiful fruits, vegetables, and flowers. Consider the several late-1970s paintings where Miss Maudell Sleet appears, sometimes with large hands indicating the largeness of her skill and, according to Bearden, her generosity.

It was in Charlotte, Bearden's birthplace, that his grade-school playmates included his cousin Charles "Spinky" Alston, who was four years older and liked to draw and dig into Charlotte's ubiquitous red clay to shape rough sculptures of human and animal figures. The cousins were very happy to re-up when

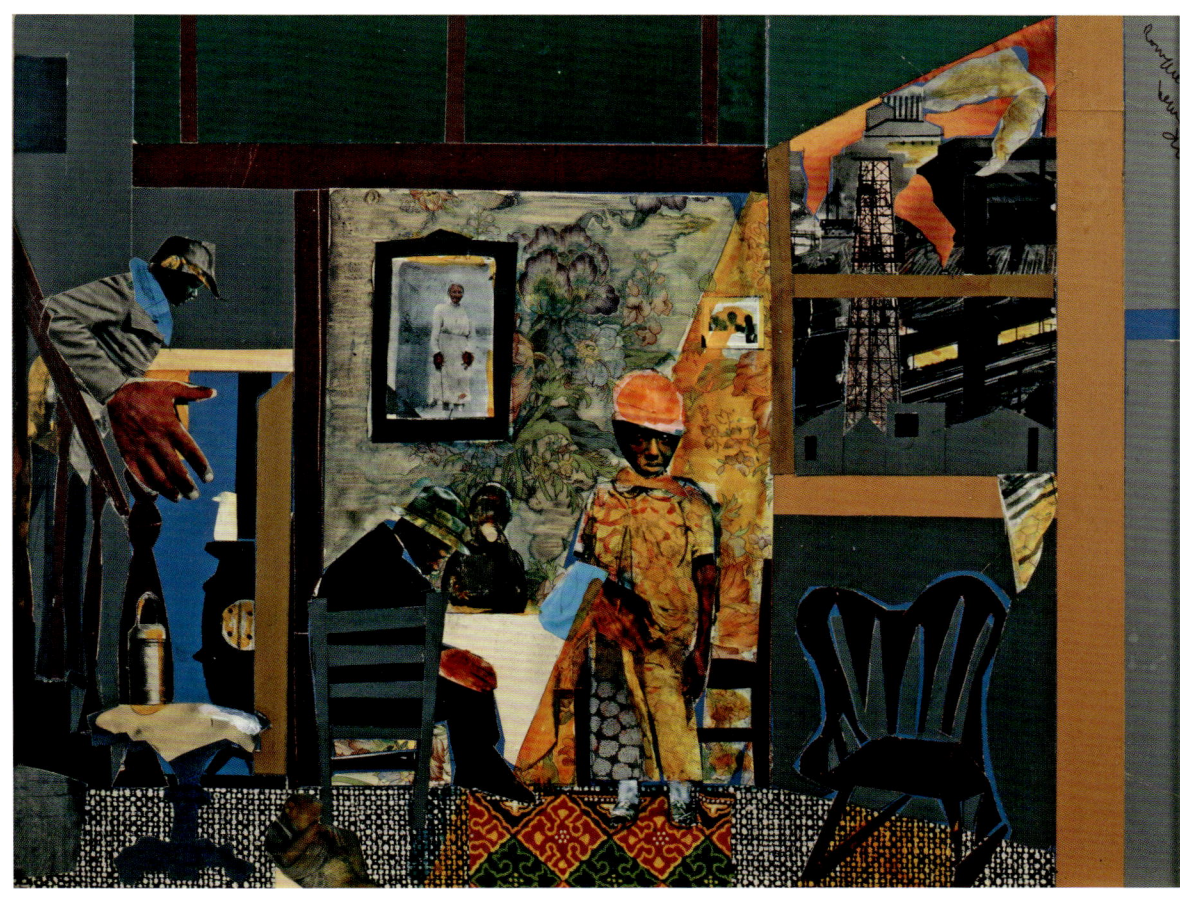

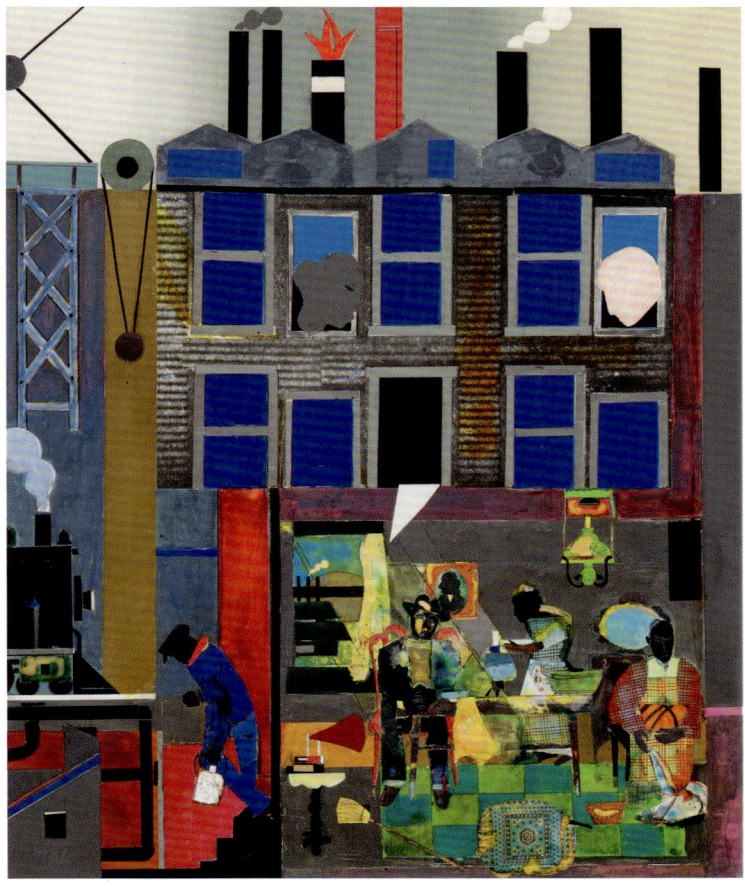

Profile/Part I, The Twenties: Mecklenburg County: Mill Hand's Lunch Bucket (Pittsburgh Memories), 1978. Collage of various papers, mixed media on fiberboard. 13 ¾ × 18 in. Cincinnati Art Museum, OH, Museum Purchase: The Edwin and Virginia Irwin Memorial and the John J. Emery Endowment

Pittsburgh Memories, 1984. Collage on board. 28 ⅝ × 23 ½ in. Carnegie Museum of Art, Pittsburgh, PA, Gift of Mr. and Mrs. Ronald R. Davenport and Mr. and Mrs. Milton A. Washington

their families moved to Harlem in the 1920s, where Alston, who eventually taught at the Art Students League, became an influential artist whose students included Jacob Lawrence and, informally, "Cousin Romy." Beauford Delaney was also influenced by Alston as one of his assistants on a Harlem Hospital murals project for the WPA.[29]

In 1933, Alston and Cousin Romy took the music impresario John Hammond on a Harlem tour that included dropping in to see seventeen-year-old Billie Holiday, who was performing at a 132nd Street club called Monette's or Covan's. Through Hammond, who became a lifelong Holiday fan, young Lady made her first recordings later that year. Alston "quite literally changed my life," wrote Hammond, "helped me to insights I would never have discovered on my own."[30] In the 1950s, Alston created expressionistic paintings honoring jazz musicians, particularly Bessie Smith, whom he adored (he recalled riding in the rumble seat of Bessie's car, en route to her gigs). As Hammond recalled, "He was in the recording studio with me during that wonderful session with Bessie Smith, during which he made sketches of Teagarden, Chu Berry, and other musicians."[31] No doubt, he remained an influence on his younger cousin.

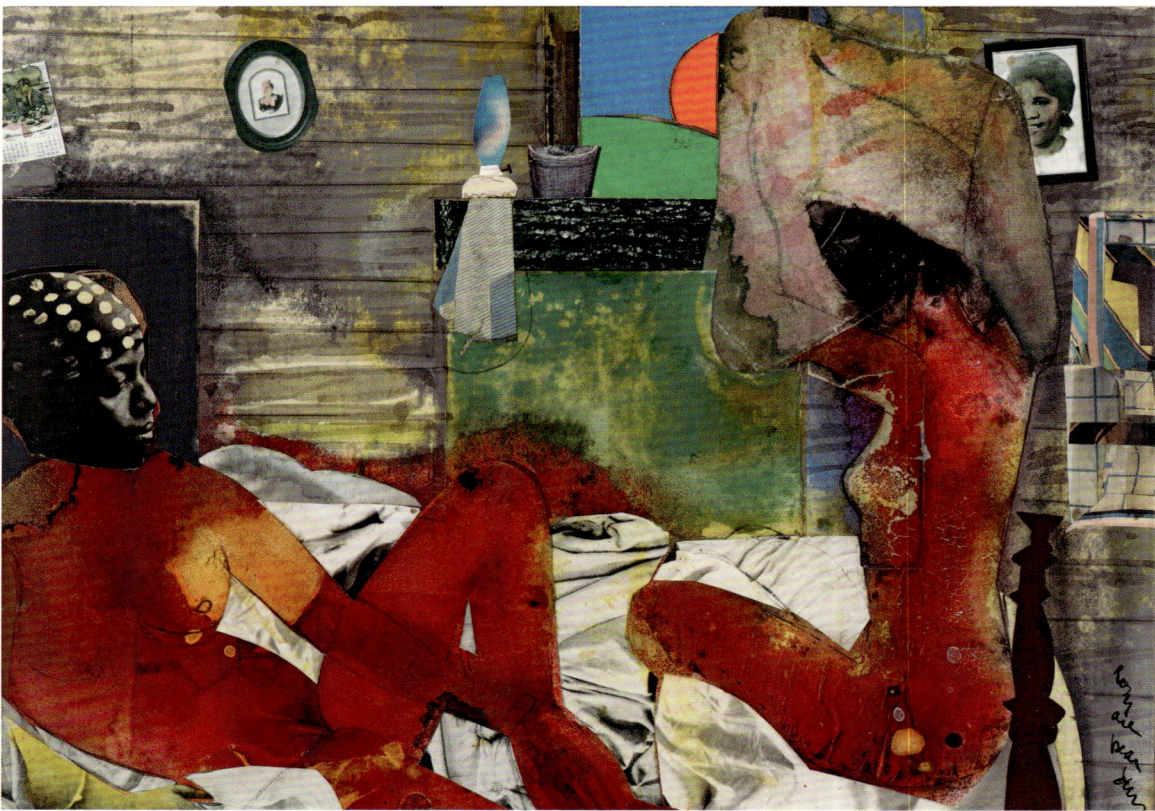

Profile/Part I, The Twenties: Mecklenburg County: Railroad Shack Sporting House, ca. 1978. Paper and fabric collage with paint, ink, and graphite on fiberboard. 11 ⅝ × 16 ⅝ in. Courtesy of DC Moore Gallery, New York

INTERLUDE IN PITTSBURGH

Before moving to New York, Bearden spent his fourth-grade year, and then summer vacations, at his grandparents' place in Pittsburgh—a major jazz city that remained a site of Bearden's creative imagination for the rest of his life. There the artist enjoyed spending time with another grade-schooler, Eugene Bailey, who, like Cousin Spinky, enjoyed drawing, and who in the summer of 1926 taught fourteen-year-old Romy how to recreate on paper the scenes Eugene secretly eyed through the floorboards of the brothel where his mom turned tricks. Often when Bearden spoke of Eugene, who died from infantile paralysis a few months after their first meeting, he would mention

that the youngster "might have been another Lautrec."[32] Of course, it is Bearden himself whose 1960s and 1970s portraits of urban life—in Harlem as well as Baltimore, Chicago, Kansas City, New Orleans, and then Paris itself—reveal traces of the influence of Henri de Toulouse-Lautrec's racy City of Light. So many of Bearden's sexually suggestive jazz-related works, including the New Orleans bordellos of *Paris Blues/Jazz*, depict parlors and boudoirs where music rang all night long—and thus where jobs for the town's many jazz musicians were steadily available.[33] And where early forms of the music could thrive without the thou-shalt-nots of official culture.

On the subject of love for sale, Bearden's *Railroad Shack Sporting House* (ca. 1978) was based on the place where the

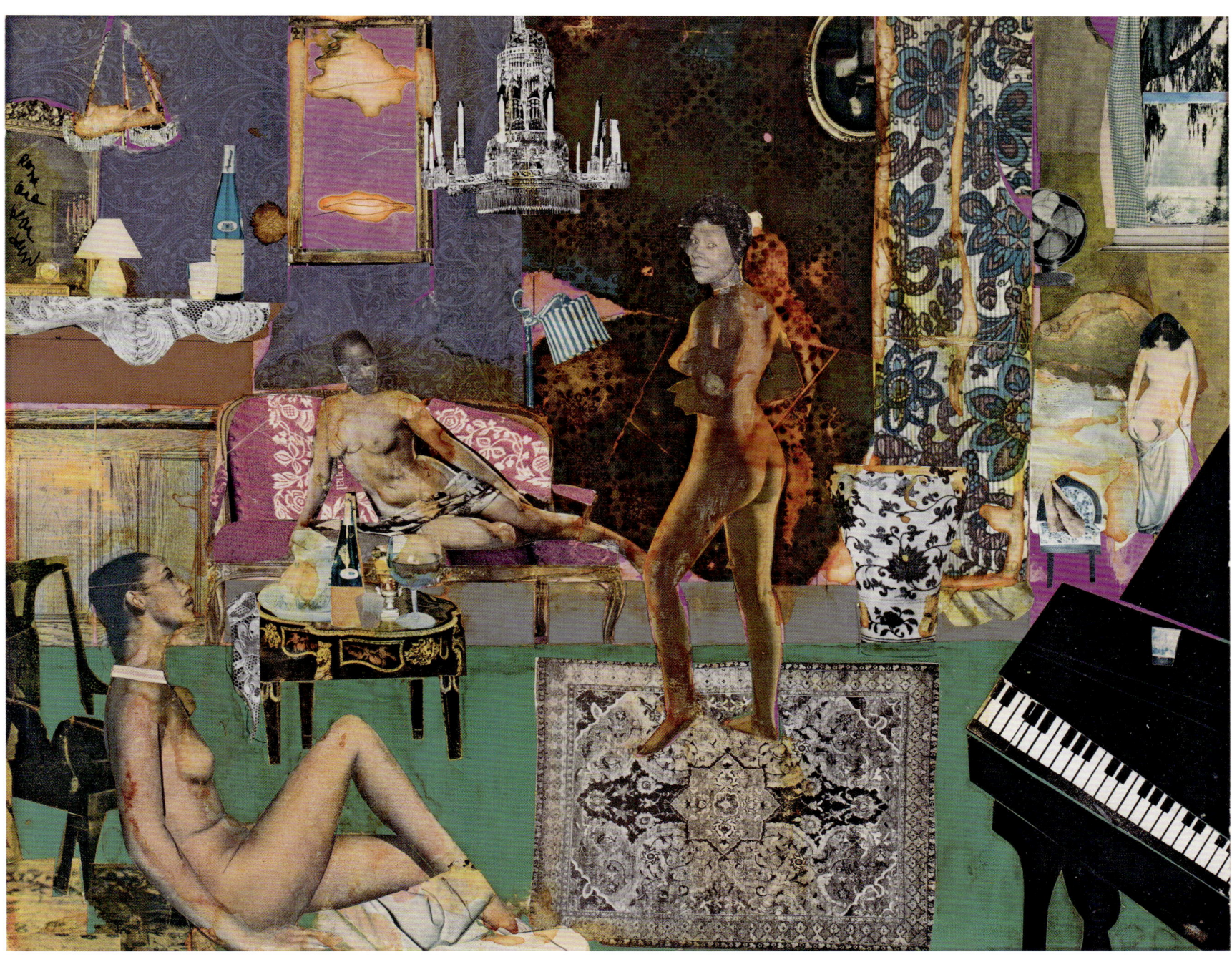

Profile/Part I, The Twenties: Mecklenburg County: Mamie Cole's Living Room, 1978.
Collage of various papers, mixed media on fiberboard. 13 ¼ × 17 ¼ in. Private Collection

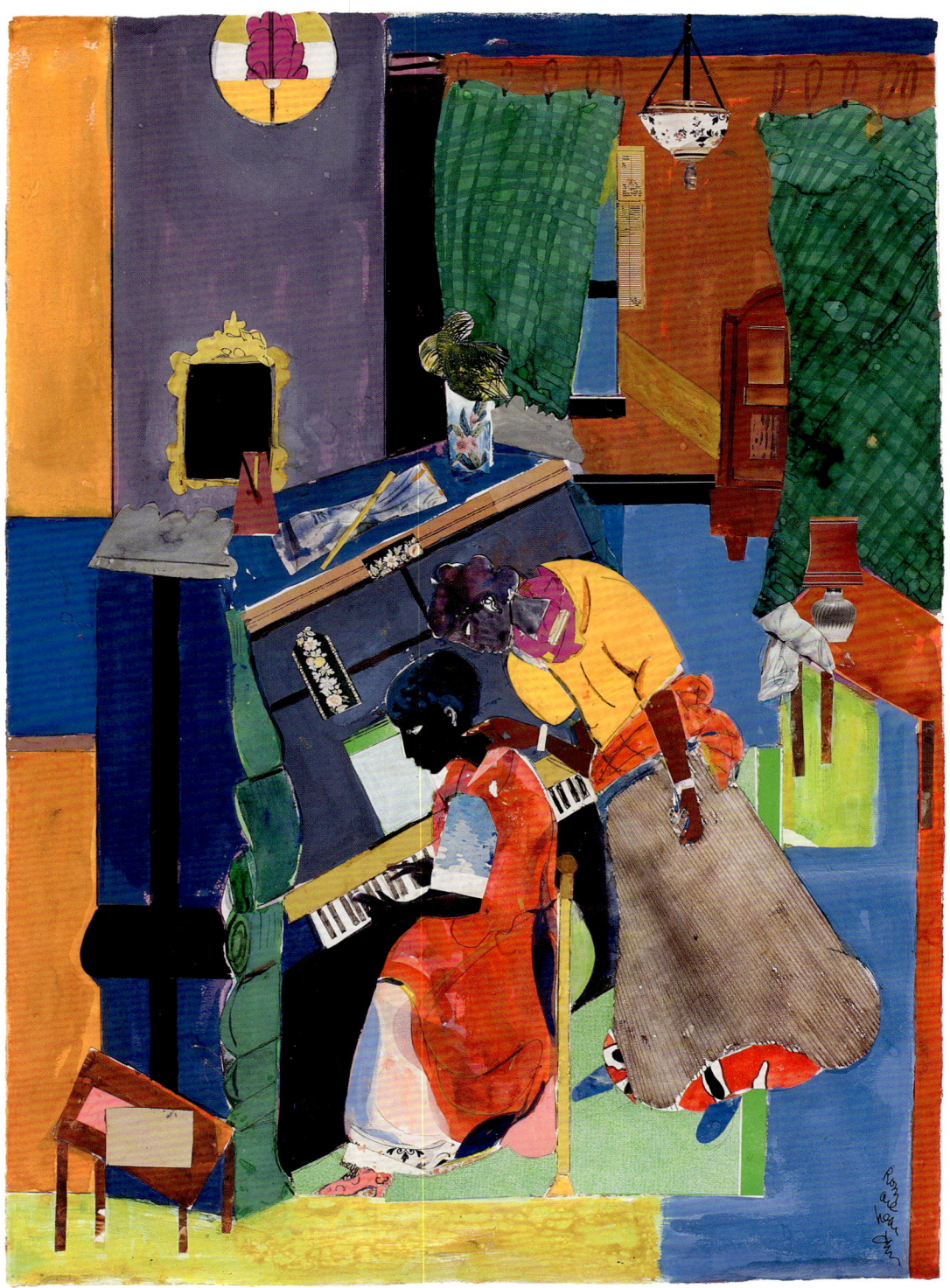

Piano Lesson, 1983. Collage of various papers, mixed media on fiberboard. 29 × 22 in. The Walter O. Evans Foundation for Art and Literature, Savannah, GA

artist's close friend Liza's mother worked. Accordingly, in this collage, Bearden places a yearbook-style portrait on the room's back wall to suggest life beyond this woman's current working world. Likewise, in *Mamie Cole's Living Room* (1978), where another scene of transactional sex is shown, wall portraits again complicate the bordello's tale. "I'd like to call your attention to the pictures on the wall," said Bearden. "I used them to show the people who were there, and that there was a definitive continuity in their lives."[34] This collage also displays a variety of textures—wallpaper, upholstery, fruits, rugs, the ladies' skin—suggesting quiltlike/jazzlike rhythmic interplay, the sense of interval that Bearden so often spoke about. The collage's shifts in pattern also recall Robert Farris Thompson's thesis in *Flash of the Spirit: African and Afro-American Art and Philosophy* (1983) that such sudden changes in rhythm, whether in Afro-musical or Afro-visual art, release cleansing, redeeming energies or "flashes" from the universe of the spirits. Think of the starbursts from the trumpet of Miles Davis in his late-career work.

It is vital to underscore here Bearden's point that it was his job as an artist to honor the dignity of every person, whatever the social class, employed or unemployed. Sometimes Bearden, who was a master storyteller, attributed this "greatest lesson in painting I've ever had in my life" to a streetwalker in Harlem and her jangling keys.[35] Of course there's a jazz lesson here, too, for the jazz band is a sort of perfect democracy where every player has a voice, and where leadership is based not on economic or political inheritances or brute force but on the achievement of a personal voice and the capacity to blend with others. Here is an art born of We-the-Band's will to make beautiful music together: *e pluribus unum* with a swinging beat! May we not call America at its best "The United States of Jazzocracy?"

It was in music-rich Pittsburgh that Bearden doubtless met the "little piano girl" named Mary Elfrieda Scruggs—later called Mary Lou Williams—who eventually became one of the music's most brilliant pianists and composers. She was an important teacher, too, counting among her tutees Thelonious Monk, Bud Powell, Dizzy Gillespie, and then, through several recorded piano-played histories of jazz, countless others. Bearden's collage *Piano Lesson* (1983) was also entitled *Homage to Mary Lou*, and as a poster image was donated to support a Williams tribute concert by the Nanette Bearden Contemporary Dance Theatre, for which Bearden's wife served as artistic director. It was this painting that inspired August Wilson to write the play *The Piano Lesson* (1987), which draws directly on the Bearden work for its characters and setting. Just as the painting helps us dig the play, the play frames the Bearden painting anew, now as a reflection on the complexly variegated piano education, formal and informal, sacred and secular, available to Pittsburgh's musicians.[36] While the play asks, *Where does Black music come from?*, it also wants to know what the music means, or (quoting Wilson): "What is the piano lesson?"[37] Under the spell of Bearden's painting, Wilson explores and celebrates the historical power of Black music, not excluding its politics, economics, spirituality, and powers to heal. Like Williams's music, his play is part of the painting's ongoing call-and-recall conversation, its "heap of signifyin'" (quoting Ellison again). For Wilson, the painting's textured shapes and colors invite us to see the cultural power plant (not the tumbleweed now) that is jazz. Let us think of Bearden hearing Mary Lou and asking himself, as an artist: What *IS* the piano lesson?!

Just to name the Steel City's major piano players whose music Bearden almost undoubtedly knew (aside from Mary Lou), consider Erroll Garner, Ahmad Jamal, Billy Strayhorn, and Earl "Fatha" Hines. As we've noted, Strayhorn, who wrote Duke Ellington's theme song, "Take the A Train," co-composed the score for the movie *Paris Blues* with Ellington. Hines warrants special notice here, too, because he is the jazz artist that Stuart Davis, one of Bearden's most important mentors—and, for many, the other dean of jazz painting—advised Bearden to study closely so as to create visual equivalents of Fatha's patterns of notes at the piano. Listen especially for the "intervals," Davis said: the patterns of movement from one single note to another, or cluster to cluster, and the spaces in between.[38] "Hines made the pauses between notes into something important and wonderful," said Bearden. "It was the precise intervals that Stuart emphasized. I began to try to do these paintings in relation to interval." "One of the things I did before I tried these pictures was just listen to a lot of music," said Bearden. "I'd take a sheet of paper and just make lines while I listened, a kind of shorthand to pick up the rhythms."[39] With this in mind, look at Bearden's abstract works of the early 1950s. And of course consider the rhythmical play of shapes and colors in the *Paris Blues/Jazz* collages.

Meanwhile, let the record show that, aside from Steel City pianists, jazz players Bearden doubtless knew from his Pittsburgh days would include trumpeter Roy Eldridge, drummer Kenny Clarke, and singer-trombonist-bandleader Billy Eckstine (about whom more shortly)—all consummate masters of musical time, space, and color.

HARLEM! (AND THE RENAISSANCE)

In 1920, when the Bearden family moved to New York City, it was one of the fastest-spinning cultural hubs on the planet. "New York!?" exclaims a character in Bearden's friend Ralph Ellison's novel *Invisible Man* (1952). "That's not a place, it's a dream."[40] "Harlem is my Paris!" declared Bearden. "It's the rhythm of Harlem, the characters, the colors—these give tremendous inspiration to the artist, creative energy."[41] This was the start of the Harlem Renaissance, which spanned the 1920s and 1930s, "when the Negro was in vogue," as Langston Hughes

put it—when bigtime publishers, producers, and gallerists in search of Black talent were a subway ride away.[42] This was a time, remarked Bearden's friend the painter Aaron Douglas, with a wink, "when [if] unsuspecting Negroes were found with a brush in their hands, they were immediately hauled away and held for interpretation!"[43] Critically, Black American intellectuals and artists of dreamscape ambition were encountering not only white friends and boosters but one another, and forming supportive Black creative communities not only in New York but also in New Orleans, Paris, London, Berlin, and other major cosmopolitan cities all over the world.[44]

The Harlem Renaissance, ultimately stretching across the whole twentieth century, strikes me as one of the central subjects of Bearden's *Paris Blues/Jazz*. Here were Black Americans of outsized talent pushing beyond any and all borders on the widest cultural highways to deliver newly vitalized Blackness to the world. In *Paris Blues/Jazz*, we see the continuation of that New Negro movement of the 1920s and 1930s into the 1970s, with Black talent continuing to generate energy for living and creating, and hope in the face of bleak times.

Teenage Bearden's family apartment on 131st Street in Harlem could rightly be called one of the Renaissance's significant *salons*. For it was in their living room that Romy and older Cousin Spinky (occasionally with Jacob Lawrence in tow) heard talks by W. E. B. Du Bois and Alain Locke, Langston Hughes and Paul Robeson. The apartment had an upright piano where Fats Waller and Duke Ellington would tickle the ivories and talk "stuff" along with serious business. (To encourage the youngster, Waller bought what Bearden called "a design . . . not really a painting"[45]; Ellington also bought an early painting.) White friends stopped through—Carl Van Vechten and John Hammond, who, as noted, eventually would be instrumental in recording Billie Holiday, but also Bessie Smith, Count Basie, and, years later, Aretha Franklin and Bob Dylan.

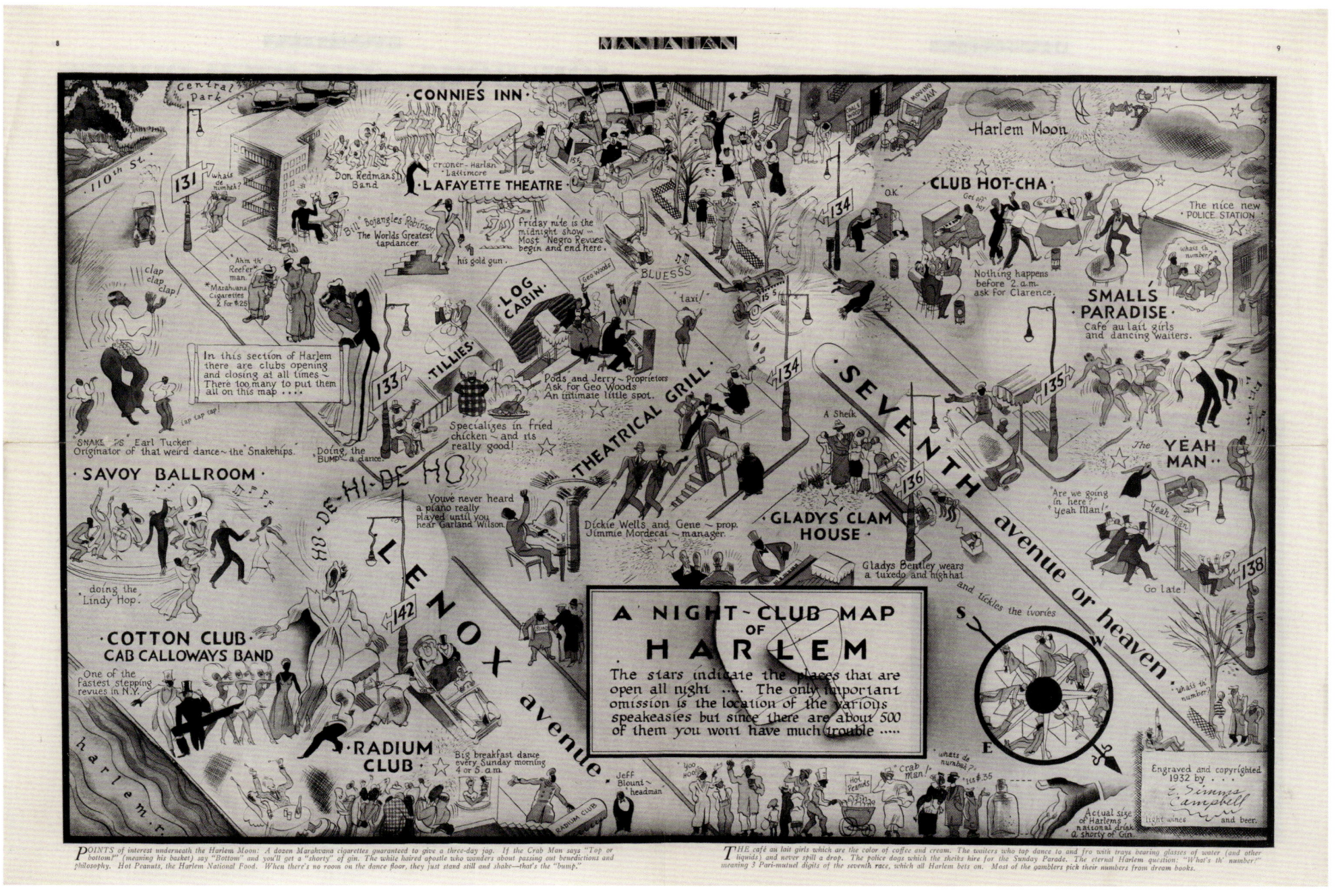

Elmer Simms Campbell, "A night-club map of Harlem," in *Manhattan–Weekly for Wakeful New Yorkers*, January 18, 1933, 13 ¾ x 22 in. Library of Congress, Geography and Map Division

Elmer Simms Campbell (1906–1971)—one of that era's only Black commercial artists to cross over into the white world of popular magazine art—renders a tongue-in-cheek version of the thickness and flavor of the nighttime/righttime street-scene young adult Bearden knew well. His family's apartment at 154 West 131st Street was located at the top of this map, near the words "Connie's Inn." Diagonally across the street from their apartment, recalled the artist, he could watch jazz players at work in a rehearsal hall located behind the 2,000-seat Lafayette Theatre, labeled here near center-top. Good time spaces above and below ground abounded, as the names of the nightspots proclaimed: the Yeah Man and Club Hot-Cha among them. Note, too, the nearness of the Cotton Club, Small's Paradise, and The Savoy Ballroom ("Home of Happy Feet"), whose manager let Bearden and other young artists in for free. Bearden biographer Mary Schmidt Campbell surmises that Bearden and his buddies may have used this map to seek out new places to hang, dance, and otherwise have fun. Check the map's centerpiece sign: *"The only important omission is the location of the various speakeasies but since there are about 500 of them you won't have much trouble."*

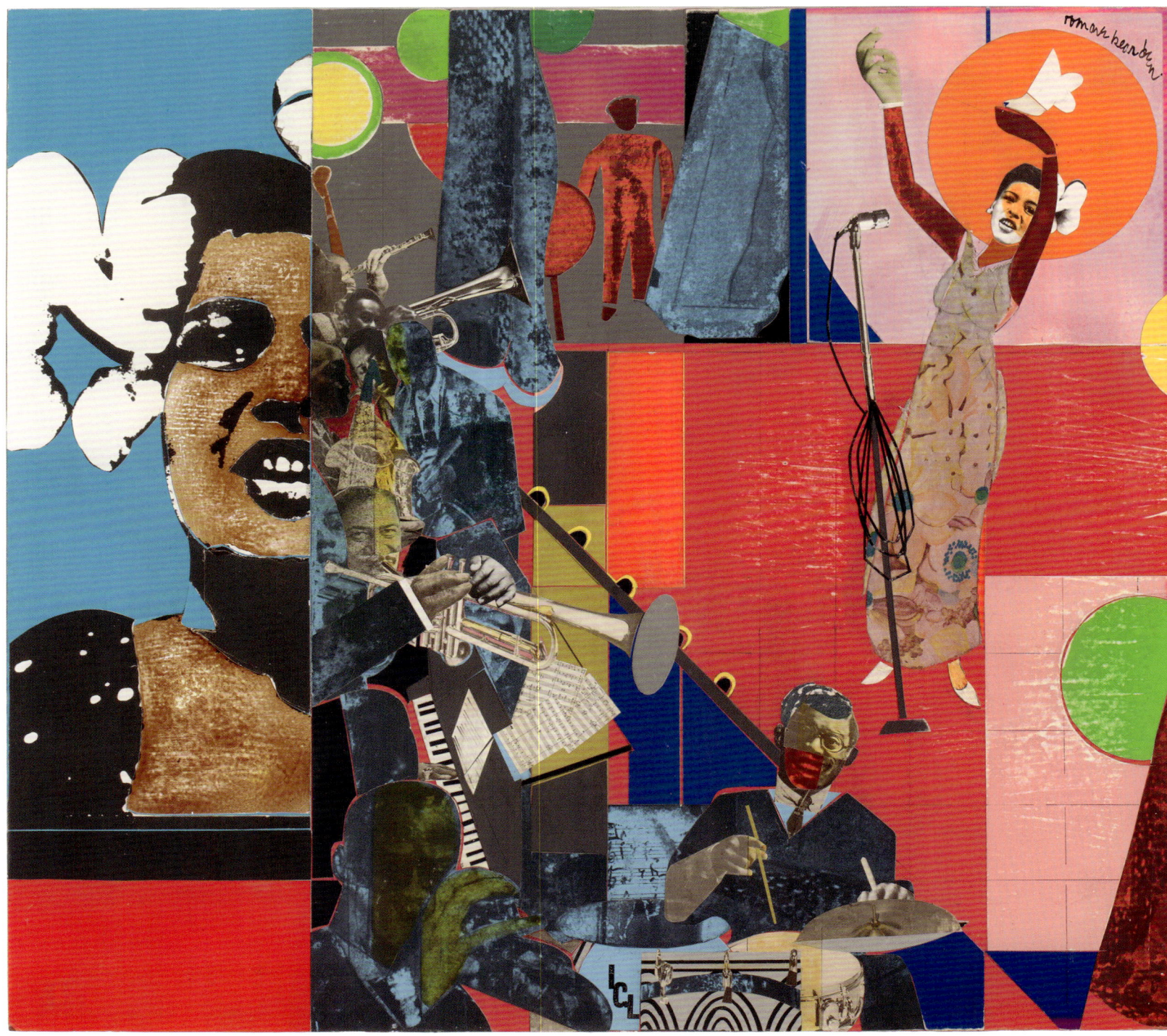

Billie Holiday, 1973. Collage of various papers, mixed media on fiberboard. 27 × 31 in. Private Collection

BILLIE: AN EARLY AND LASTING MUSE

Per Hammond, Billie Holiday's first recording sessions were with Benny Goodman (along with Chu Berry and Jack Teagarden), and then with other all-star units led by Teddy Wilson. During this period, Romy and his cousin regularly saw her at her day job as receptionist in the 125th Street Apollo Building studio of the photographers Marvin and Morgan Smith, near Bearden's own studio. Starting in the 1960s, Bearden created pictures of Lady Day over and over again, including a shimmering mosaic, unveiled in 1982, in a Baltimore metro station not far from where she'd grown up. For Bearden, as for Roy DeCarava, James Baldwin, Amiri Baraka, Gayl Jones, Elizabeth Hardwick, Thelonious Monk, Jayne Cortez, Miles Davis (among others), and ALL contemporary singers, Holiday was a muse: standard-bearer in the tradition of soulful Black expression and Harlem Renaissance woman if ever there was one.

In 1973, Bearden created a collage as cover art for the retrospective album *Billie Holiday: The Original Recordings*. Here, as usual, Bearden depicted Lady Day as a joyous goddess. He knew that her triumph was in the shapes, textures, and potent silences of her music (its intervals), and in the way she confronted the shipwrecked-blues without forgetting that humanity is not defeated by them. In a rightly praised 1957 televised performance of "Fine and Mellow,"[46] Lady's musical conversation with saxophonist Lester Young offers a gesture toward perfection in human relations—toward clairvoyant understanding and care, love beyond words, toward true grace—glowing directly in the face of the lyrics of a troubled song. *I hear what you're saying*, Lester says in fluent saxophonese. *I hear you baby, and I'm there for you—I got you!* Jazz as a more perfect union.

THE 306 COMMUNITY

A very major meeting spot in Harlem was "306," nicknamed for the building at 306 West 141st Street where many Harlem notables lived, and where Charles Alston had a top-floor studio. Here's Bearden on the cultural melding that went on there:

> Harlem then resembled a small town. Almost all creative people in the arts knew one another, as well as the leading ministers, physicians, lawyers, business leaders, and national political figures like James Weldon Johnson and W. E. B. Du Bois. Alston began inviting people he knew from the WPA to social parties. These turned into intellectual discussions, and 306 rapidly became a unique community institution. It particularly attracted artists, writers, musicians, actors, dancers, and designers, who were excited to discover one another's talents and views. Even Philadelphia, Washington, and Chicago artists showed up—and sometimes Alain Locke. On payday, the partying and discussions at times spilled over into the huge studio classroom. What black artists achieved in one field stimulated all the others, creating deeply satisfying waves of appreciation that went beyond mere applause.[47]

At 306 Bearden would routinely see Claude McKay and Ralph Ellison, both of whom became lifelong friends. Like Hughes, these novelists wrote brilliantly about Black musical culture and tried to capture on their pages something of the note and trick of the music itself. McKay's *Home to Harlem* (1928) is a paean to the Upper Manhattan neighborhood, and his *Banjo* (1928) narrates the efforts of Afro-musicians from across the diaspora to form a band together in Marseille that accentuates their common Black culturalisms: like Bearden's *Paris Blues/Jazz*, it tells of an ongoing international Harlem

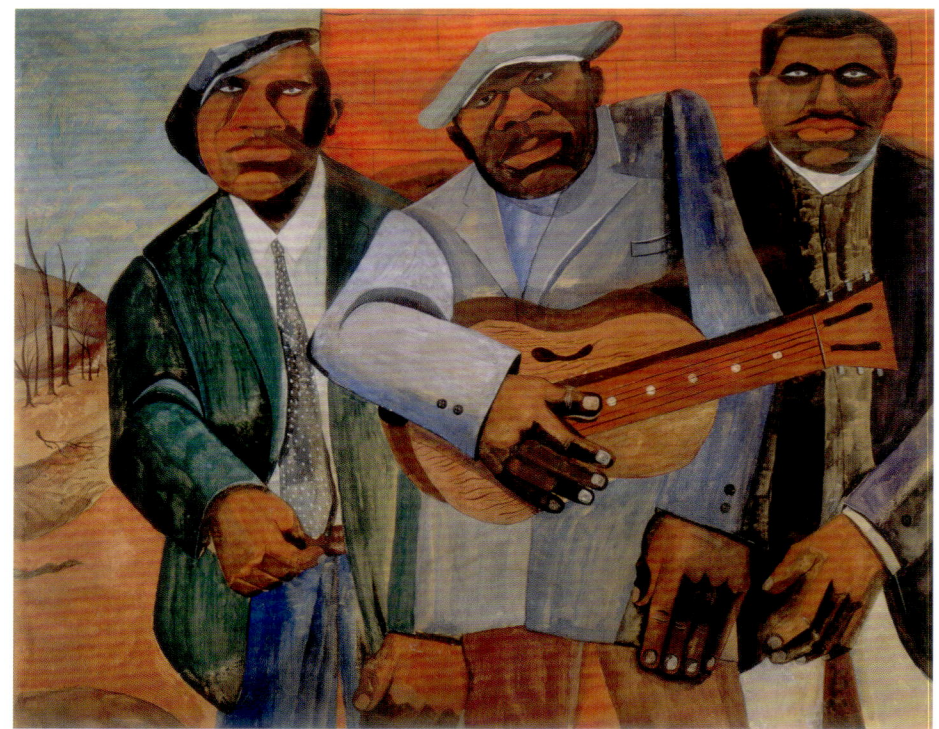

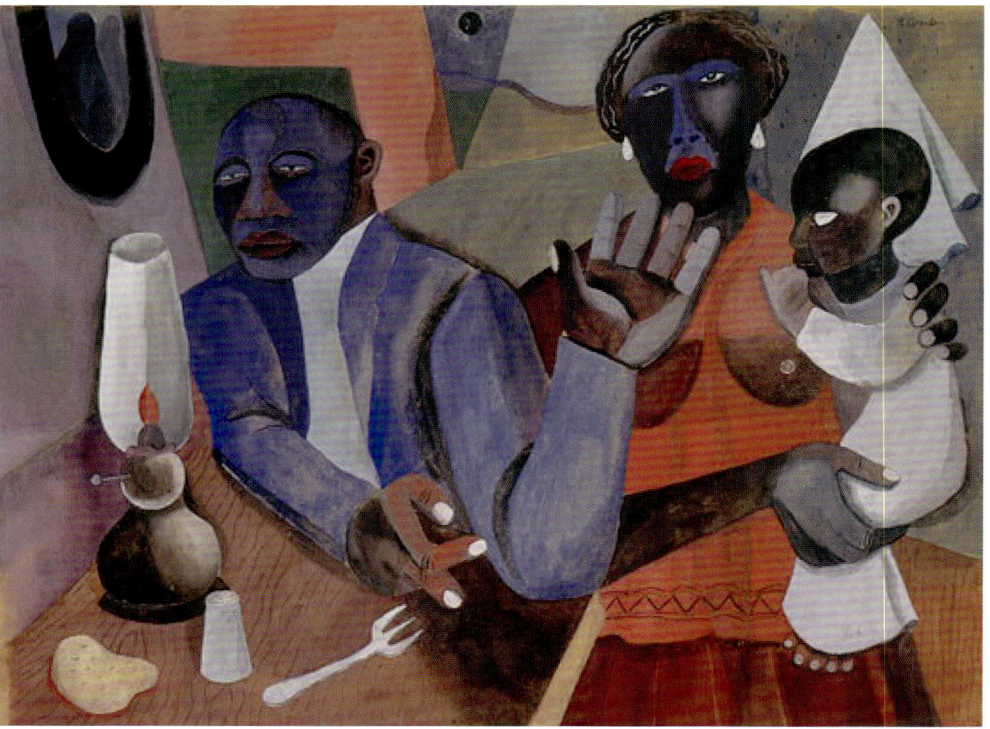

Folk Musicians, 1941–42. Gouache and casein on kraft paper. 35½ × 45½ in. The Curtis Galleries, Minneapolis, MN

The Family, ca. 1941. Gouache, ink, and graphite on paper. 29⅛ × 41¼ in. Collection of Earl Hyman, Promised gift to the National Gallery of Art, Washington, D.C.

Renaissance, accent on Black dance and music not just in America but *en France*.

Ellison eventually wrote one of the most comprehensive contributions to Bearden studies. His exhibition-catalogue essay of 1968 speaks of Bearden's ways of creating collages in language that could apply to the modernness of Ellington, Armstrong, or Lady Day: Bearden's "combination of technique is in itself eloquent of the sharp breaks, leaps in consciousness, distortions, paradoxes, reversals, telescoping of time and surreal blending of styles, values, hopes and dreams which characterize much of Negro American history. Through an act of creative will, he has blended strange visual harmonies out of the shrill, indigenous dichotomies of American life, and in doing so has reflected the irrepressible thrust of a people to endure and keep its intimate sense of its own identity."[48] In a final public reflection on Bearden (delivered at the artist's memorial service in 1988), Ellison asserted that Bearden's collages tell the story of America as "a collage of a nation."[49] Very attuned to jazz ("My strength comes from Louis Armstrong,"[50] Ellison said), he recognized Bearden's use of collage as suggestive of jazz performances and the complexly nonlinear mystery-in-history stories they tell.

THE VISUAL JAZZ ARTIST EMERGES

In the mid-1940s, Bearden—by now in his thirties and with an NYU degree, studies at the Art Students League, and military service (1942–45) under his belt—was a practicing artist. In

December 1946, his gallerist, Samuel Kootz, organized a group exhibition called *Homage to Jazz* that included three paintings by Bearden. One of them, *A Blue Note*, was an abstract work suggesting the shapes of jazz instruments and players and the play of colors in the music. The pamphlet essay accompanying that show, by Bearden's friend Barry Ulanov, the Barnard College professor and editor of *DownBeat* magazine who that year had released his fine biography of Duke Ellington, linked the flatness of so much modern painting to jazz music's flat key signatures. "Even as the painters had robbed parallel lines of their converging point, even as they flattened houses, and faces, and guitars, jazzmen had reduced the value of notes, flattened them. And to ears which would hear, a richer music was made."[51] Building on Ulanov, art historian Donna M. Cassidy declares mid-century jazz the direct source of Abstract Expressionism: "Jazz, which during the 1940s and '50s was becoming increasingly abstract and improvisatory in the hands of John Coltrane, Miles Davis, and others, [is] the source of this new American art."[52]

Jazz historian John Szwed cites drummer Max Roach's idea that once you erase Renaissance art's reliance on one-point "perspective"—the idea that someone (often the subject of the work or its patron) sits comfortably front and center while others are barely seen—the entire jazz band may be regarded as *all up front all the time*. Here is the jazz orchestra as the embodiment of multiple perspectives—not even the conductor, if there is one, always takes the lead. When it comes to soloing (or driving the band's tempo to swing harder), sometimes, in the words of James Brown, "you gotta give the drummer some!"[53] As a model for democracy in action, this Roach idea that members of the jazz band are equals puts artists "up front of the Civil Rights/Omni-American struggle"[54]—that is, of everybody's struggle, with the rich sharing equal elbow room with the tired and the poor, all yearning to live and breathe more freely together. This new view of the "United States of Jazzocracy" is made vivid

in Bearden's musical cutouts: each piece having its say before waiting patiently for the others to speak.[55]

Step by step, Bearden began to consciously incorporate jazz modes into his artistic process. In 1947, at the Manhattan studio of Spanish painter Joan Miró, Bearden saw a jazz connection in Miró's technique. Bearden reflected:

Here he was fixing two compositional positions across the canvas from each other, around which, like a jazz musician, he began to swing his rhythms and improvisations. So what he was coming up with had little to do with the original small sketch, just as the improvising jazz musician's "continuing thesis" has little to do with the original melody. This is not a method for everyone, and I certainly did not feel capable of doing what Miró did at the time—because it calls for sureness, a confident feeling that everything is going to turn out all right, and a way in which a kind of playfulness is kept moving throughout the composition.[56]

PARIS: "MORE THAN ONESELF"

Urged by the artist Carl Holty and his novelist friend Claude McKay, in 1950 Bearden took off for Paris, spending seven months there on the G.I. Bill of Rights. In a letter, Holty told Bearden he needed to leave the easy familiarity of the New York art scene. "What you need is banquet after banquet for your eyes,"[57] Holty told the younger artist. "You are what you are, but one *has to be more than oneself*" (my emphasis).

In February 1950, Bearden booked passage on a ship to Paris; soon after landing, he rented "a nice studio on the same little street where Cezanne once lived."[58] "It was my first time in Paris," said Bearden, "and of course I thought I'd go first to

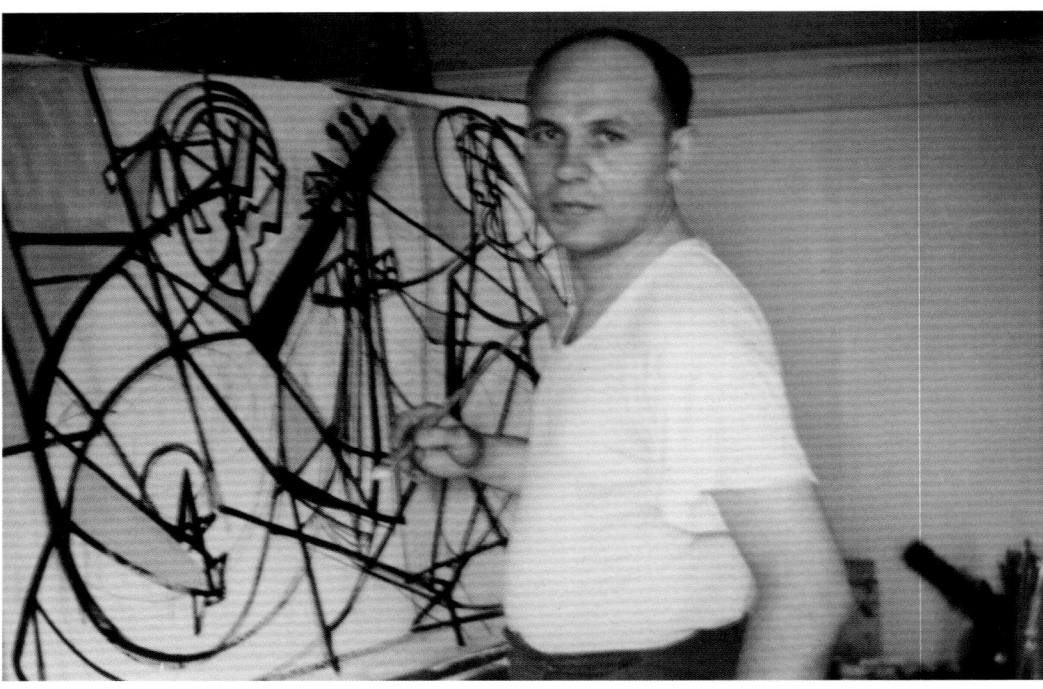

Romare Bearden with artwork, c. 1946, Romare Bearden Papers, The Wildenstein Plattner Institute, Inc.

the Louvre, but it was sort of like Kafka's Castle, I could never bring myself to go there . . . This was the place that I mainly wanted to see but there was always something to do." When, three months into the trip, he finally made it to the museum, "I only got there by accident. I happened to be in that vicinity one day."[59] Nor could Bearden get himself started on new paintings. Instead, this first trip to Europe offered a welcome sabbatical from the clatter of New York, a stretch of time to reflect on his direction as an artist, to reset.

As required under the G.I. Bill, he'd enrolled at the Sorbonne. But Bearden's Paris of 1950 was less a place to study than to party. The war was finally over. "I guess it was a little like the Renaissance after the Dark Ages," he said. "There were all those explosions and general liveliness. There was so much to do and see, just walking the length and breadth of Paris.

It was another life altogether."[60] Like Harlem, Paris offered "a life lived outdoors." He recalled that one night he heard familiar music flowing from an apartment. "It didn't sound like French musicians, so I went up, knocked on the door, and there inside the room were Sidney Bechet [saxophonist/clarinetist], and Roy Eldridge [trumpeter], and Minto Cato, [mezzo-soprano singer] . . . and several others. I knew them! They were just having fun by themselves. . . . Finally at three in the morning they made us leave, and we ended up continuing the party out on the street, music and dancing, it was wonderful."[61]

It was in a Saint-Germain café that Bearden first met Albert Murray, who became a lifelong friend and frequent collaborator. Both were insiders on the U.S. jazz scene, and Murray was just beginning to develop his jazz fiction and theories of jazz (as heroic action in the face of entropy and other

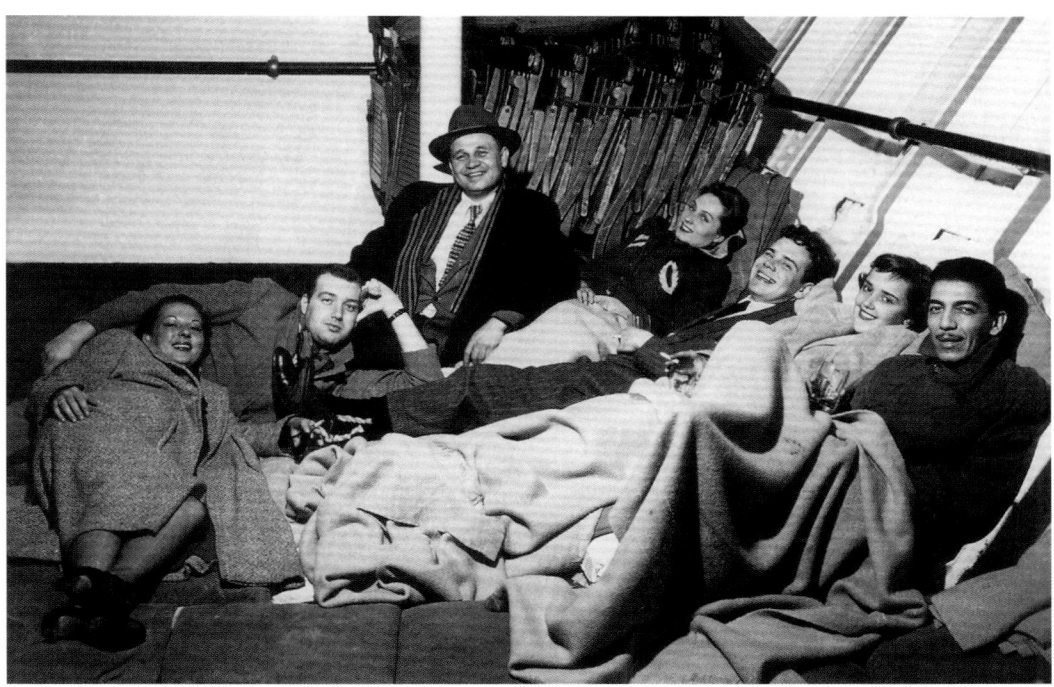

Morgan and Marvin Smith. Bearden (wearing a hat) and friends, USS *America* crossing, 1950

"dragons") that affected Bearden's own art and perspectives on the music. "We all learn from Mann, Joyce, Hemingway, Eliot, and the rest," wrote Murray in a headnote accompanying his first published fiction (1953). "But I'm also trying to learn to write in terms of the tradition I grew up in, the Negro tradition of the blues, stomps, ragtime, jumps, and swing. After all, very few writers have done as much with American experience as Jelly Roll Morton, Count Basie, and Duke Ellington."[62] Within a few years the two men would work together on a wide variety of projects, including Bearden's two-part series *Profile* (1979, 1981), for which the novelist assisted with the works' titles and accompanying sentences—and the *Paris Blues/Jazz* project.

It was also in a Saint-Germain-des-Prés café where Bearden met James Baldwin, who, after two years in Paris (from Harlem and Greenwich Village), was beginning to hit

his stride with a first novel, *Go Tell It on the Mountain* (1953), from which Bearden heard him read when the manuscript was called "I, John."[63] In an interview, Baldwin recalled that as he was struggling to understand the secrets of French menus and rapid conversations in French cafés—"in that silence," Baldwin said—he finally began, as he put it, "to hear another language"—*his own*.[64] From the distance of the Left Bank and Montmartre in Paris, he heard his father's sermons as if for the first time, and the voice of Bessie Smith (like Armstrong's horn and voice, Bessie Smith seemed to call so many artists back home). "I was listening very hard to jazz," wrote Baldwin, "and trying very hard to translate it into language."[65] Soon it would be Romy trying just as hard to translate the music of Bessie, Duke, Strays, Waller, Holiday, and yes, Mary Lou, into lines and tones that everybody, not just the musicians, could

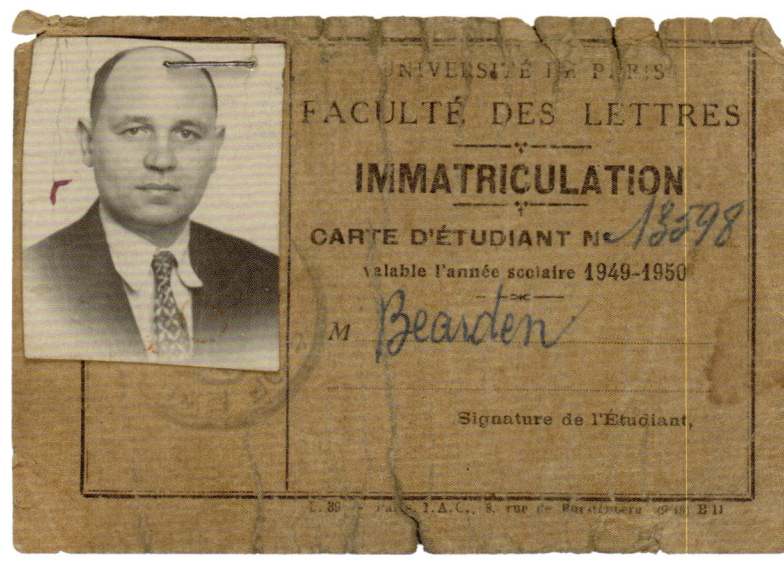

Temporary Resident Card, France, 1950–51. Romare Bearden Papers, The Wildenstein Plattner Institute, Inc.

Université de Paris Faculté des Lettres, Immatriculation, Carte d'étudiant [University of Paris Faculty of Letters, Registration, Student ID card], 1949–50. Romare Bearden Papers, The Wildenstein Plattner Institute, Inc.

see. Perhaps it's fair to say that for all its exciting distractions, above all Paris offered Bearden a "silence" or the running-space of a creative interval. Fair also to say that in the silence of the City of Light, and with artists of every category conducting experiments all around him, Bearden began to figure out what it would mean to find a new sense of direction, to be "more than oneself."

In Paris, Bearden liked to hang on rue Jules-Chaplain at Chez Honey, the club his friend, the painter Herbert Gentry, had bought and named for his wife, the singer Honey Johnson. Art gallery-salon by day and watering hole by night, Chez Honey gathered an international party of artistic movers and shakers—club regulars included Jean-Paul Sartre, Orson Welles, Juliette Gréco, Sam Middleton, Boris Vian, Duke Ellington, Sidney Bechet, Roy Eldridge, Kenny Clarke, Zoot Sims, and Don Byas. Gentry's claim that "modern jazz was born in my place in Paris" overblows the case; but Chez Honey was a club where musicians and other artists partied and

jammed with and against one another, encouraging experimentation beyond boundaries—hearing other languages as well as their own.[66]

A conceptual artist who said he liked to let his images float from deep within his mind, Gentry was one of the first painters, Bearden said, to introduce "the American concept of gesture, free invention and the vivid dissonances of color" then known in Paris as "'the school of the Pacific' and in this country [the U.S.] of course as 'Abstract Expressionism.'"[67] "All these traits," Bearden continued, "are attributes of jazz."[68] In Paris, Bearden felt the strength of jazz's influence on contemporary painting far more in the work of Americans and other expat newcomers to that city than in the art of the French themselves. "A lot of these painters painted with jazz sounds filling their studios," Bearden told an interviewer. Certainly this was true of the brilliant African American painter Beauford Delaney. What must it have meant to Bearden, back in New York after splitting Paris—actively in search of ways to introduce color into

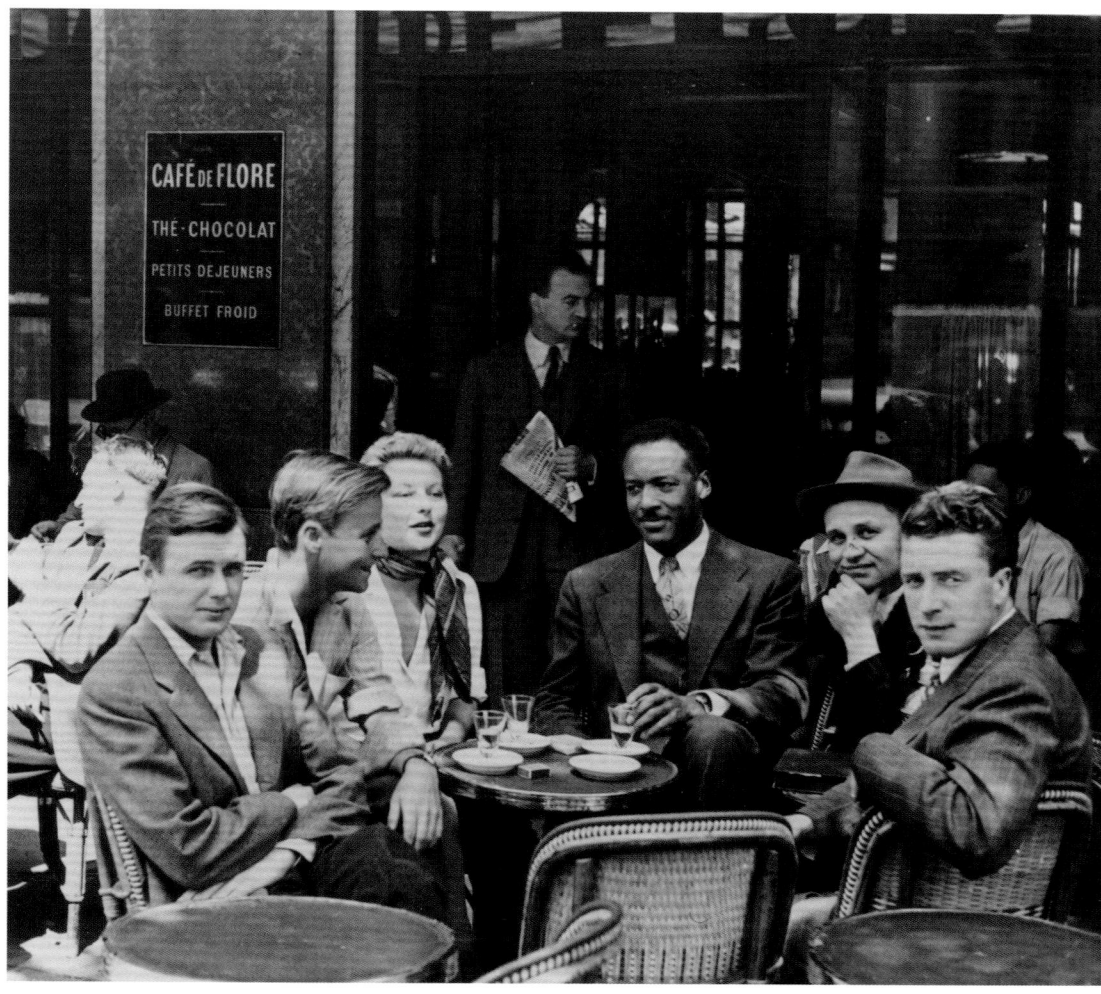

Romare Bearden (second from right) and a group of friends at a café in Paris, 1950. Photograph and Prints Division, Schomburg Center for Research in Black Culture, The New York Public Library

his work—to recall the thick strokes of color in Delaney's 1941 portrait of James Baldwin, for example, and his other boldly colored works of that era that were likewise vibrant enough to light entire rooms? Abstract Expressionism was "an indigenous American way of seeing," Bearden said. Black, brown, and beige American artists, in Paris and then back home, were exploring the U.S. cultural terrain not with images of cattle ranches and oil rigs but "through one of the most positive elements in American culture—its music." Something about the music had to do with color and motion. "In America," said Bearden, "it was the *speed* that was different from other countries, the speed, the dissonance, the movement, the traffic lights and everything: *Abstract Expressionism!*"[69] He and other Abstract Expressionists sought to represent these qualities of the American scene (at its best), Bearden says, by using "color dissonance: throwing, say, violet against orange, and the concept of improvisation, letting oneself go, acting on the canvas itself—in a word, *jazz*."[70]

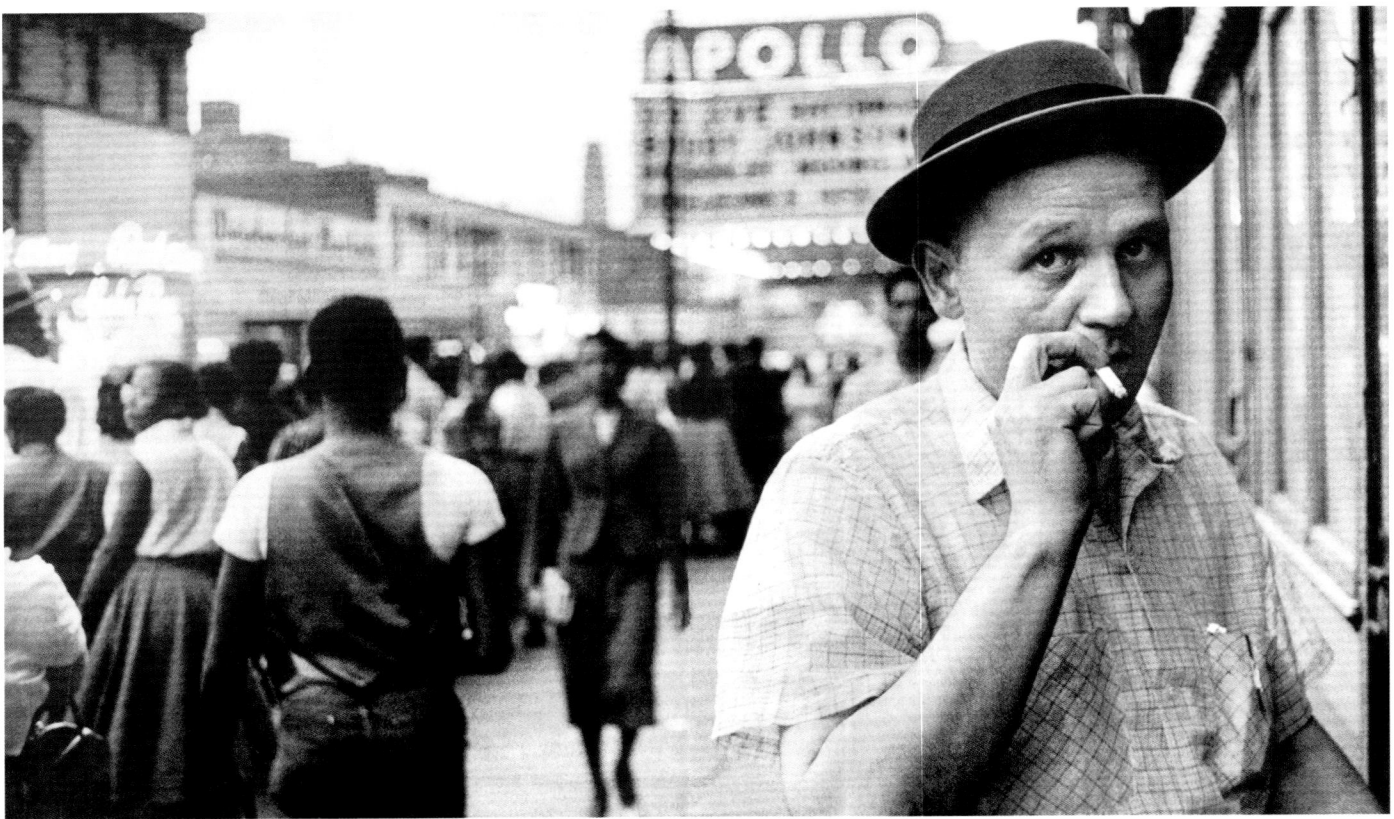

Sam Shaw. Romare Bearden, Harlem, New York City, 1952

RETURN TO NEW YORK: MUSIC VS. PAINTING

While it's a stretch to call Bearden a jazz composer, it is true that when the party was over (for him) in Paris, and he had to return to New York, he wondered how hard it could be to write a song that could bring a big enough payday to get him back to Europe. With this goal in mind, Bearden eventually sat in with musician friends at an upright piano in his Harlem studio, fitting together his lyrics and their tunes.[71] In the end, Bearden, whose journals showed he liked to experiment with writing poetry, was credited as the lyricist for about twenty published songs. One of these, "Seabreeze," was recorded by the singer (former jazz bandleader and trombonist) Billy Eckstine,

Bearden's Steel City homeboy, and then used as the theme song for Seagram's gin. The song caught on with other jazz artists, and was recorded by Dizzy Gillespie, Oscar Pettiford, Tito Puente, Yusef Lateef, and (in a twenty-first-century tribute to Bearden) Branford Marsalis.

Yet by the early 1950s, with close friends warning him that if he didn't get back on the case he'd never paint again, Bearden put aside these songwriting distractions as well as the persistent hope of returning to dreamland Paris, and buckled down to mos'-def painting. "Perhaps as a sign of the artistic ideas developing in Bearden's mind," writes art historian Tracy Fitzpatrick, "on the day he left France he'd 'spent the whole day buying paper. . . . All kinds of drawing

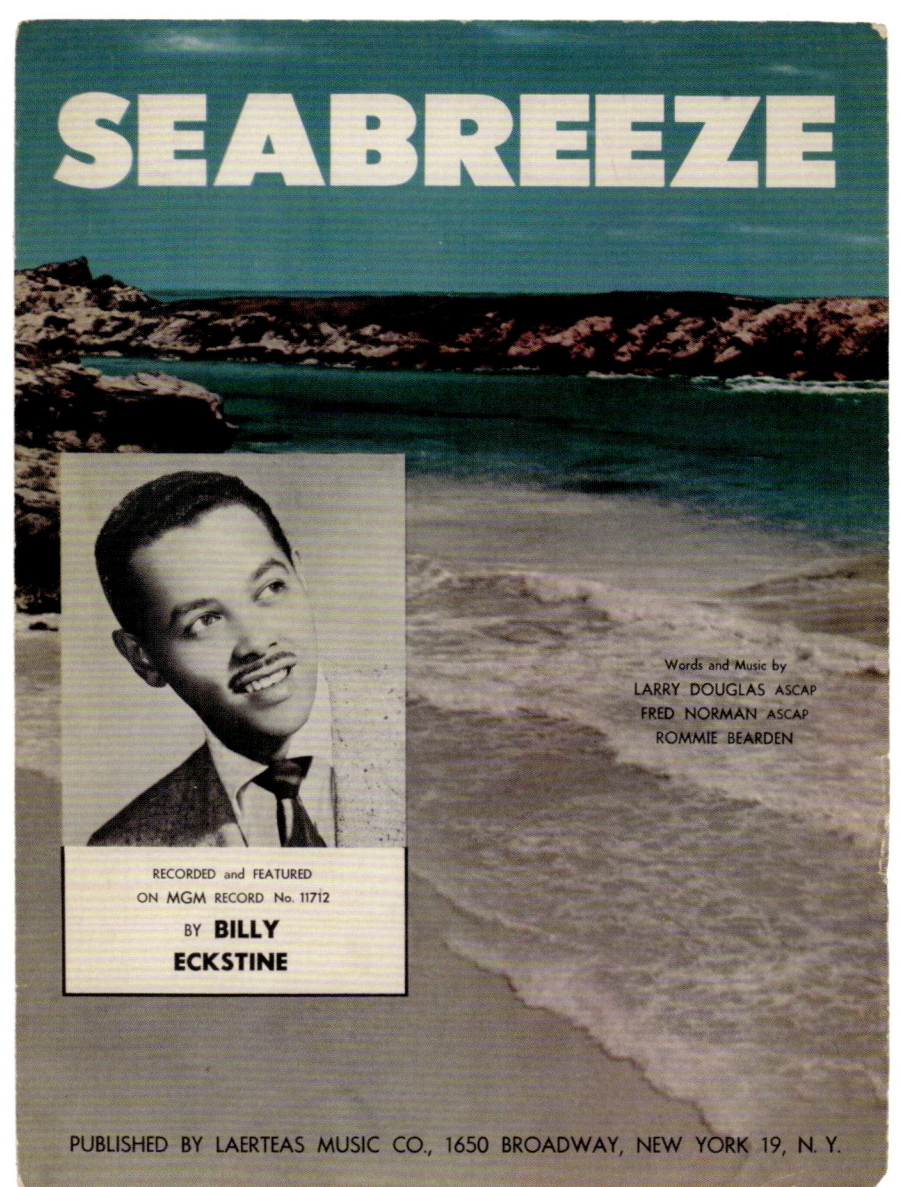

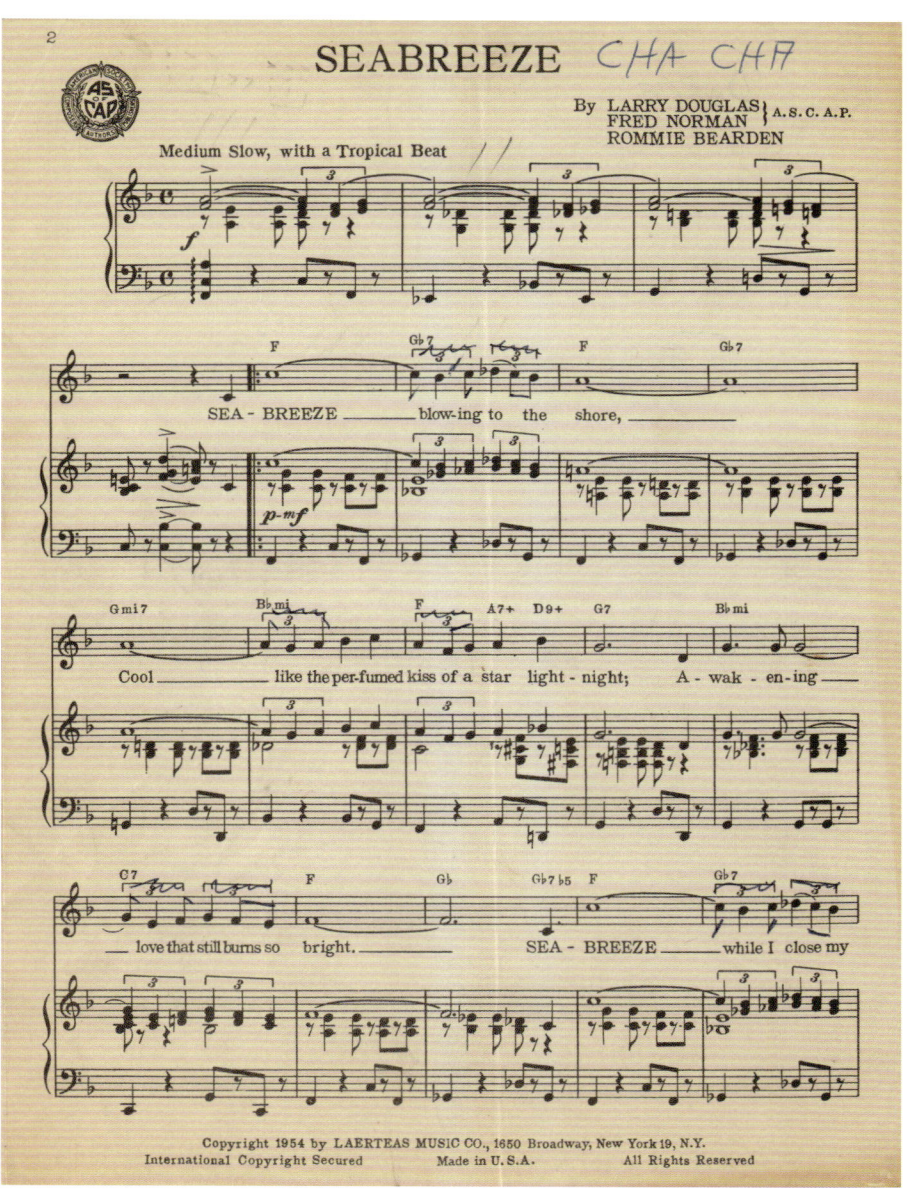

Sheet music, "Seabreeze," words and music by Larry Douglas, Fred Norman, Rommie [Romare] Bearden (1954). Romare Bearden Papers, The Wildenstein Plattner Institute, Inc.

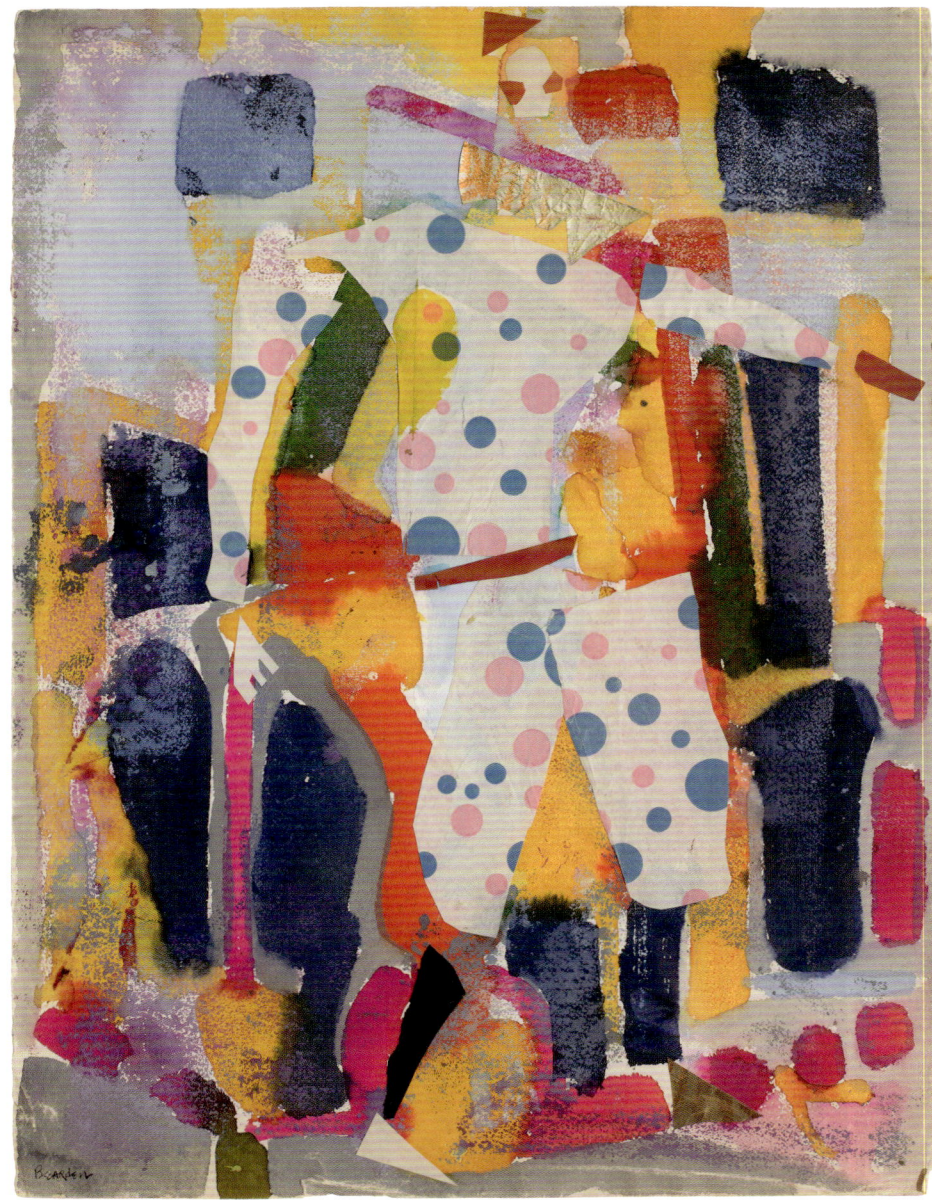

44

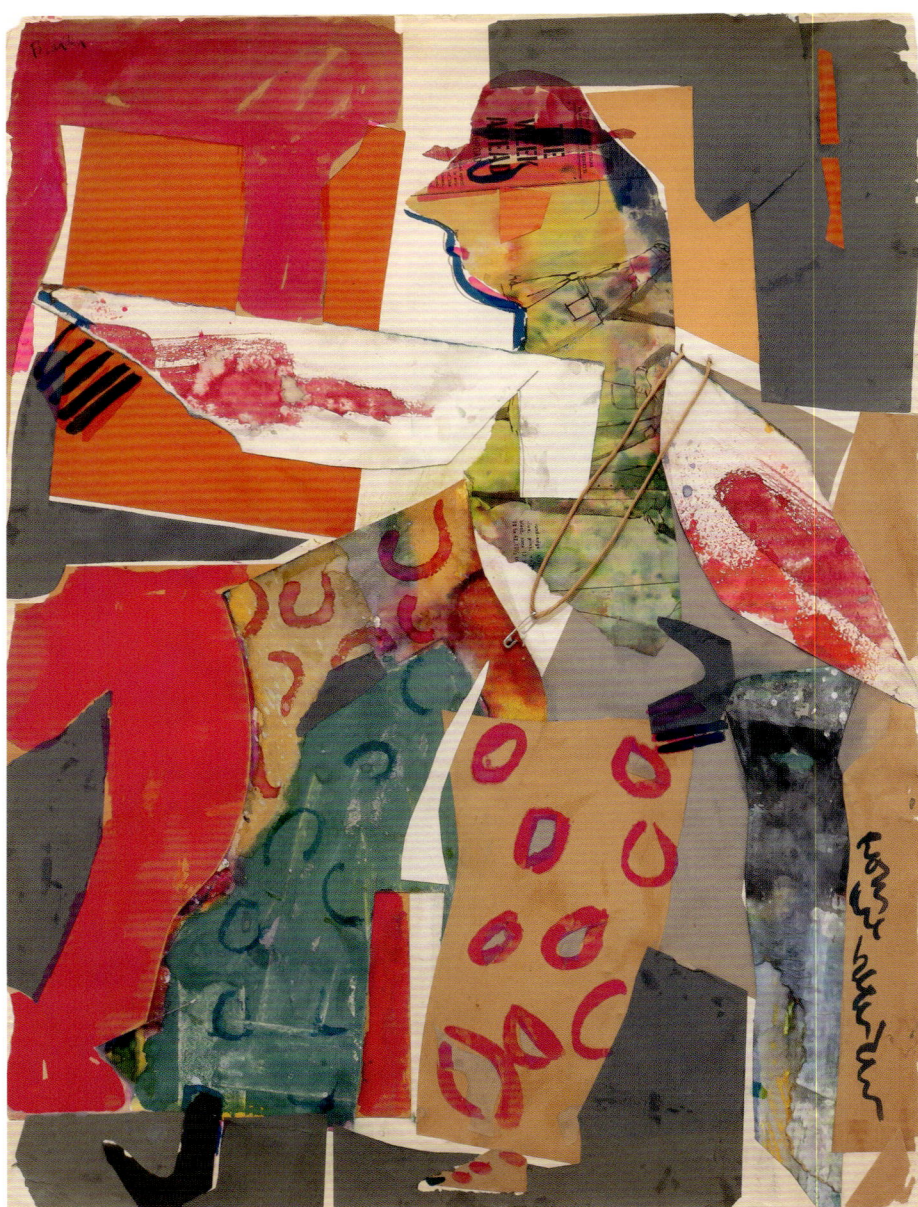

Untitled, ca. 1956. Mixed media and foil collage on paper. 26 × 20 3/16 in. Courtesy of the Nanette Bearden Trust and DC Moore Gallery, New York

Untitled, n.d. Mixed media with twine and safety pin on paper. 26 × 20 1/4 in. Courtesy of the Nanette Bearden Trust and DC Moore Gallery, New York

papers—rice papers, special sizes and surfaces, different colors,' as recalled by Bearden's friend Albert Murray."[72] Those multisize colored papers would provide Bearden with a bridge to his new artistic experiments in deliberate abstraction and colors that were more and more bold. "I'd avoided colors, I wasn't sure what to do with them," said Bearden. "But I always knew that when the colors came in they would walk around like big men!"[73]

STUART DAVIS & MR. WU

As noted, lessons learned from Stuart Davis in particular informed Bearden's back-from-Paris work. He had met the American painter in the early 1940s, as he was turning from the political cartooning of his college years and his subsequent social realism experiments. Davis emphasized color as an aspect of structure. Bearden:

> "[I] gradually got back to painting again. And when I did, I found I had very definite ideas about color. I began to just put color down in big marks and I found that using the color in this mosaiclike way destroyed the form . . . opened up the form. So my color work became then increasingly non-representational as I allowed this color to give itself free rein. And I felt by using these tracks of color up and down and across the canvas, that I learned a great deal about the color's action."[74]

Davis also emphasized color as part of his works' musicality. "Davis's paintings showed a way of getting right to the essence of what color could express about America, and its unique art form—jazz." "His art has that kind of quality," said Bearden. "The lettering—*jazz*."[75]

Also, as noted, Bearden found listening to Earl Hines's improvisations on the piano, as Davis advised, to be "very helpful to me in the transmutation of sound into colors and in the placement of objects in my paintings and collages. I could have studied this integration and spacing in Greek vase painting, among many examples, but with Earl Hines I ingested it within my own background. Jazz has shown me the ways of achieving artistic structures that are personal to me, but it also provides me continuing finger-snapping, head-shaking enjoyment of this unique, wonderful music."[76]

Chinese art is also part of Bearden's back-from-Paris story. After moving to Canal Street, by chance Bearden met a bookstore owner, Mr. Wu, an expert on the history of Chinese art, including calligraphy. Conversations with Wu extended Bearden's exploration of artistic "intervals"—in this case the spaces between the brushstrokes of each calligraphic character. Bearden was especially taken by the Chinese technique of an artwork's "open corner," a section, often in the upper right corner, left blank as an invitation to viewers to complete the work in their imagination—thus to participate in its meaning. Mr. Wu's lessons on aspects of perspective in Chinese painting were also quite significant for Bearden, who said, "The great [Chinese] landscapes usually use three perspectives: the lower part as if you were looking down upon it; the middle part as if you were looking at it straight on from the front; the mountains at the top as if you were looking upward at them." Here again the aesthetic of flattened space confirmed lessons from certain European moderns and from jazz: the flatted notes and egalitarian sense of the jazz band's ways of making art, with no one player or instrument always in the spotlight. Like jazz, the flatness and open spaces in Chinese art "allowed me to free myself," Bearden said.[77]

THE TURN TO COLLAGE

Because Bearden's collages are so strong, it is easy to forget that his prior jazz-inflected abstract works marked a vital phase in his artistic development toward collage, and that his abstract works are fantastically alluring in their own right. "Between 1952 and about 1963," writes Fitzpatrick, "Romare Bearden created a large body of abstract watercolors, oil paintings, and collages. Some titled, some not, they ranged in height from over seven feet to just under three inches. Exhibited with success at the time of their execution, these artworks are little known today, yet they directly inform the collages for which he is now best known."[78] Jazz is a bridge here. Consider *River Mist* (1962), for example, a work informed by Bearden's listening to Earl Hines records "over and over again," as he repeatedly said. The artist divides this work into three roughly equal sections—a trio or three-note chord/keyboard or waltz-beat presentation of color strips (cut and torn swatches of linen on canvas) framed as variations on one another, blue notes with abundant overtones. Here, one might say, is a funky version of Mondrian's clean-line geometrical works:[79] shapes of things to come as Bearden moves further into collage in living color and begins also to reintroduce the figure, often singing in a Harlem club or holding a jazz horn.

While Bearden had experimented with collage prior to leaving for Paris, it was on his return to New York that, along with abstractions in watercolor and oil, he began in earnest to work in collage. "In one early collage," says Fitzpatrick,

> he took a large sheet of the *New York Times*—a page about gardening dated January 15, 1956—glued it to a sheet of heavy paper, and then tore parts of it away. The process is formally known as *déchirage*, and refers to distressing the paper by tearing or peeling it away once it has dried after gluing. On top of the newsprint, Bearden pasted

harlequin figures, a common theme for him at this time, created from collaged cut-and-torn colored papers as well as paint. The harlequin motif may have been inspired by Picasso; there were numerous Picasso exhibitions in 1956 in celebration of the artist's seventy-fifth birthday.[80]

Then again, laughing to keep from crying and wearing "the mask that grins and lies" while the world "dreams otherwise"[81] are longstanding tropes (and strategies) in Black America. "The tears of a clown," as Smokey Robinson put it.[82]

These little-known harlequin collages by Bearden also strike me as having a jazz aspect: in their free-style playfulness (their "serious" or "divine" playfulness, Bearden liked to say), their sheer let's-have-a-party joyousness of spirit. No wonder such masked figures of fun (and of the reversal of official power relations) reemerge in Bearden's *Paris Blues/Jazz* collage *Jazz with Armstrong* (1981). Their upside-down carnival world is suggested as well in *Cirque d'Hiver* (1981), also from that series—one of several Beardens recalling Matisse's folio of collages titled *Jazz* (1947). (Here I second Albert Murray's assertion that jazz is fundamentally a comic form of expression—the comedy sometimes feigned, sometimes hiding the real tragedy—a goodtime music designed for settings where listeners come to flirt, dance, and chase the blues away.[83])

Note again that Matisse was immensely important to Bearden, who owned multiple copies of *Jazz*, and with them a long row of books about the major French modernist. While Matisse's *Jazz* is not explicitly about the music, its playfully rhythmical imagery and freshly juxtaposed colors, its dancing figures, big-tent performance scenes, and tilted lettering all confirm the book title's announcement that the subject here is jazz. Perhaps above all it is the book's spirit of fresh, ongoing improvisation, suggested by elements affixed one way that might have been affixed differently (the originals, with

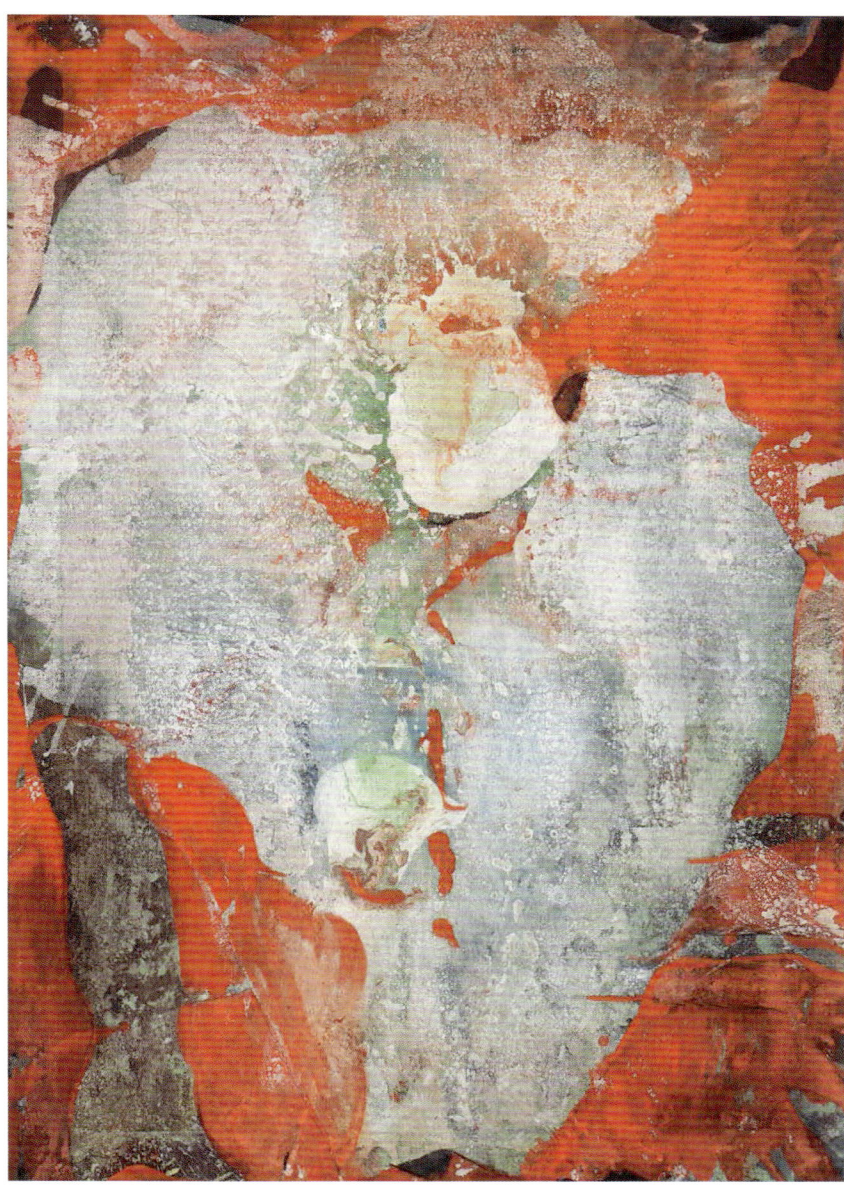

The Silent Valley of Sunrise, 1959. Oil and casein on canvas. 58⅛ × 42 in. Museum of Modern Art, NY, Given anonymously

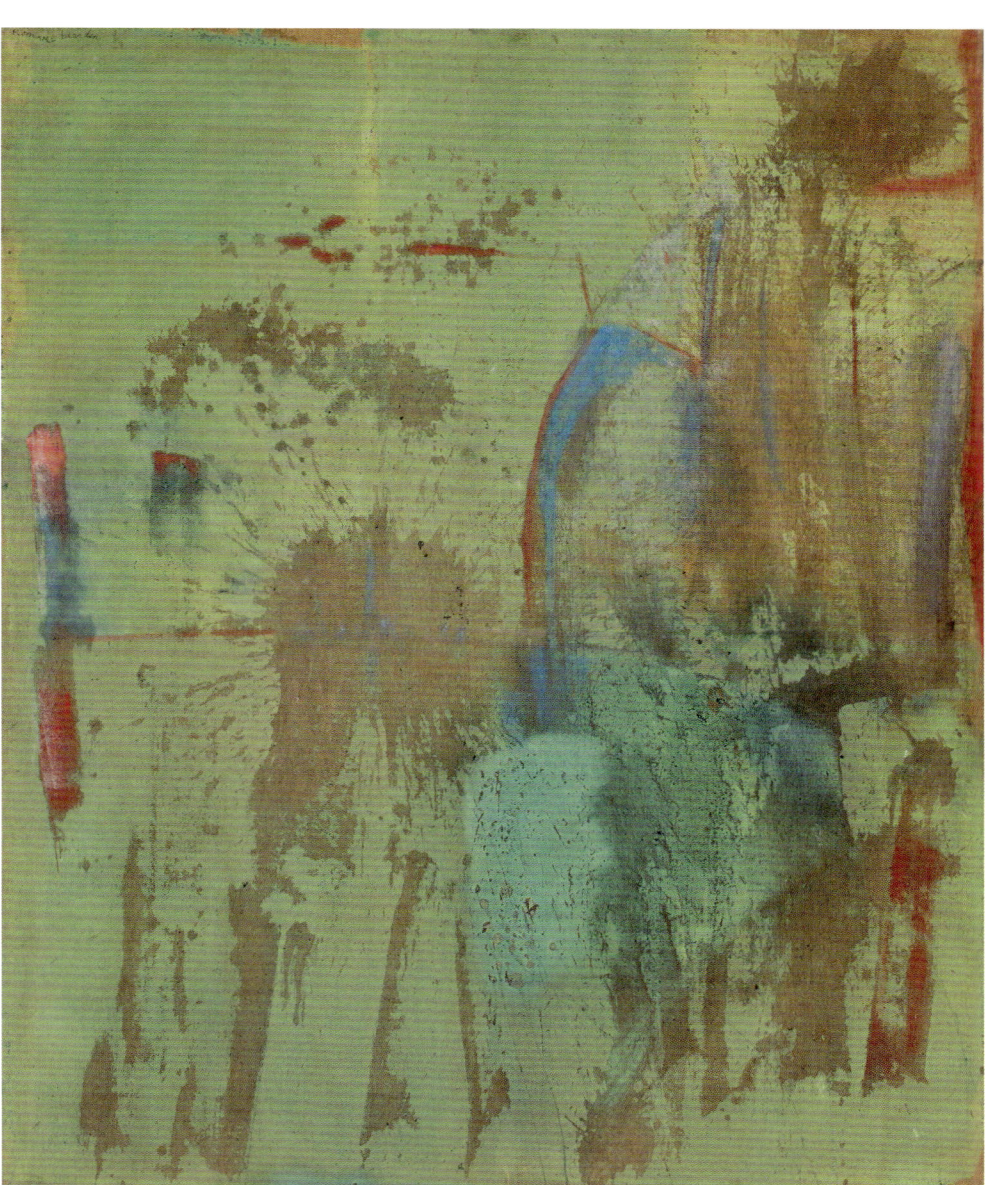

Green Torches Welcome New Ghosts, 1961. Oil on canvas. 60 × 50 in. Courtesy of the Nanette Bearden Trust and DC Moore Gallery, New York

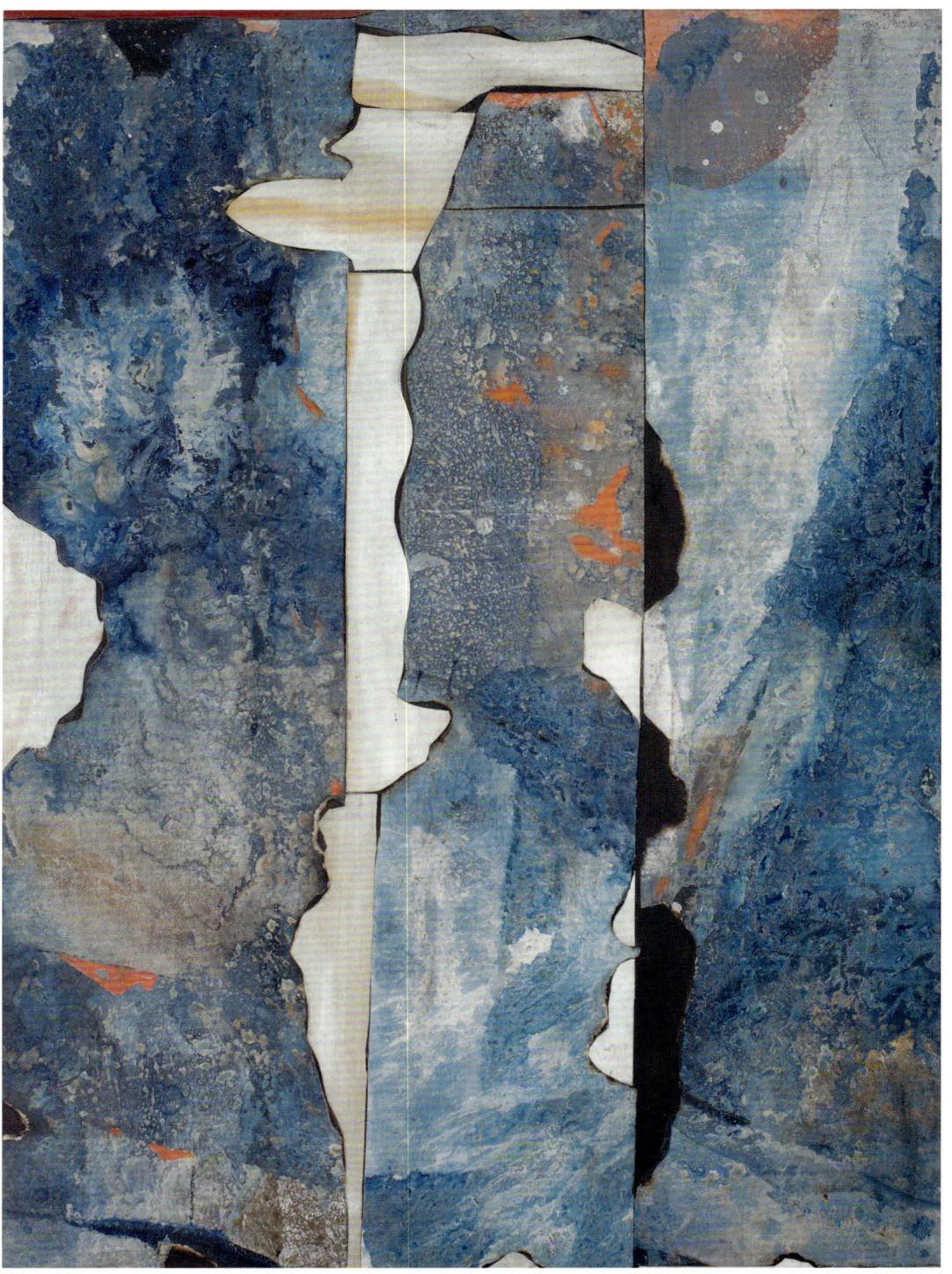

River Mist, 1962. Oil on unprimed linen, and oil, casein, and colored pencil on canvas; cut, torn, and mounted on painted board. 54 ¼ × 40 ⅞ in. Neuberger Museum of Art, Purchase College, State University of New York

their pinholes, suggest experiments in one direction and then another). For Bearden, as for Matisse, the music's shapes, colors, and silences suggested worlds to be created in cutting sessions, so to speak, where less is almost invariably more. "Seven notes, with slight modifications, suffice to write any score," said Matisse. "Why is it not the same for the visual arts?"[84]

SPIRAL

In the history of Bearden as a jazz collagist and painter, the Spiral collective stands out for exemplifying the synergies of the Harlem Renaissance. Of course Spiral is very much an organization of the 1960s, but it also offers dynamic proof that the Harlem Renaissance did not end in 1929 or 1930, as many argue, but continued through the long twentieth century into our own. Spiral was one of the dynamic fulfillments of the Renaissance's ongoing "sophisticated moment," when Black Americans worked hardest to earn positions of leadership across many categories—in the case of Spiral as leaders in the field of visual art.

A month before the 1963 March on Washington for civil rights, Bearden helped convene Spiral as a group of Black artists in his Canal Street apartment, in Lower Manhattan. He proposed the session "for the purpose," as noted in his journal, "of discussing the commitment of the Negro artist in the present struggle for civil liberties, and as a discussion group to consider common aesthetic problems."[85] When the group was slated to have its first show, Bearden apparently suggested they make a large collaborative work—a collage. He provided a collection of cutout materials, mostly photographs, but the other members, invited to do likewise, lost interest. Cultural scholar Brent Hayes Edwards comments: "I am less concerned with the fact that the collaboration was aborted than with the way that collage for Bearden starts in collaboration—not just

as an improvisational mode of composition, not just as an engagement with the documentary elements of photography, but also as an impulse to work together. Even later, Bearden would sign one of his earliest collages 'Spiral Group.'"[86]

Bearden's 1963 suggestion that the Spiral group work jointly on pictures for an exhibition represented a step into an aesthetic/political realm that was new and fateful for him. Can we say that he proposed forming a band and making art as if they were the Duke Ellington Orchestra? And that when the idea of a literal band of artists composing pieces as a group did not crystallize, Bearden opted to continue composing such improvised pictures on his own? (After the big band era, Charlie Parker and others, now in quartets and other small combos, continued playing as if fifteen or more players were still backing them. Some of this accounts for the speed and density of the solo work of Parker and Gillespie—and of Mary Lou Williams, who played the piano as if it were a full band.) "Collage is almost by definition an improvisational form," writes Myron Schwartzman.[87] The artist gathers bits and pieces from disparate sources and assembles them into a coherent whole, as if they (the artist working with other artists) were Count Basie or Art Blakey. "I paint out of the tradition of the blues," said Bearden. "You start a theme, and you call and recall."[88]

ANOTHER WORD ON BEARDEN'S JAZZLIKE PROCESS

On the subject of his jazzlike process of working, Bearden has also famously said:

You have to begin somewhere. So you put something down. Then you put something else with it, and then you see how that works, and maybe you try something else and so on, and the picture grows in that way. . . . Once you get going, all sorts of things begin to open up. Sometimes something just seems to fall into place, like the piano keys that every now and then just seem to be right where your fingers happen to come down. But there are also all those times you have to keep trying something over and over and then when you finally get it right you wonder what took you so long.[89]

In a television appearance with Herb Gentry, we are made privy to this jazzlike process—or, more accurately, to a performance of it. With Basie's rhythm section driving Johnny Griffin on sax and Milt Jackson on vibes—all sounding from an old-school boom box from the back of their studio—Gentry and Bearden bounce on their feet as they start to paint broad lines of color on white rectangular paper, no subject or theme evidently prearranged. As they get going, Bearden sees "something like African sculpture," and begins to outline an African mask and an imposing female figure. "You take it," says Gentry, as if on the bandstand as Bearden continues, solo. "We didn't paint this," says Gentry, as they finish up. "*We danced it!*"[90]

The *New Yorker* writer Calvin Tomkins asked Bearden about his processes of building a collage: *When working on a very large piece, where do you begin?* "Say the ratio of the picture is four by five," replied the artist:

I start by dividing the surface into rectangles, usually having some proportion. I believe that the art of painting is that art of putting something over something else. . . . By shifting the planes you can get volume and still keep the flat surface. But you must keep the relationships. Then, as things go down in this ratio, it gives me some ideas of what might happen in the picture. What I do first is to unify the painting in this way. . . .

This rectangular device has advantages and disadvantages. It makes for a very classical method. But it isn't baroque and—moving. When I did the jazz series, I had to modify this a bit in a few things, to get that other thing, the sense of movement.[91]

On another occasion, Bearden used musical language to advise a young art student: "You must become a blues singer," he said, "only you sing on the canvas. You improvise—you find the rhythm and catch it good, and structure as you go along—then the song is you."[92]

Bearden's landmark series *Projections* (1964), that first release of his collages inspired by the Spiral encounter, was jazzlike in its modes of construction, and featured a few works depicting people and places of jazz culture, including *Jazz: (N.Y.) Savoy–1930's* and *Jazz: (Chicago) Grand Terrace–1930's*. As the idea of working as an improvising composer using cutouts to play the tilted-rectangle canvas continued to take shape in his mind, Bearden cut, pasted, and painted more and more works with explicitly named jazz themes.[93] Drawing with his scissors, he gathered and sometimes painted papers and pictures and found objects (one of the *Paris Blues/Jazz* collages has a French Metro ticket pasted on) and put them over boards and canvases and over one another. That's what art is, he said: "Putting something over something else."

It's important to note here that Bearden routinely used photography in his creative process, almost from the very beginning. Too shy, he said, to sit in museums and copy artworks whose structure he admired, he had favorite works photographed and blown up so he could study them at home. Then came the *Projections* works, created by photographing collages made from a mix of photographs trimmed from newspapers and magazines along with other materials. Bearden explained:

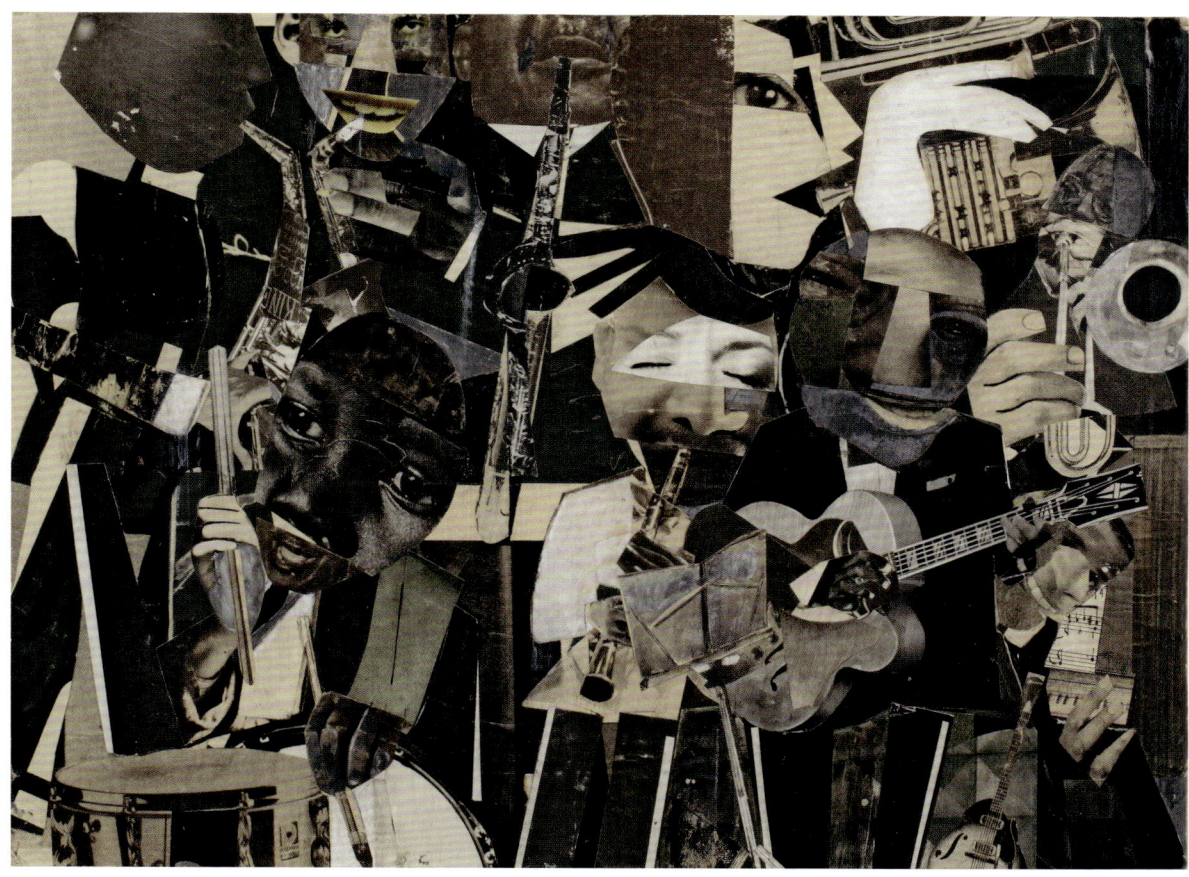

Jazz 1930s—The Savoy, 1964. Collage of various papers with paint on board. 10¼ × 15 in. Nelson-Atkins Museum of Art, Kansas City, MO

I don't use photographs the way many people suppose. Many of my faces and hands are made from mosaics. I might use the photograph of pavement to form a face; a picture of grass for hair and another photograph of marble for the eyes. These constructs of figures and objects must fit and interact evenly and exactly on the boards. It took a great deal of study and several years of experimentation with glues and cutting devices to prevent the boards from warping. I no longer begin with the idea of what I'm going to compose. The interaction of huge rectangles of color overlaid on the board suggest the idea.[94]

As another example of this freed-up approach, in May 1986, Bearden and jazz musician Jackie McLean jointly performed "Sound Collages and Visual Improvisations" at the Wadsworth Atheneum in Hartford, Connecticut. In a tour-de-force presentation, Bearden painted while McLean played percussion, piano, and alto sax. The performance was followed by a conversation between the two men where Bearden spoke of his brief time writing songs and of his efforts to capture the sound-of-surprise improvised play of the music in his work as a visual artist.

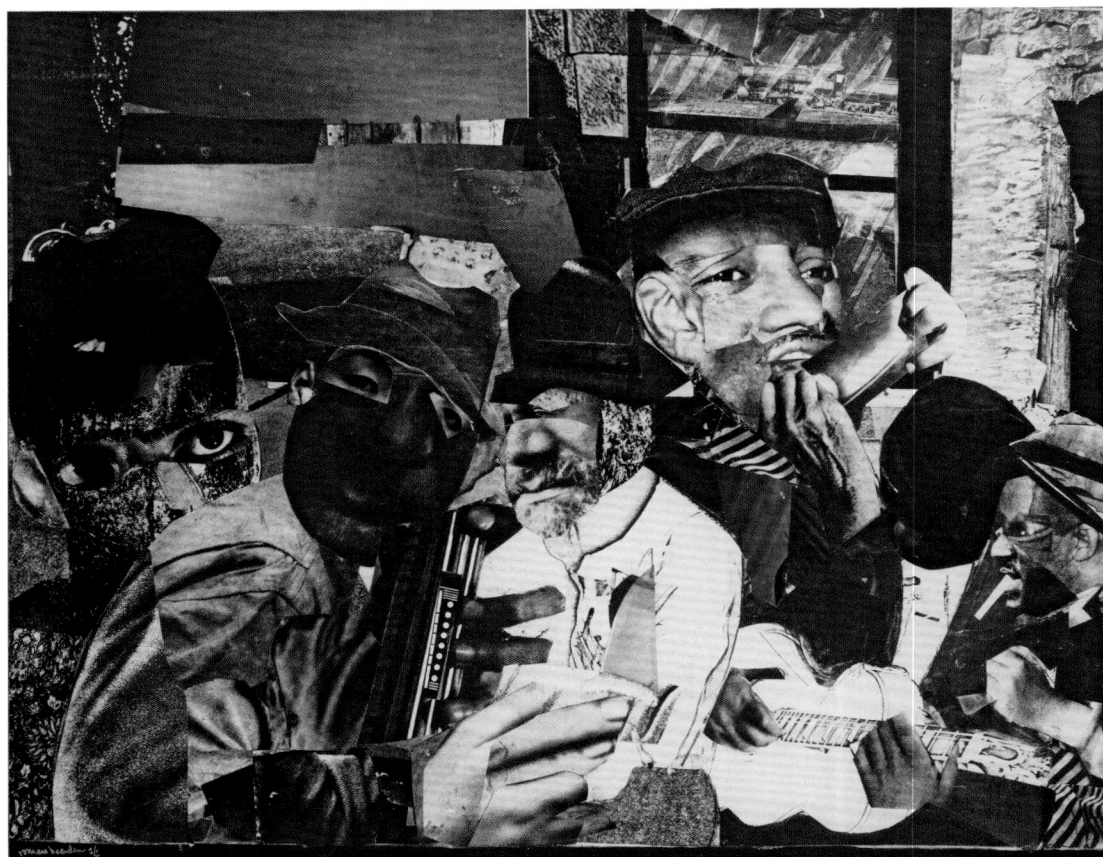

Train Whistle Blues No. 1, 1964. Gelatin silver print (photostat) mounted on fiberboard. 29 × 37 ½ in.
Museum of Modern Art, NY, Acquired through the generosity of Agnes Gund

JAZZ MASTERWORKS

During the period when Bearden created his visual jazz masterworks, certain series stand out: *Of the Blues* (first and second "choruses," comprising two gallery exhibitions) in 1975; *Romare Bearden: Jazz* in 1980; and the landmark autobiographical *Profile* paintings (1979, 1981), where music and musicians tell much of the story of Bearden's development as an artist. In these jazz/blues shows, one after the other, what became increasingly clear is that Bearden was formulating a specific vocabulary of images, some first seen in the *Projections* series: musicians, bathing women, trains,

African masked figures, birds. He would reshuffle and present these again and again in new works, like a novelist whose favorite characters show up repeatedly in different contexts and stages of life. Bearden told an interviewer, "[My] same characters may reappear in different pictures, like the Nick Adams character in those stories of Hemingway's."[95] (Note that Bearden's friend Albert Murray called Hemingway a "blues writer" whose heroes demonstrate the fundamental quality of readiness to improvise in all circumstances with personal flexibility and blue-steel toughness.[96]) We can compare Bearden's improvisatory remixing process to Dexter Gordon's or Ella Fitzgerald's, both of whom could turn

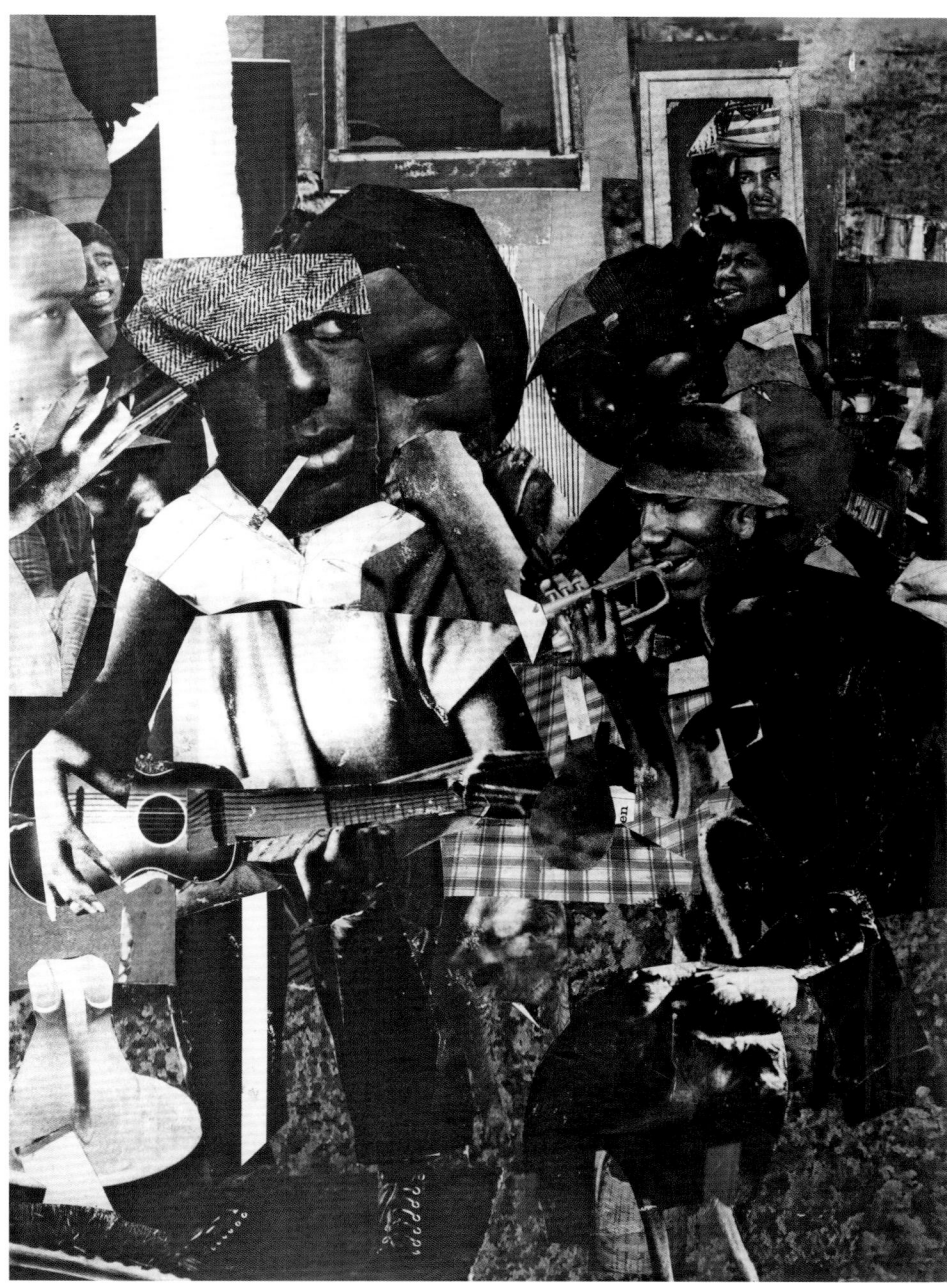

Train Whistle Blues No. 2, 1964. Gelatin silver print (photostat) mounted on fiberboard. 39 × 29 ¼ in. Courtesy of the Nanette Bearden Trust and DC Moore Gallery, New York

certain favorite phrases in freshly inventive ways with each performance of the same song—or who'd quote one song (perhaps now re-composed) inside another. Or compare the jazz painter to a bandleader/arranger/composer assigning solos to players whose sounds and styles of playing work in multiple contexts. Anyone doubting Bearden's improvisational use and reuse of characters and images is invited to view the Bearden files at the Library of Congress, where a large collection of his mix-and-match cutout papers survives. What an exhibition just these colored puzzle pieces would make—paralleling a recent show in Paris of cutouts by that other master collage improviser (and, as noted, one of Bearden's key models), Henri Matisse.

With remixing core vocabulary in mind, look at *Mysteries* (also called *The Train*), with its portrayal of blues women and girls. According to Bearden scholar Camara Holloway, "'Mysteries' was made as a collage in 1964, with some Projections [photos of the original collage, now blown up or *projected*] also created that year. In 1974, he used photos of that original 1964 collage to assemble a new collage—this time with color added—now called 'The Train'. Then he used the new collage to make 12 prints called *The 12 Trains series*."[97] One by one, Bearden printed these twelve identical images, first in one color and then another, including one in sun-bright yellows, another in soft rainbow pastels, the next in grays so dark that at first glance you could not see the forms or figures: *The Train* by day, *The Train* at night, The train, which may be the single most resonant symbol in this artist's created world, usually runs North, as Bearden's family had done, following promises of greater freedom. His cutout, drawn, and painted locomotives, typically flying in the background, may signal the time of day—as some of his train-work titles indicate. Some hint at a certain uneasiness—"a mind to ramble" or "to make my getaway"—as blues ballads often signify. Many of these paintings

53

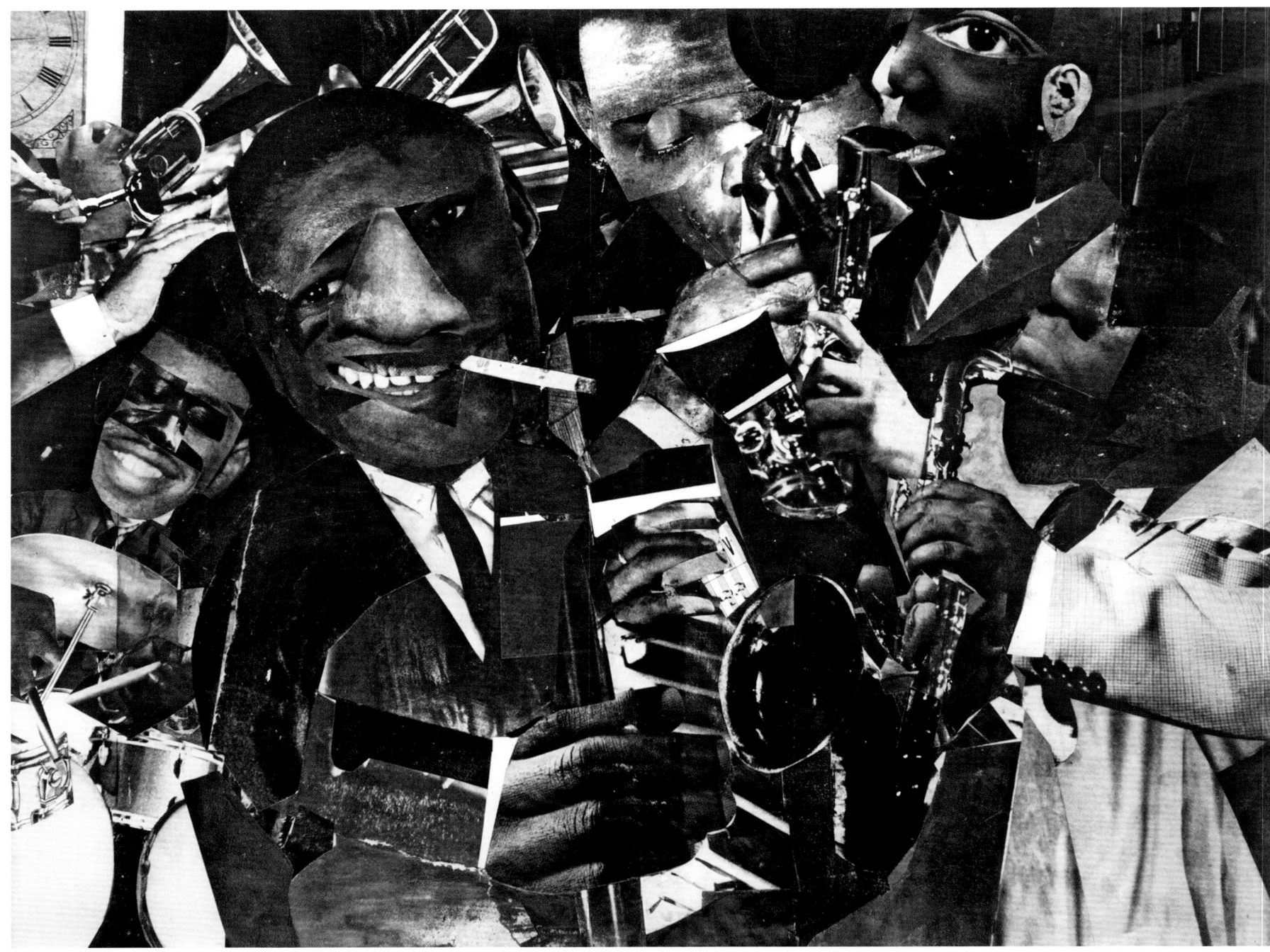

Jazz: (Chicago) Grand Terrace—1930's, 1964. Gelatin silver print (photostat) mounted on fiberboard. 34 ⅞ × 47 in. Private Collection

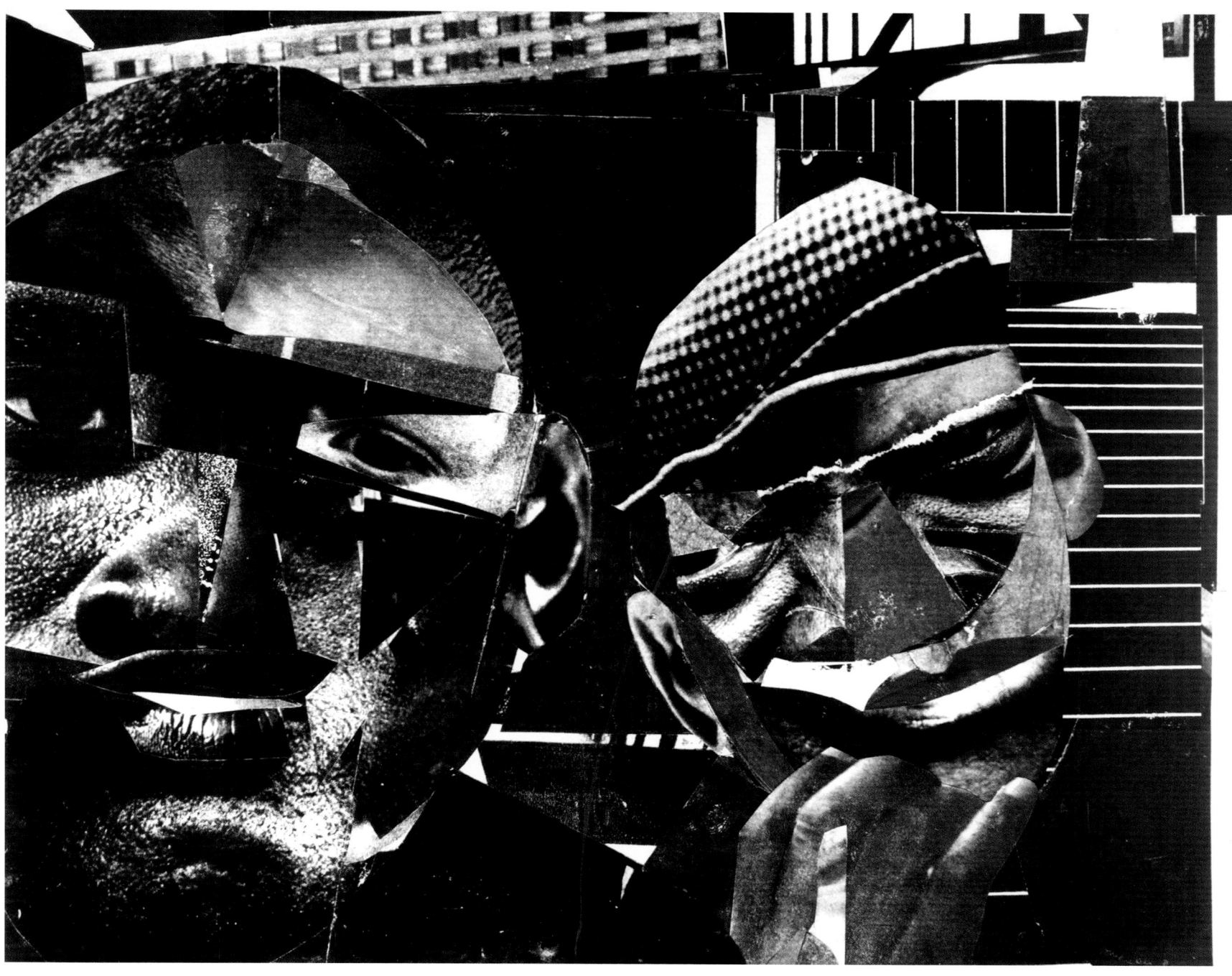

Pittsburgh Memory, 1964. Gelatin silver print (photostat) mounted on fiberboard. 27 ¼ × 35 ½ in. Tate Americas Foundation

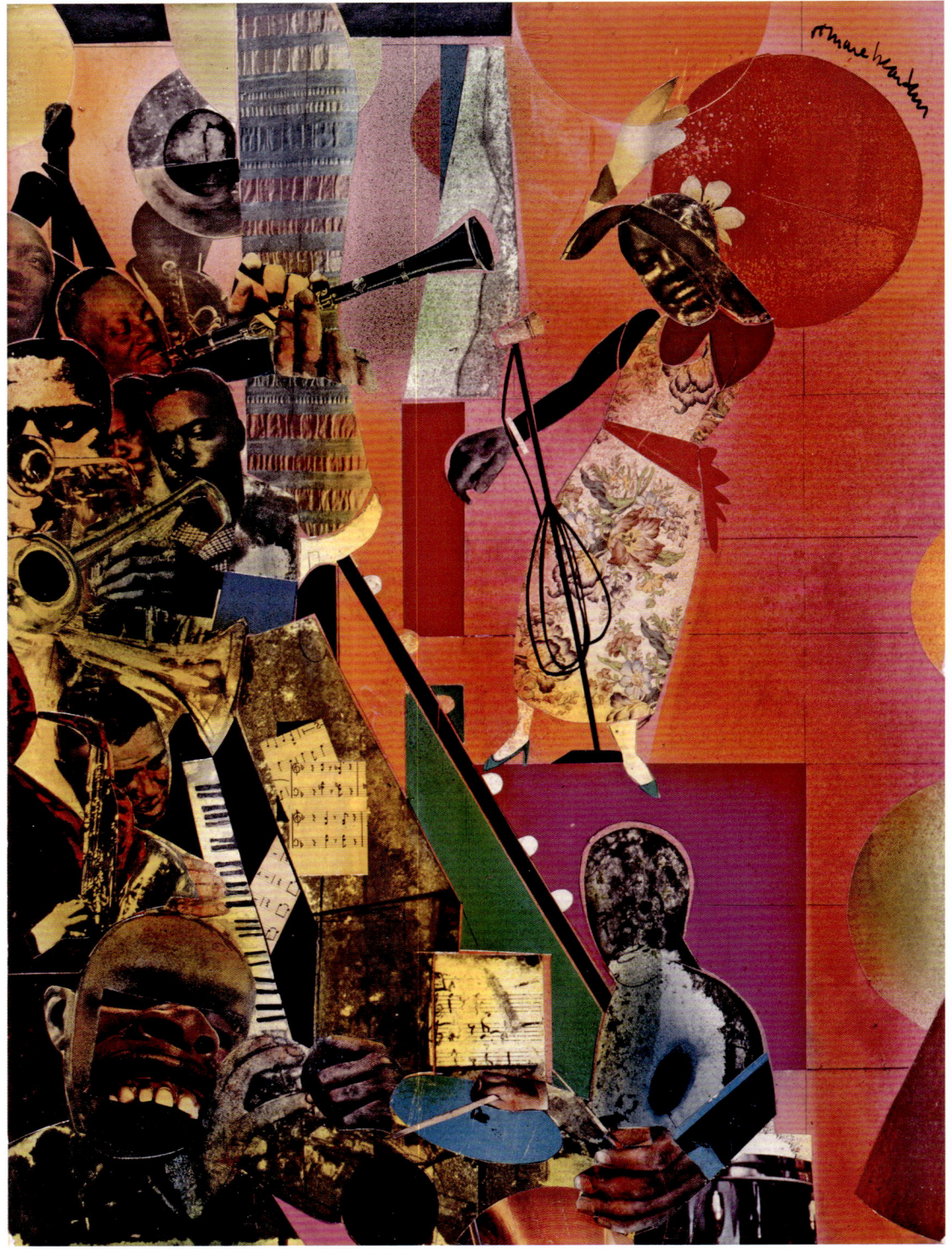

The Blues, 1975. Collage of various papers, mixed media on fiberboard. 24 × 18 in. Collection of the Honolulu Museum of Art, HI, Gift of Geraldine P. Clark, 1977 (4451.1)

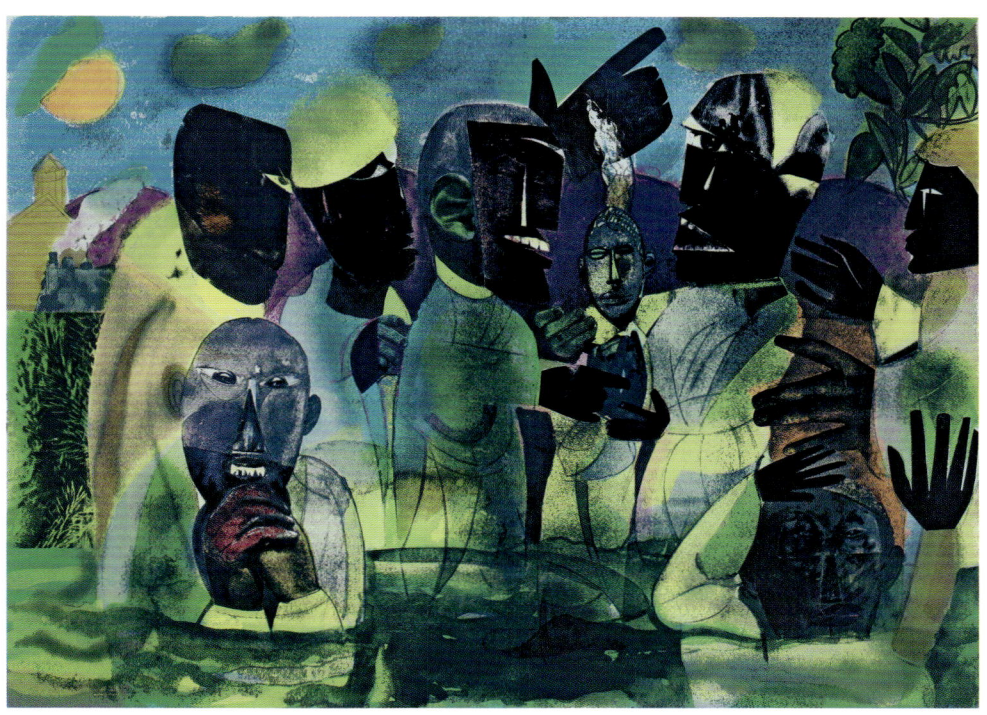

The Baptism, 1975. Screenprint on paper. 32 × 45 in. Edition of 50. Courtesy of DC Moore Gallery, New York

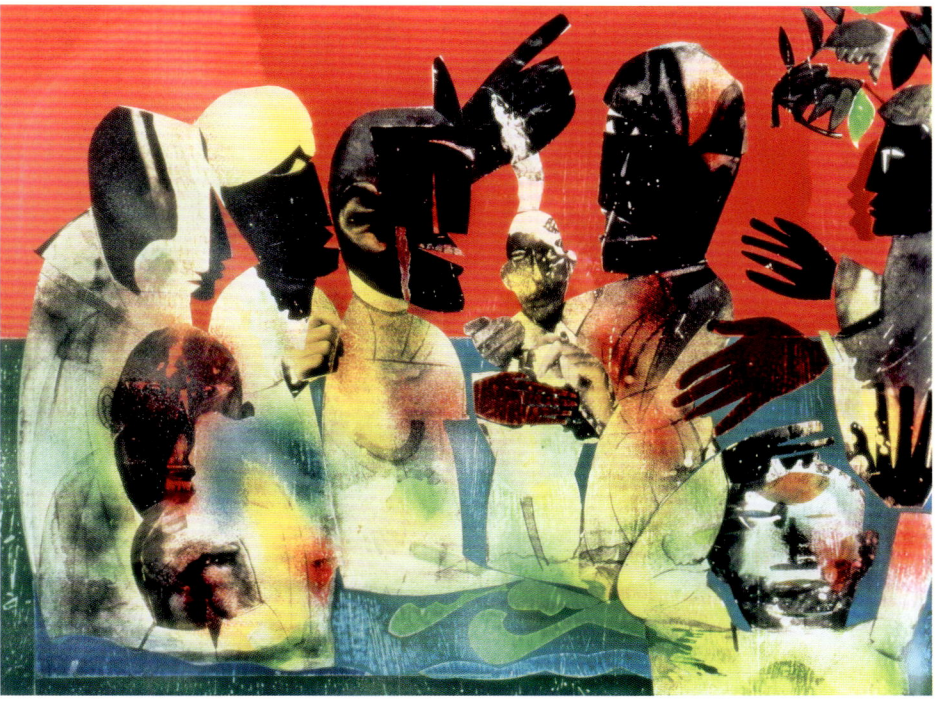

Of the Blues: Carolina Shout, 1974. Collage of various papers, mixed media on fiberboard. 37 ½ × 51 in. Mint Museum of Art, Charlotte, NC, Museum Purchase: National Endowment for the Arts Matching Fund and the Charlotte Debutante Club Fund

imply the joy of movement itself, the irresistible pull of kinesis: the pleasure of finding oneself most at home on the road or flying on a dance floor, free as a bird.

Bearden's practice of remixing images recalls Billie Holiday's telling a reviewer, "I never sing the same song the same way twice—tonight it's a little brighter, tomorrow it's a little slower."[98] Holiday could turn a joyous love song like "I Thought About You" into pure romantic fun, and then the next set into a bitter dirge or accusation. Carmen McRae, perhaps her best student ever and a very great singer in her own right, said that a song's melody as written meant little to Holiday; she could turn "that fella" around anytime.[99] What McRae (and Holiday) cared about were good lyrics. But if the words got in the way she could parody them or otherwise alter their meaning; or she could drop them altogether, scat them

to smithereens, her voice as horn or spirit figure speaking in tongues, depending on her feeling about them, night by night.

Calvin Tomkins was fortunate to visit Bearden just as he had completed a new work, created for the artist's first one-man show in Paris in May 1975. According to Tomkins's rough notes to himself,

Before starting . . . he got together a lot of raw material, which he unrolled. Blowups of older paintings, from which he may cut a whole face, an eye, etc. . . . [He was] using elements cut from magazines, elements cut from photostatic blowups of former Bearden paintings, a scrap of red and white checked cotton fabric, and a good deal of painting. . . . He doesn't have any specific ideas for paintings in mind at this stage, but knows he can use such and such images. [He may start with] an old painting of a cabin [that now he] reproduced in black white, reversed—[a] woman holding a candle [to convey a] quality of starkness he likes.[100]

The artist also repeatedly told interviewers that it became important to him not to "close down" a painting too quickly—instead, to leave it open to new possibilities for improv. He did not try to finish a work at the end of a work session; instead he'd leave himself a place to start the next day, at least one corner open as an invitation. Finally, he said, he learned not to try too hard to finish a painting but instead to let it go, to "relinquish" it.[101]

On this subject of Bearden's creative processes and moves between one format and the other, take *The Baptism* (1973). Here is another canonical Bearden work first created as a collage, this one later transformed into a screenprint washed in shades of watery blues and seaweed greens, in keeping with its first subject of religious cleansing and renewal. Then (perhaps discovering the work's double or layered meaning as he progressed) he used the same images to create a new collage, *Carolina Shout* (1974). With the original collage's pictures of riverside immersion and religiously ecstatic upraised hands still in place, the new title directed the viewer's attention to the Deep South, specifically to the Carolinas (and his birthplace, Charlotte), and to Black church shouts of religious possession and revelation. But because the title *Carolina Shout* is borrowed from the most famous composition by Harlem stride pianist James P. Johnson, now these holy images are associated with Deep South juke joints, Harlem rent parties, and other spots of loud party people. Of course, Bearden would also be aware of the "shout" as a dance-and-music form brought North by Afro-immigrants from the South (including from the Global South) and performed in a range of settings, private and public, sacred, secular, and borderline.[102] "The Northern towns had a hold-over of the old Southern customs," recalled James P. "I'd wake up as a child and hear an old-fashioned ring-shout going on downstairs. Somebody would be playing a guitar or Jew's harp or maybe a mandolin, and the dancing went to 'The Spider and the Bed-Bug Had a Good Time' or 'Susie.'"[103] Here it's also significant that Johnson's "Carolina Shout" is a famously complicated piece to play, a "finger-buster," in the lingo of the 1920s, and test piece for those wishing to impress Harlem's elite ragtime piano "gladiators."

The idea of jazz as antagonistic, or competitive, as well as collaborative is key to Bearden's work. An example is the collage *Sitting In at Baron's* (1980), from the *Profile* series, in which a man sits at an upright, playing and looking out at us (the audience). The caption reads: "When you sat down at the keyboard you knew very well you would play only so long as you kept Willie the Lion Smith, J. P. Johnson, Lucky Roberts and Fats Waller interested in what you were doing." This word-and-picture combination is especially significant for its reference to Baron's, the predecessor, in the 1910s and 1920s, of Minton's in Harlem, where piano virtuosi showcased styles eventually called "Eastern ragtime" or "Harlem stride." The four named in *Sitting In* were among the most famously demanding house pianists at Baron's, where the young Duke Ellington jammed with and against them. These clubs were "safe spaces" of a very particular sort—safe for high-speed, risk-ready artists forever in training who came to play hard and work hard; safe for young aspirants to "sit in," but only until their mentors decided they were done.

Such competitive scenes may have suggested to Bearden a world where he also was testing himself against the great painters of his time (of *all* time?), the soulful "finger-busters" of the canvas. Would he have been able to keep Picasso and Matisse and Benin's master carvers interested in what he was doing?

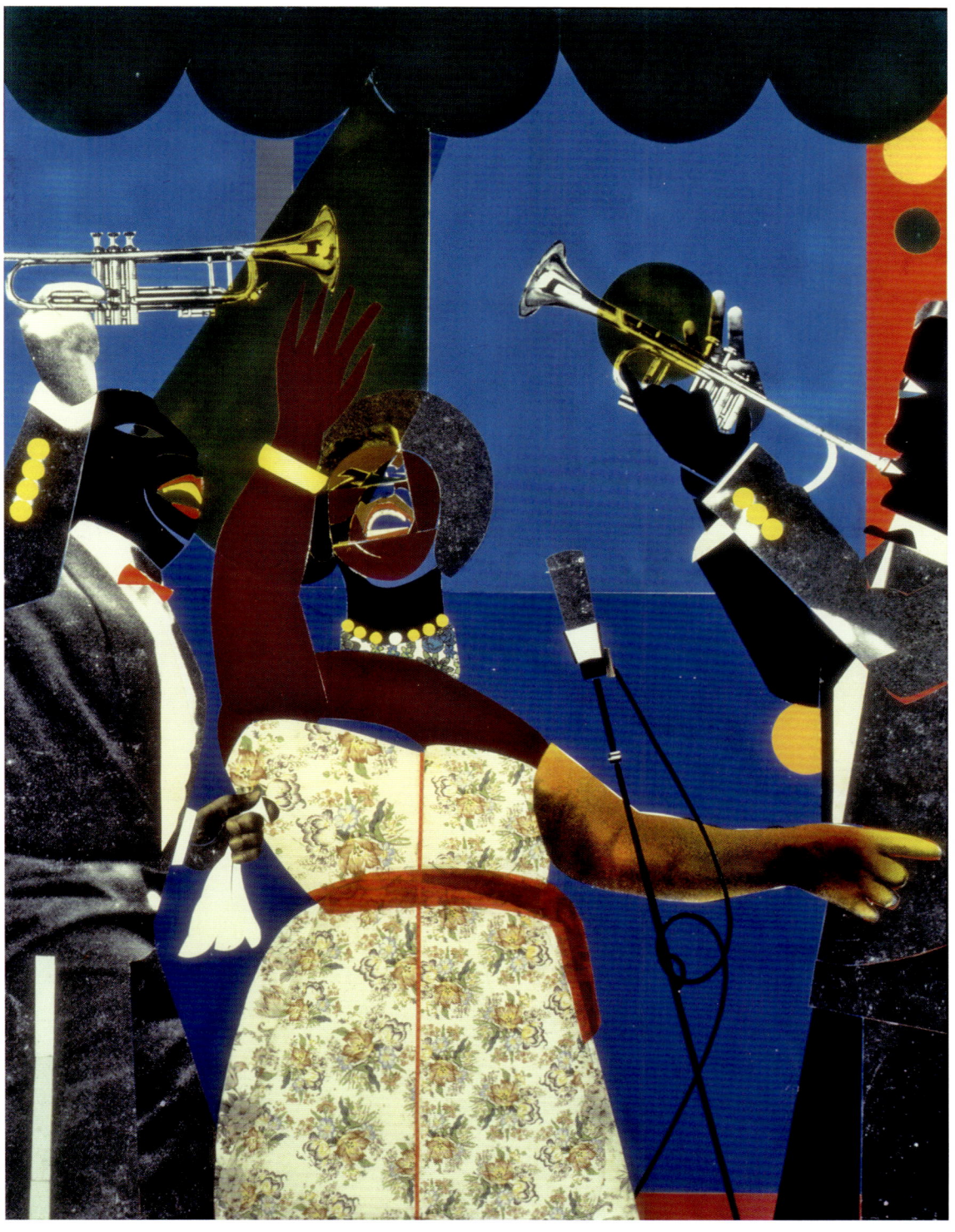

Of the Blues: Showtime, 1974. Collage of various papers, mixed media on board. 50 × 40 in. Crystal Bridges Museum of American Art, Bentonville, AR, Gift from the collection of Candace P. and W. Michael Humphreys, 2024.89

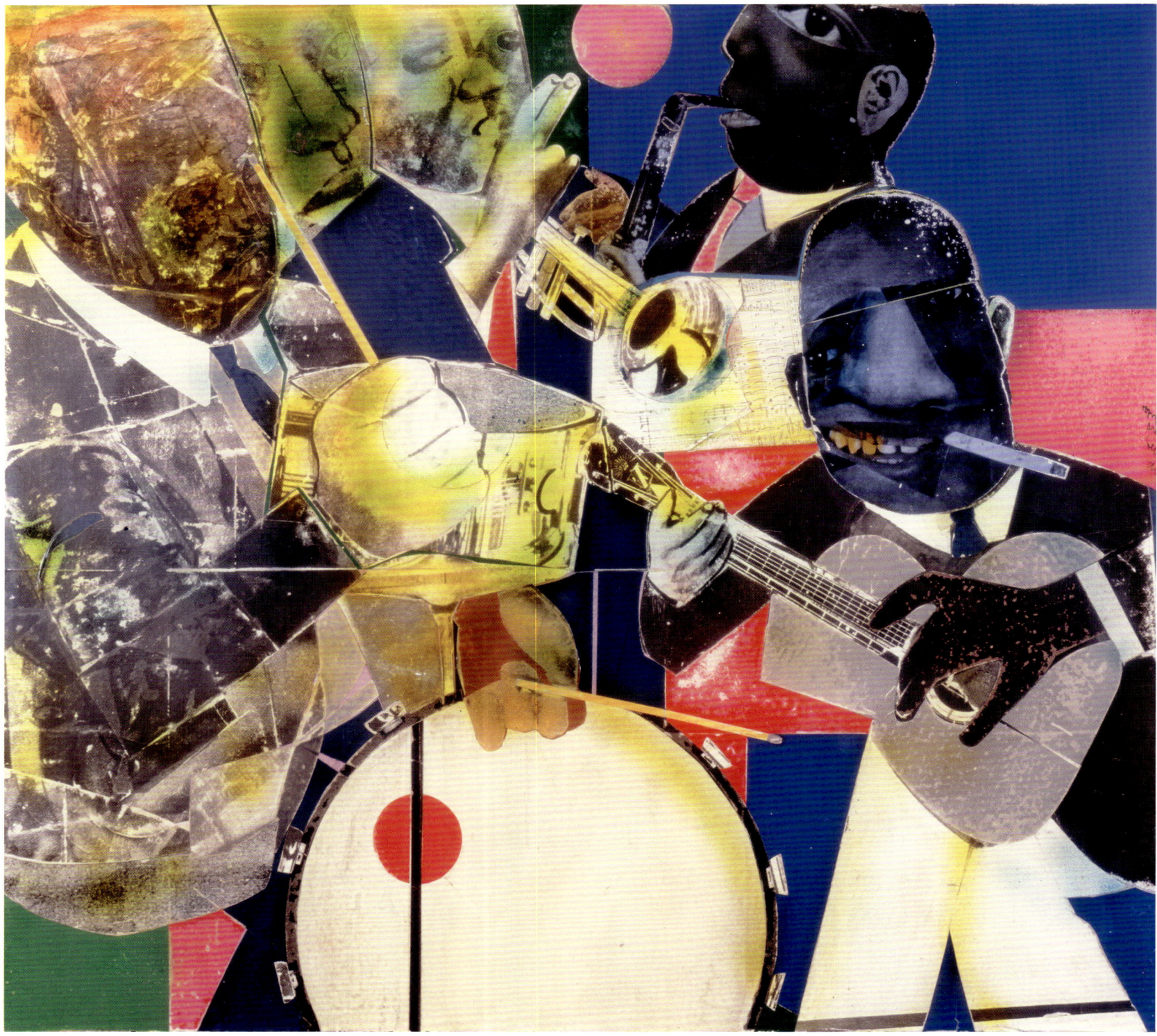

Of the Blues: Kansas City 4/4, 1974. Collage of various papers, mixed media on fiberboard. 44 × 52 in.

JAZZ PLACES / JAZZ EVERYWHERE

Bearden's jazz collages refer to many specific jazz places beyond Harlem and its clubs, *Kansas City 4/4* (1974), *Jazz (Chicago) Grand Terrace* (1964), and *Baltimore Uproar* (1982) among them. Before turning to this book's masterful *Paris Blues/Jazz* series—with jazz collages zeroing in on Paris, New Orleans, and, yes, Harlem—one has to take in the reality that once he started his jazz works, nearly *everything* Bearden did had a blues/jazz aspect. That includes the Caribbean Obeah works, suggesting the magical and sometimes enigmatic women of the blues, and the *Black Odyssey* series, where not Odysseus but the improvising, shape-shifting goddess Circe takes center stage. I love including these latter works in the jazz category. Albert Murray joked that the painting entitled *Odysseus Leaves Circe* (1977) (one of the several *sorry-but-I-can't-take-you* collages in this series) could just as easily be called "Circe's Empty Bed Blues," echoing a Bessie Smith title. In certain *Black Odyssey* works, the consummate shape-shifter Odysseus is a heroic figure making his way home to his Penelope; but just as often Bearden leaves him as a background villain—unseen thief, colonial intruder, reckless man with no plan. Perhaps what's most important here is that, like Homer himself and his "man of many ways," Bearden himself is a brilliant improviser, the artist of many ways who recasts what's often called the greatest story ever told as a brilliantly colored solo-song with meanings cut out for today.

In one little-known precursor of the *Odyssey* series, *The Cyclops* (ca. 1968), Bearden suits up his version of Homer's one-eyed "monster" as an Afro-Caribbean spirit figure who is all set to use force, if necessary, to maintain good order. A ghastly, Klansman-like specter—evidently a modern Odysseus, stripped of all heroic trimmings—threatens this Cyclops and his lush green home. But this time the collaged Afro-figure stands at

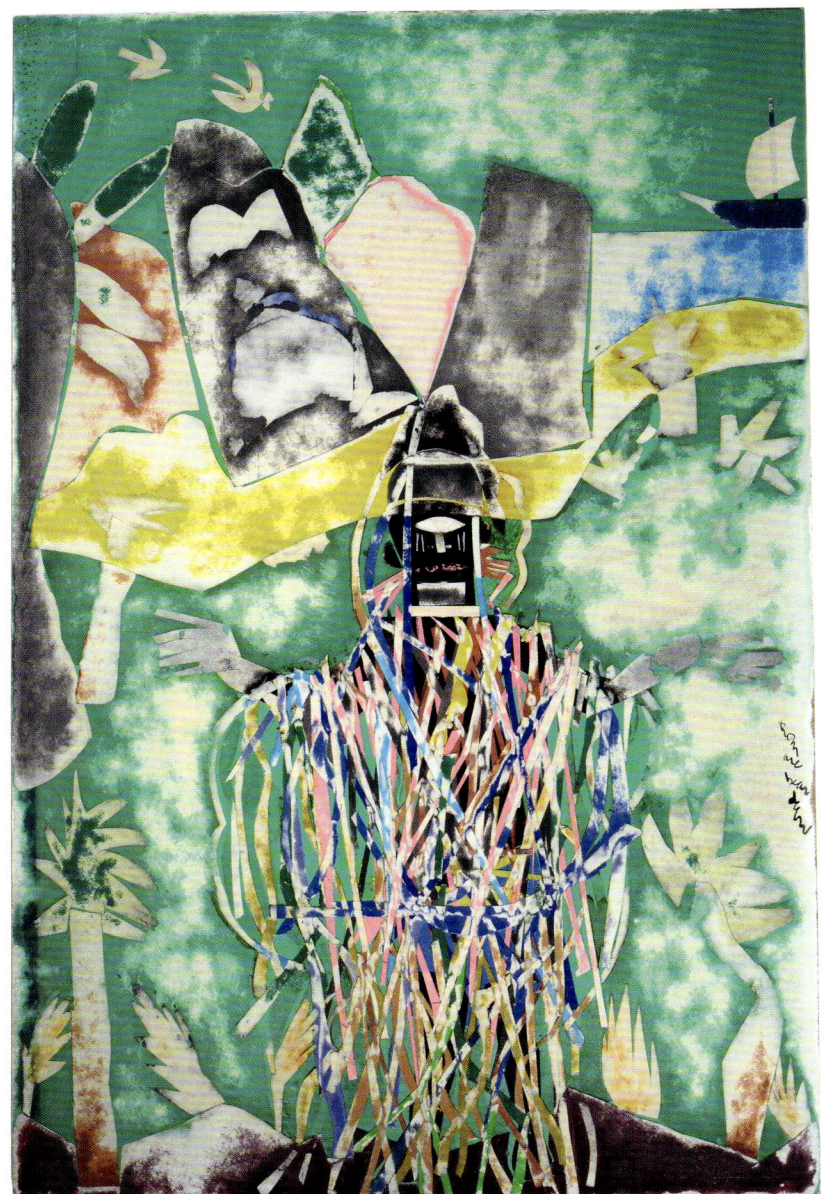

The Cyclops, ca. 1968. Collage of various papers, mixed media on fiberboard. 18⅛ × 12¼ in. Private Collection

the ready, channeling Black spirit traditions from east and west, ancient to the future. His single-eyed face is a thumb piano or *mbira*, from an ancient African family of instruments often associated with marshaling the ancestors, showing the son of Poseidon as a Black Power king. He is possibly related to Pitchy Patchy, a figure from early Jamaican carnival who usually wears a many-colored suit of tattered cloth and is charged with keeping the festivities orderly.[104] Perhaps the outstretched arms of this Bearden Cyclops are meant to evoke Kongo gestures of authority and ecstasy. K. Kia Bunseki Fu-Kiau says that this gesture communicates "feeling ready to fly with inherent spirit."[105]

With Afro-thumb piano as his masklike head, this layered figure sets the stage for Bearden's *Paris Blues/Jazz* series. Like the collage, the series is music-centric, insistent on its own brand of unruly Black cosmopolitanism that stars improvising artists as members of powerhouse bands, as highly flexible guides beyond our world of trouble to worlds of possibility and—to use the word Bearden repeatedly used to express the purpose of art—redemption.

Opposite: Frank Stewart. Romare Bearden in his studio, c. 1980–81

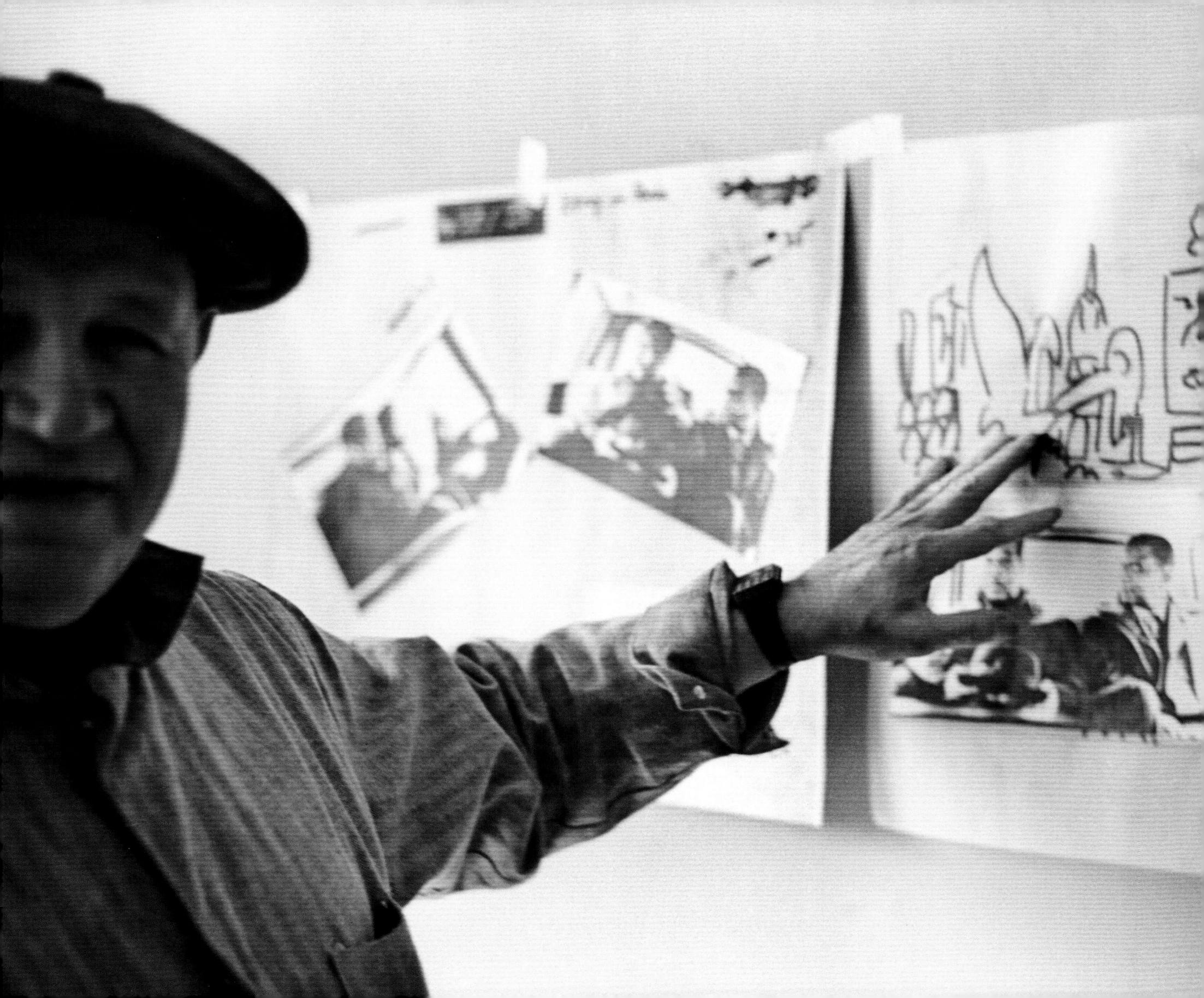

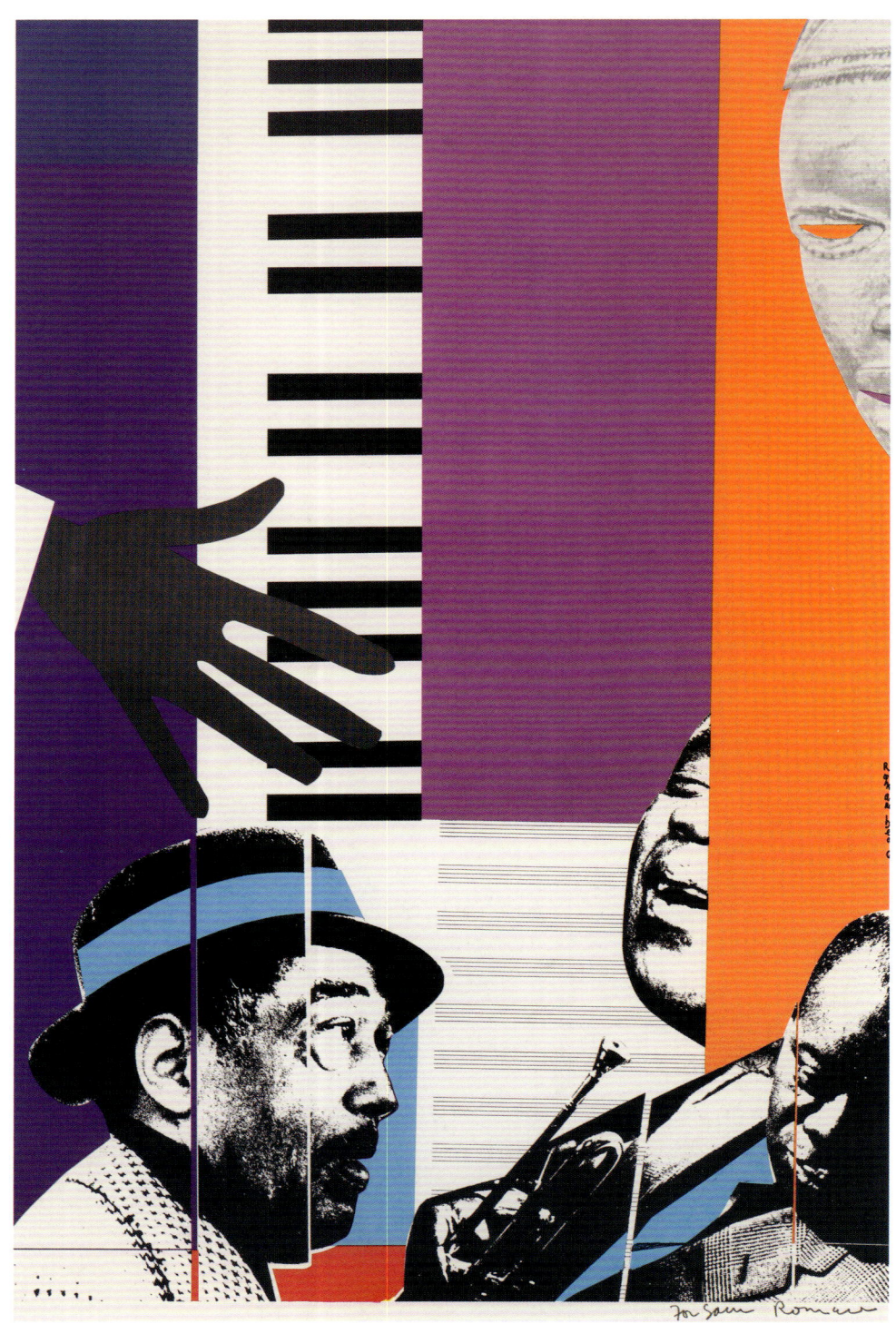

Ellington and Armstrong, ca. 1975. Offset lithograph on paper. 26 ⅝ × 17 ¼ in.
Courtesy of DC Moore Gallery, New York

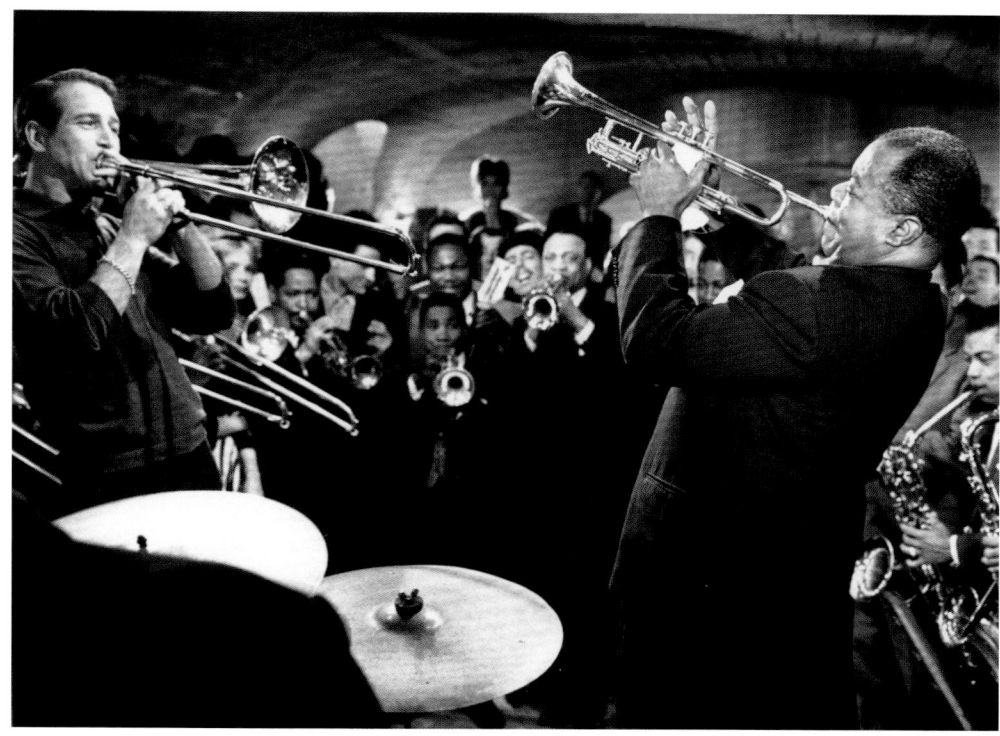

Paul Newman and Louis Armstrong in *Paris Blues* (Martin Ritt, 1961)

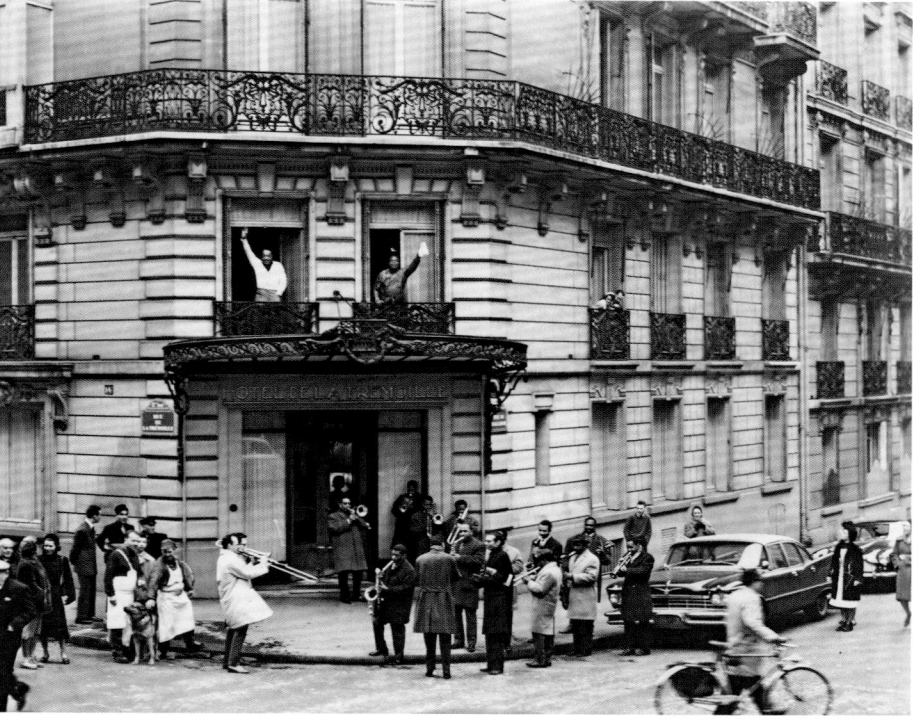

Jacques de Potier. Duke Ellington and Louis Armstrong on a balcony in Paris while filming *Paris Blues*, 1961

ON THE PARIS BLUES/JAZZ PROJECT

As described at the outset of this book, the *Paris Blues/Jazz* project emerged from a collaboration between Romare Bearden, Sam Shaw, and Albert Murray. This trio aimed to create a large-scale book of collages riffing on the 1961 movie *Paris Blues*, which Shaw had produced but which disappointed him and Bearden, whose stories of his Paris days, as told to Shaw, were the origin point of the film. Together with Murray, who dismissed the movie as "Hollywood pulpfare," they would redress its wrongs; but more than this, they would present a vision of Black creativity and cosmopolitanism, with the real jazz heroes at the fore.

I've been stressing that jazz is a music defined by collaboration. The ambition of Bearden, Shaw, and Murray to "colabor" like a jazz band was crucial to the *Paris Blues/Jazz* project. There was individual assertiveness involved, as in all

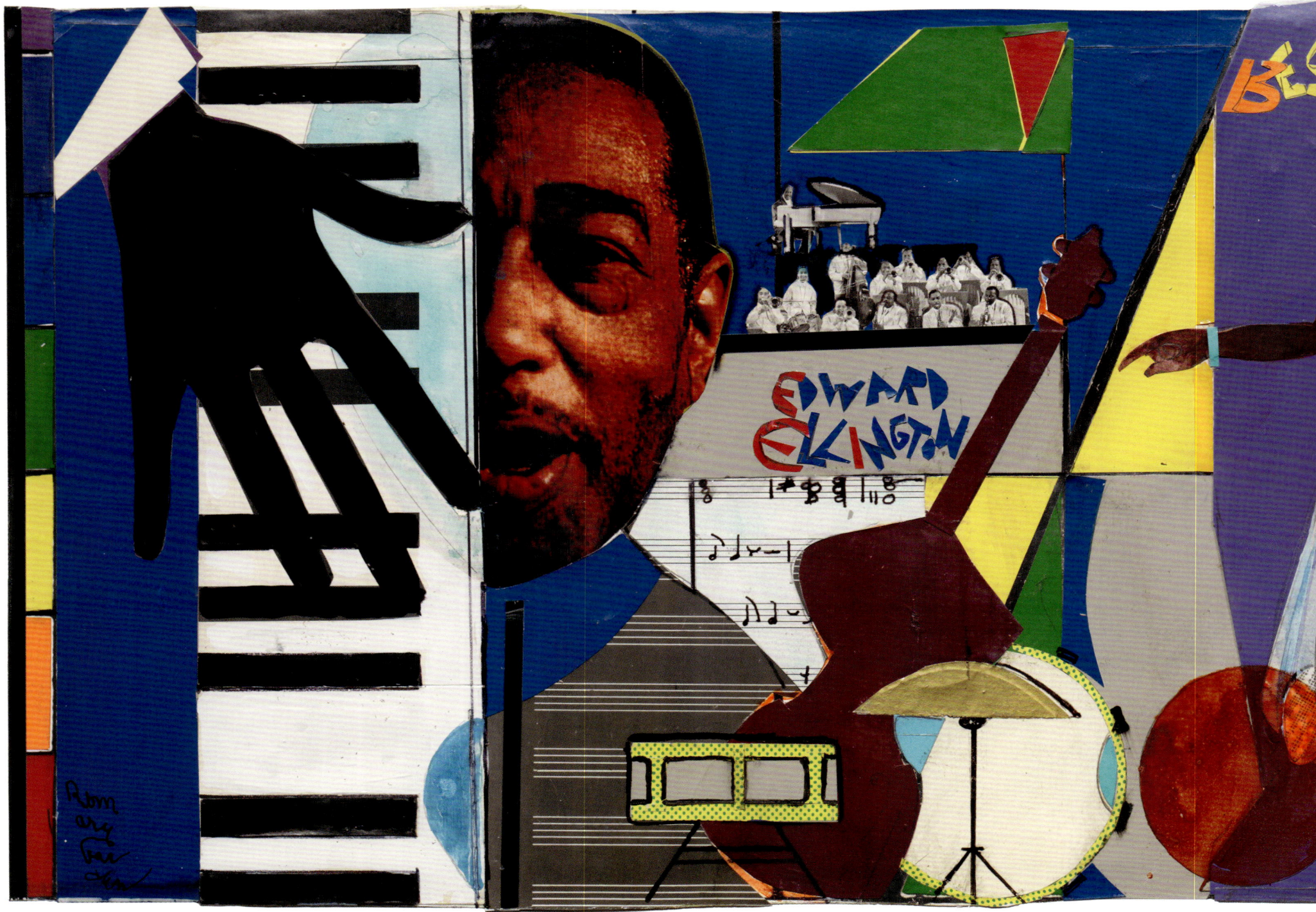

66

Bessie, Duke, and Louis, ca. 1981. Collage of various papers, mixed media on fiberboard.
12 ¼ × 43 in. Courtesy of the Nanette Bearden Trust and DC Moore Gallery, New York

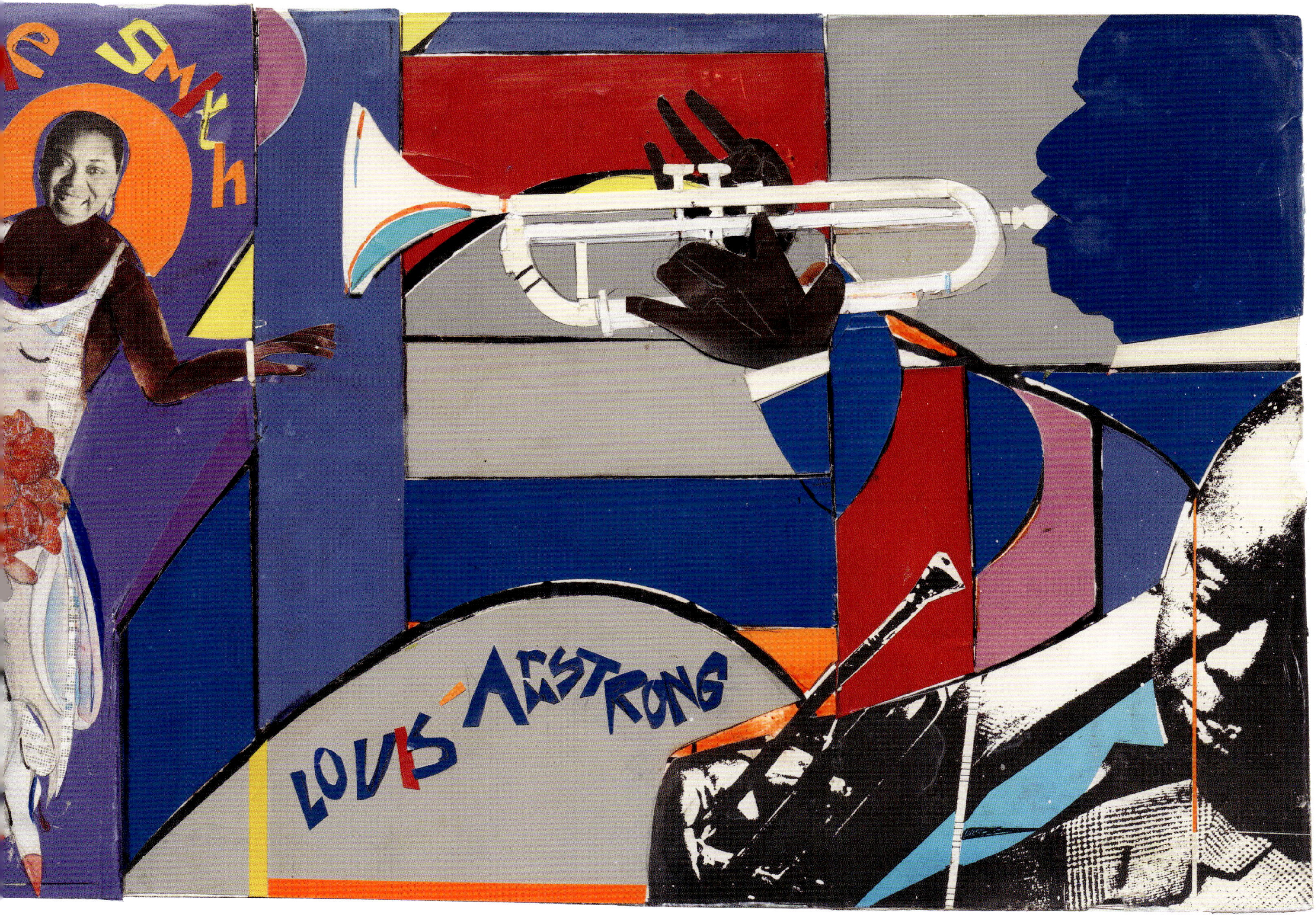

serious art, as well as the paradoxical fact that no art is *ever* one person's alone. Someone provided the paper, paint, and scissors (Bearden), someone the writing (Murray), and someone almost all the photos (Shaw); ideas emerged in concert. If we step back, this partnership reminds us of poet-philosopher Édouard Glissant's proposition that the African American's journey "from slavery to freedom" (Frederick Douglass's ringing phrase[106]) is, at its most profound level, a trip from narrow individuality—from the enslaved person's confinement, with personhood legally denied—toward the multiplication of personal roles, interactions, and travels, as the free person steps out (becomes "more than herself or himself"). For our trio's project, it is also significant that one of Glissant's ultimate models for post-slavery flights to freedom is the jazz band. And rightly so. For like the contemporary poet-philosopher Fred Moten, Glissant uses jazz to posit a multiplied sense of self—playing with personal style while dedicated to playing with-and-against others, checking, balancing.[107] Self, selves, communities.

Both these brilliant thinkers, Glissant and Moten, also lift up the jazz band as a model for democratic community as a whole. The jazz band's ideal is that its members swing in coordination, really hearing one another as they call and recall, call and countercall, as a unit. It's with this in mind that Moten calls the music of Ellington "the sound of love."[108] And music by Duke Ellington the composer, like the *Paris Blues* film score, was also always *co*-composed with his writing companion of decades, Billy Strayhorn, and/or with the band's instrumentalists and singers, some of whom joined the band and stayed there the rest of their lives. The band also worked with (and sometimes against square) audiences that, at their best, included dancers, all of them part and parcel of a dynamic coproduction of great creative momentum. Self among selves. Self among selves creating the always unsquare sound of love. Strayhorn called it "Something to Live For."[109]

With all this in mind, we assert again that the collage is by definition jazzlike. As a creative mode, it's both improvisational and collaborative. It's a rhythmical assembly of pieces and parts from a variety of sources, from work by many hands, layered and held together (the word is from *collé*, French for "glued") in a way that can result in forms that look like music. In a Bearden collage, the music you see is unmistakably jazz.

To map out the *Paris Blues/Jazz* book, the three met periodically at Bearden's Long Island City studio. Shaw's archives show drafts of pages produced there, many of them numbered, as the book took shape. Some pages contain sketches by Bearden based on Shaw's cache of photos of Paris, especially, but also of New Orleans and New York. Some sketches and pasted photos refer to Shaw's own *Paris Blues* storyboards leading to the design of the movie (of figures climbing steep staircases in Montmartre, for example)—along with many Shaw photos of Ellington and Armstrong. Shaw's bulging New Orleans and Harlem photo files also proved inspiring to Bearden, who trimmed Shaw pictures and/or made drawings based on them. In the arrangements of materials and the overall point of view of the book-in-progress, one ever feels the presence of Murray, some of whose notes toward captions for these collages (and anticipated collages) eventually found their way into a 1994 Smithsonian Traveling Exhibition Service show on Louis Armstrong, and, later, the essay "Armstrong and Ellington Stomping the Blues in Paris."[110] Shaw was enthusiastic about his photos in the context of collages—so much so that he created a few collages himself, a fact which, according to Murray, helped doom the project. Bearden was delighted to use Shaw's fine pictures in his collages but was not amused by the prospect of sharing pages or credits with Shaw as collage maker.

There's no archival record of exactly what they talked about as they worked. But obviously there was much about *Paris Blues* the movie that the Bearden-Shaw-Murray team

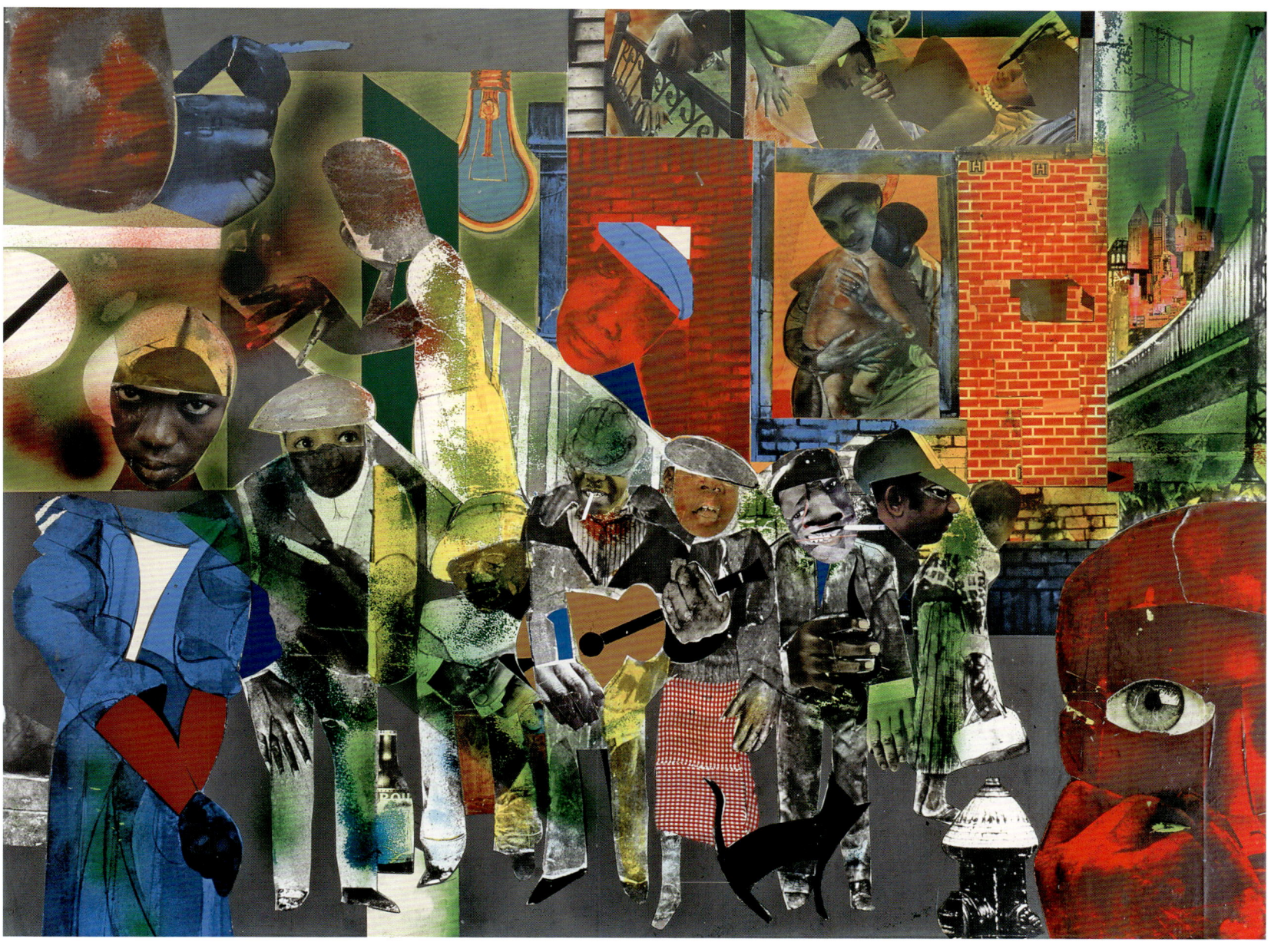

The Street, 1975. Collage of various papers, mixed media on board. 37⅝ × 51⅛ in. Private Collection

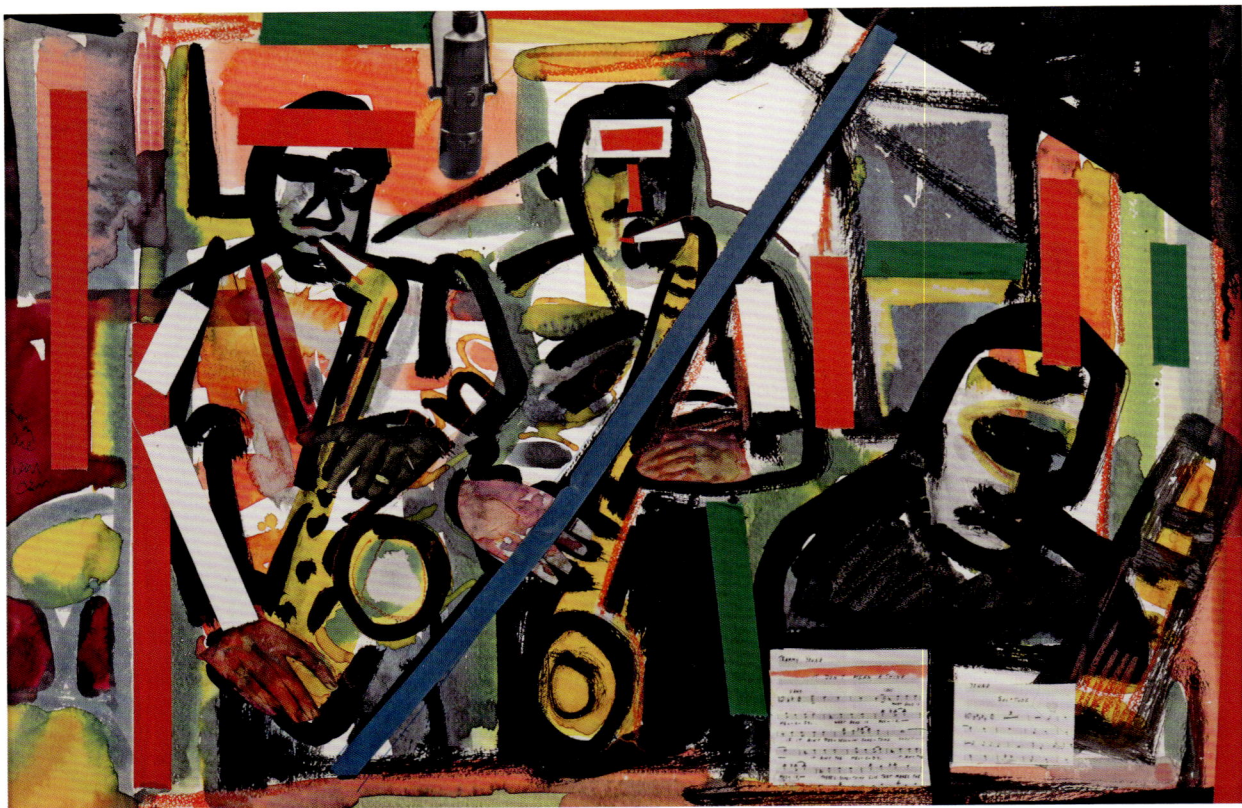

Profile/Part II, The Thirties: Rehearsal Hall, 1981. Collage of various papers, mixed media on board. 16 11/16 × 25 in. Private Collection

aimed to modify, contradict, or just expunge. To begin with, no white lead actor (Paul Newman) would carry the storyline in place of the young Romare Bearden in Paris. And rather than two talented journeyman musicians (the Newman and Sidney Poitier characters), the stars of the Bearden-Murray-Shaw book would be none other than Louis Armstrong and Duke Ellington, with occasional appearances by longtime Duke collaborator Billy Strayhorn. Armstrong had been cameoed in the *Paris Blues* movie, and the Ellington-Strayhorn team had provided its score. Because Duke, Strays, and Louis had spent time in Paris around the movie set (and, sometimes with Shaw, partying on the town), Shaw had formal and informal photographs of them. For Ellington and Armstrong's prominence in the *Paris*

Blues/Jazz project, there's no stronger evidence than the pair of works *Graffiti (Duke Ellington)* and *Graffiti (Louis Armstrong)* (1981), consisting entirely of signaturelike letters, spelling "L-o-u-i-s-A-r-m-s-t-r-o-n-g" on one page, and "D-u-k-e-E-l-l-i-n-g-t-o-n" on the other, implying that these two great ones cosign this version of the *Paris Blues* story.

The big collage book's presentation of Louis Armstrong explodes the rap sheet of African American male stereotypes offered in Harold Flender's novel *Paris Blues*, and of certain aspects of "The Wildman," as the Armstrong character is called in the novel and then the movie. As Shaw must have told Bearden and Murray, there was tension between Armstrong and the movie's director, Martin Ritt, on the *Paris Blues* set.

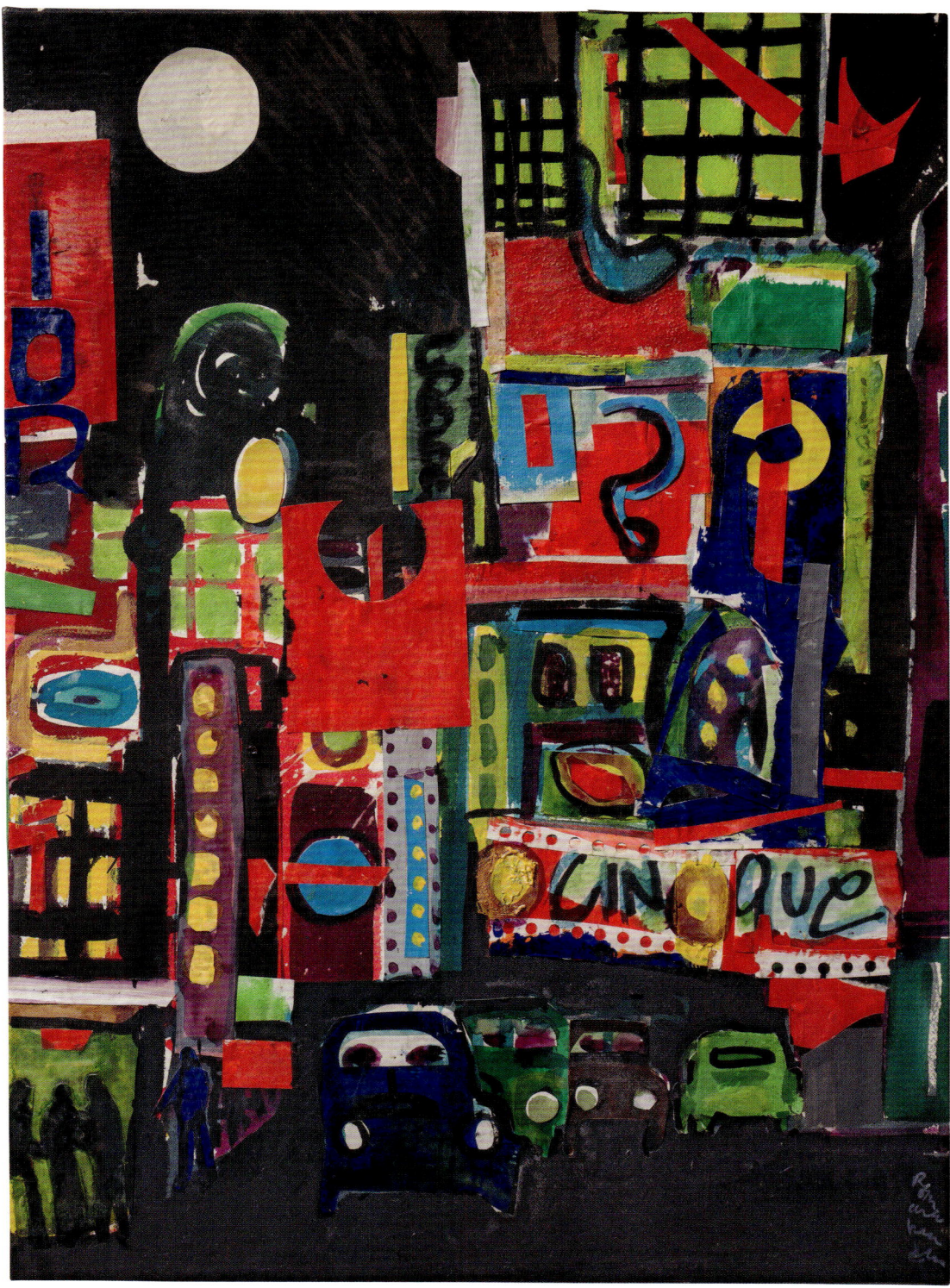

Midtown, 1982. Collage of various papers, mixed media on paper mounted to board. 27 ½ × 20 ½ in.
Courtesy of DC Moore Gallery, New York

Whenever Louis arrived for the day's work, the French musicians and actors there (Black and white) burst into spontaneous applause. Here was the great man himself, flesh and blood! Between scenes, Pops would relax with extras on the set with a little shake-a-leg jitterbug dancing of their own. (Armstrong was well known in the business as one of the exceptionally talented musicians who liked to dance.)[111] "The director couldn't understand," Armstrong told an interviewer. "He said, 'Why all this? Who do you think you are, the star of the show?' I said, 'No, that's just my cats up there.'. . . He was an American director. They don't let nothing happen in America."[112] The fact that no dressing room had been set aside for him intensified the frostiness. Maybe it was on the set, too, with this draft already in the air, that Armstrong finally had time for a closer look at the script and its antecedent novel. What did it mean to be cast (certainly in the novel) as a screeching, howling wild man, a sellout in contrast to the urbane sophisticates played by Newman and Poitier, by Carroll and Woodward? Whichever slight tipped the scales—the script, the novel, Ritt's tone, or the missing dressing room—suddenly Armstrong had had enough and walked off the set (he "raised," as they used to say in Harlemese) to hail a cab back to his hotel.

Shaw later said that it was only because he promised Armstrong that he could have his (Shaw's) dressing room, and that Armstrong wouldn't be annoyed again by proximity to Ritt, that he returned to finish the movie. But Satchmo remained on edge—something conveyed by portraits by Shaw and Herman Leonard, another brilliant photographer on the set. Here was motivation enough for our *Paris Blues/Jazz* trio to overlay both the novel and the film's imagery of the Black artist in Paris—utterly false to Bearden's own experience there, and to Armstrong's—with images of the Armstrong and the music they knew as well as complex truths about Black Americanness and art, at home and abroad, as they had witnessed and/

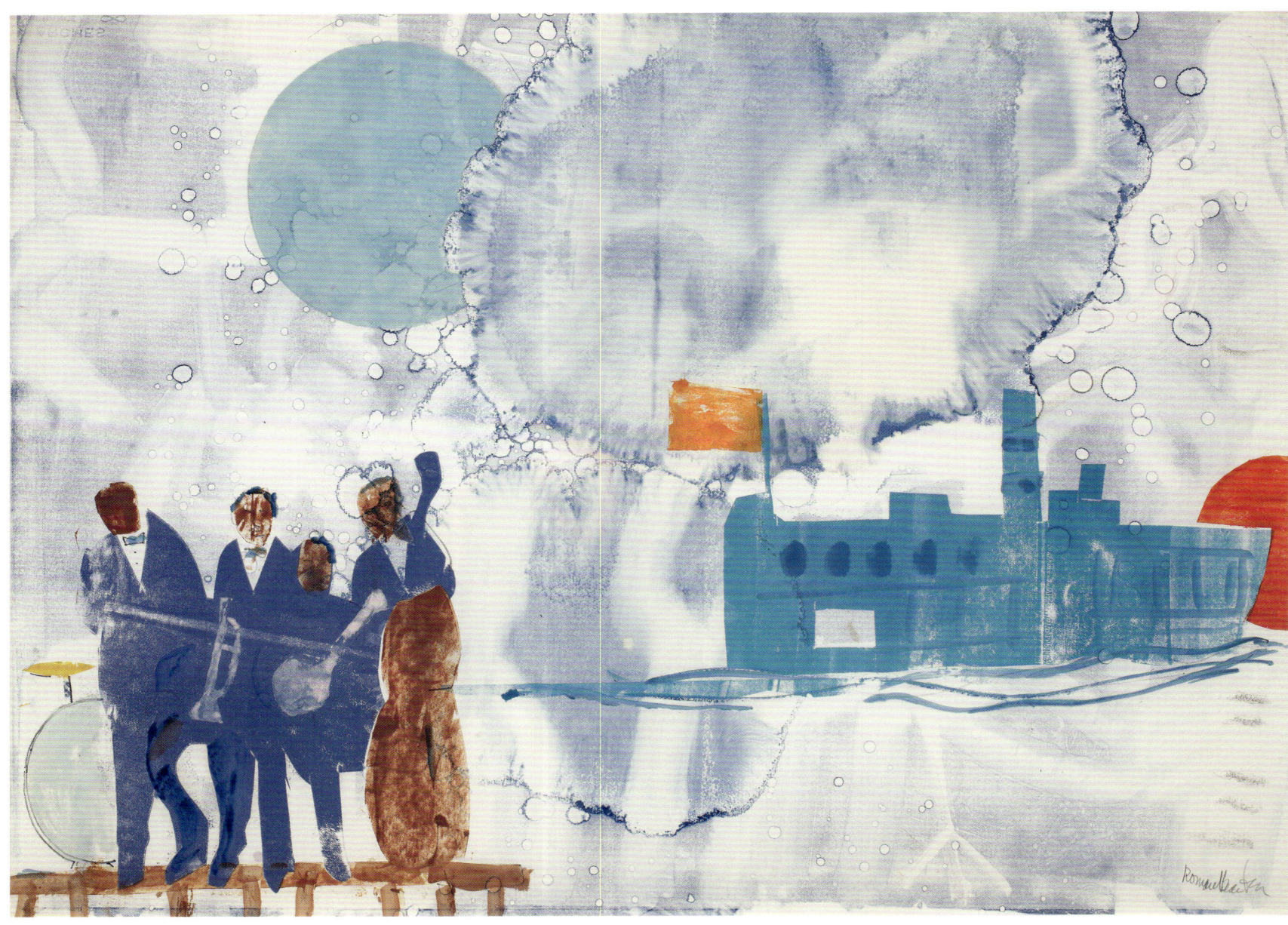

Riverboat Musicians, 1984. Monotype on paper. 29 × 41 in. Courtesy of the Nanette Bearden Trust and DC Moore Gallery, New York

or lived it themselves. This time Bearden's own Paris story of 1950 would come through in collages he made in the late 1970s, when he was at the summit of his artistic powers.

In their version of the Black American artist in Paris, the Bearden-Shaw-Murray trio shed the movie's whitewashed plot: in the collages, no racially aligned spring-break flings force choices between love and art (Newman and Joanne Woodward), or between escape in socially freer France and vaunted return to Negro credit-to-the-race obligations back in the States (Poitier and Diahann Carroll). Bearden's collages seem to say that love and artistic inspiration are where you find them (see *Lovers in Luxembourg Garden* [1981], race unspecified), and responsibilities to social justice are everybody's, everywhere, all the time. (As the old spiritual says, "There's no hiding place down here." But as Bearden, Baldwin, and many other Black travelers beyond our borders have discovered, escapes from the anvil of American oppression can invigorate the creative mind.) Neither is the focus here on the movie's false divides between formal musical composition and improv, or conservatory training and "ear cat" modeling and mentoring. Instead, in the collage series, Armstrong, Ellington, and Strayhorn are no-doubt-about-it master jazz artists unequivocally committed to the majesty of their art, including its robust collaborative and improvisatory dimensions.

Enlisted for life in the music's never-ending development, Satchmo, Duke, and Strays move from gig to gig, town to town, learning all the time, sometimes from conservatory-trained cats, sometimes from "ear cats." And as we have seen, Bearden was an avid student of art in the same category as wondrous patchwork quilts: art forms that surrounded him in childhood, from African American artists-in-motion—Lindy Hoppers on the dance floors of Harlem—to the experimental canvases and boards of Picasso, Matisse, and Aaron Douglas. For Armstrong, Ellington, and Strayhorn, musical creation was a matter of collaboration as well as individual labor, improvisation as well as written scores. These categories blur in jazz, in any case: the scores of Ellington and Strayhorn show that, along with blank "ad lib" sections, they wrote out many solos note for note, expecting the players to play them precisely as written but to make them sound freshly improvised. As the *Paris Blues/Jazz* series underscores, for Bearden and his collaborators, making art involved formally and informally learned interplay and improv, reflecting their subject: jazz. For all of them, Bearden and Co. and Satchmo and Co., art thrived in certain art-rich places—it definitely took off in Paris, New Orleans, and New York; and it was pushed forward by the artists' will to travel crisscrossing circuits through running spaces and roads high and low, country and city: jazz art is unafraid and unprejudiced. It *moves*.

And so, the *Paris Blues/Jazz* collages trace artistic movement, visit legendary circuit stops, and pay homage to the urban centers that foster the arts. In so doing, the series would reframe the movie's version of jazz, defining it not as a youthful escape for fledgling American music makers playing at being cool (Newman and Poitier), but as an essential American modern art—some would call it THE essential modern art form. Because location is key to the collage series—Paris, New Orleans, and New York being its focal points—understanding how Bearden and his collaborators understood cities is essential.

CITY SPACES: INTERIOR AND EXTERIOR

When it came to choosing American cities as homes along the way, New Orleans and New York—or specifically, Harlem—were the places to return to, both physically and in the musicians' minds.[113] Each town had special significance as a Black space and jazz space. On the international circuit, certainly Paris offered special turns: it was, at least comparatively, an open city where the arts were revered, a shining beacon. And hence its role in Bearden's life, in the movie (originally based on his life), and later in the book project. In the *Paris Blues/Jazz* collages, all three urban centers offer the sense that anything is possible, whether implied by the acrobats of the Cirque du Soleil (will they next leap through a hoop from the back of a galloping horse?), the frolicking party people of New Orleans at Festival Time, or the light shining from the composer's fingers in Harlem as dancers take to the air. Each city has its own flights (some of them up what seem like Paris's stairways to the stars), accents, and flavors. And each has an international horizon, too, the will among its inhabitants to move as citizens of the planet.

In truth, Paris is not the only international city depicted in Bearden's collages. Through the twentieth century, as now, one could hear non-English talk all over Harlem and NOLA (see the landmark study *The World That Made New Orleans*).[114] All three cities have been sites of international confluence and connection: places where artists and intellectuals run into their counterparts from all over the planet; places where, as the philosopher Alain Locke put it, "peoples meet."[115] (There's something really good about Locke's pluralizing the mutually welcoming *peoples*.)

And yet, as much as Harlem, New Orleans, and Paris are cosmopolitan centers, they are not only citified but *countryfied* places—much more so than is generally noted. There's a layered country-in-the-city aspect to them and to Bearden's art—Armstrong's and Ellington's, too. The Great Migration of the early twentieth century set millions of Black Americans flowing from the rural South to the urban North.[116] One of his paintings of 1981 depicts a Southern sister, with a caption composed by Bearden and Murray that reads: "The trains in the stories she told always ran North."[117] But trains also were running to the urban South, to cities such as Birmingham, Mobile, Atlanta, Baltimore, and Washington, DC, as well as New Orleans. Furthermore, many

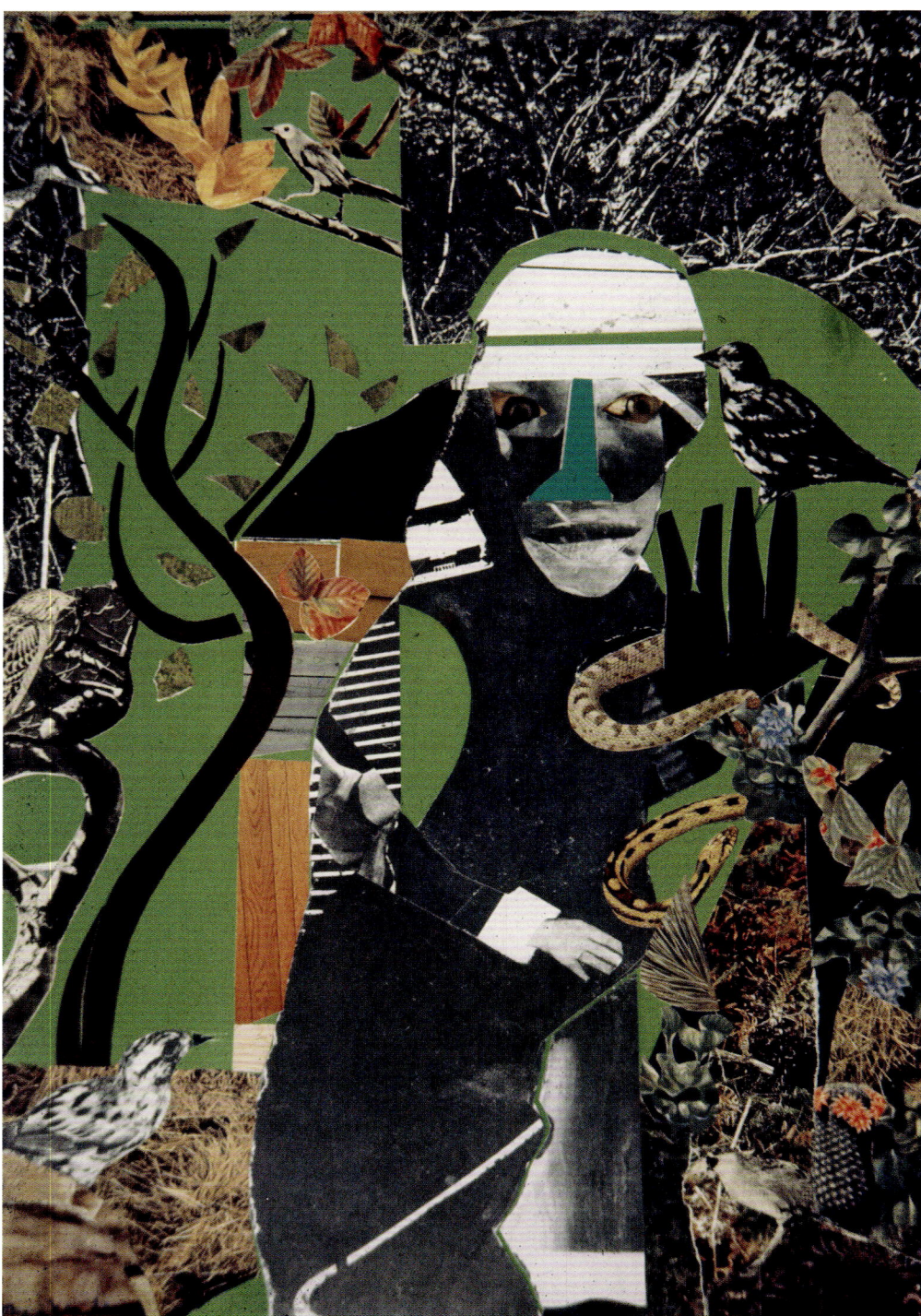

Conjur Woman, 1971. Collage of various papers, mixed media on board. 22 ¾ × 16 ¾ in.

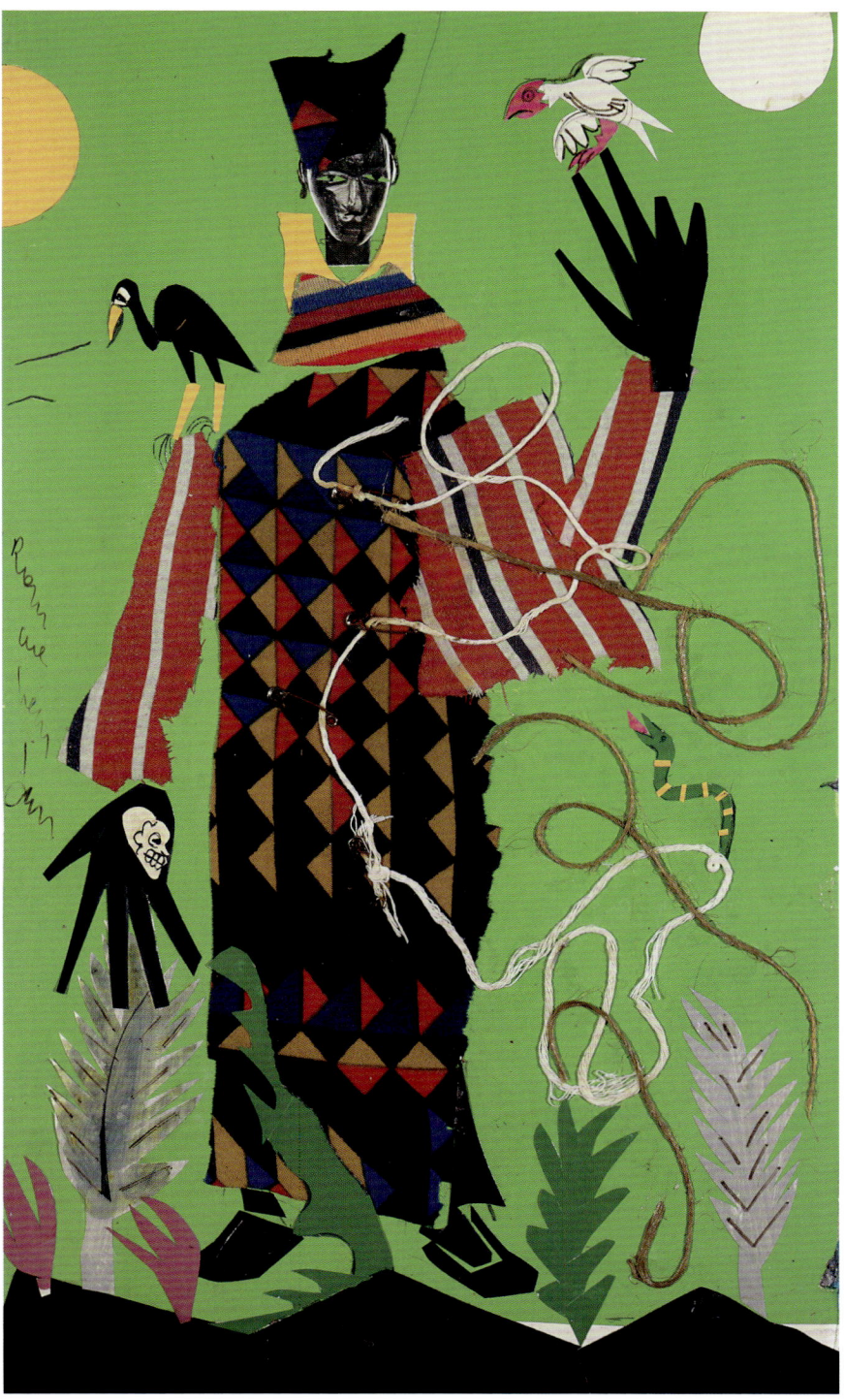

The Conjur Woman, ca. 1979. Collage of various papers, mixed media on board. 23 × 15 in. Private Collection

blues songs record instances of Black migrants taking off for the North and then turning back home, "to a simpler place and time."[118] According to bluesman Jimmy Rushing, "Broadway's all right, and the lights shine nice and bright / I'd rather walk down home by my little lantern light."[119] And Bessie Smith sang, "Goodbye North, Hello South / It's so cold up here that the words freeze in my mouth!"[120] Another Smith song (1924) announces the singer's determination to leave the United States altogether: to make her way from the "work-house" (the women's labor-prison she's in) "to the Nation" (the native lands beyond the United States). She's "going to the Territory."[121]

In Bearden's *Paris Blues/Jazz*, New Orleans stands for the Global Southernness and Indigeneity of jazz, along with its country-in-city character and its internationalism. And rightly so, as greater New Orleans has been shaped by its many Native nations; its variety of African populations, slave and free, including people from Cuba, Haiti, and throughout the Global South; the periods of French and Spanish colonization prior to the Louisiana Purchase in 1803; and the twentieth-century surges of migrants from Italy, Germany, Holland, and especially French-speaking Canada, the so-called Cajuns.[122]

Another angle on Southern places concerns some of the enigmatic ironies of heading back home—or finding one's Southern country-home somewhere in the North or overseas. Bearden spent his first years in Mecklenburg County, North Carolina, his birthplace, while his *Paris Blues/Jazz* collaborator Albert Murray spent formative years (through college) in semiru-ral Alabama. Further, the roster of leading jazz musicians from the Carolinas alone includes Max Roach, Dizzy Gillespie, John Coltrane, Nina Simone, and Thelonious Monk. Sun Ra hailed from Birmingham, Mary Lou Williams from Atlanta (and then Pittsburgh and Kansas City), and Lester Young from Mississippi. Philadelphia—where so many musicians, regardless of where they were born, met other students of the form and learned to play jazz—lies only thirty miles northeast of the Mason-Dixon Line, providing "the city access to Southern and rural traditions in addition to the urban and Northern forms that one would expect."[123] And similarly, Newark, although nowhere near as close to the Mason-Dixon Line, was nonetheless a Deep South city in the urban North—up-South home to Willie "The Lion" Smith, Sarah Vaughan, Wayne Shorter, Woody Shaw, and too many more major jazz artists to name. For years, Black residents of Washington, DC, circulated the joke on themselves that "DC" stands for "De Country"!

The point is that in the United States—but not only there—Northern and Southern, country and city cultural elements love to mix and mingle; and that one detects this quite boldly in jazz, so stirred by its ongoing migrations and immigrations, and likewise in the *Paris Blues/Jazz* series, whose subject is the music. And therefore what we think is urban is often more than a little rural. Kidd Jordan, the big-tone avant-garde saxophonist and composer, grew up not in New Orleans, as some sources claim, but miles outside that city. This tenor sax man's signature blur of notes gave sound to a wide variety of experiences, as he told an interviewer, including faraway train whistles, the countryside's chorus of tree toads and crickets, and his wild, high-register neighing conversations-in-song, as a schoolboy, with favorite horses on his family's farm.[124] The New Orleans marches, etcetera, sounding through his music came later.

Likewise, in Bearden's *Paris Blues/Jazz* collages, country lights glow in each city's background. Let us consider the collages featuring the Ellington band, which was originally The Washingtonians (first formed, in other words, in De Country), whose major members, at the beginning and then all through the years, hailed from all over the nation, and beyond. Note in particular the presence in Duke's band of the growling mute work of trumpet player James "Bubber" Miley, born in Aiken, South Carolina, alumnus of blues queen Mamie Smith's Jazz

Hounds and then of King Oliver's Creole Jazz Band. Alongside Bubber, consider Joe "Tricky Sam" Nanton, the trombonist born in New York City whose parents were Garveyites from the Caribbean. These two were vital creators of the signature sound of Ellington's Harlem-based band—thus, like Armstrong's Mardi Gras–tempered trumpet, the sound of modern city sophistication! Ellington and Armstrong's presence throughout this collage series indicates a country-citified walk through the world.

Prior to the *Paris Blues/Jazz* collages of New Orleans, Bearden drew a corner of that city as a place where people were on their way out of town: *Riverboat Musicians* (1984). This monotype depicts what Toni Morrison has called "a row of Preservation Hall–type musicians, standing before a riverboat. . . . For the first time in a representation of black jazz musicians, I saw stillness—not the active, frenetic, unencumbered physical movement normally seen in reproductions or renderings of musicians, but the quiet at the center. It was, in a word, sacred, contemplative. A glance into an otherwise obscured aspect of their art."[125] Here are travelers enjoying an interval of contemplative peace in a zone that's neither quite country nor city.

The subject raised in this work is among the most persistent of the series: Where does this music come from? (What is the piano lesson?) That it comes from New Orleans, where music was (and still is) played not just for tourist entertainment but for community rituals operating at profound levels, certainly is part of the answer. It's with these deeper levels in mind—not excluding rituals involving comic larks as well as slow, somber marches—that Bearden reminds us that, like all art, New Orleans music flows from the quiet place at the artist's center. Body and soul music from soul and body, in motion and here, uncannily, in stillness. This artwork also reminds us that Morrison said, yes, of course she was trying to write prose with a musical feeling; but don't forget she also had her eye on painters, Bearden in particular.

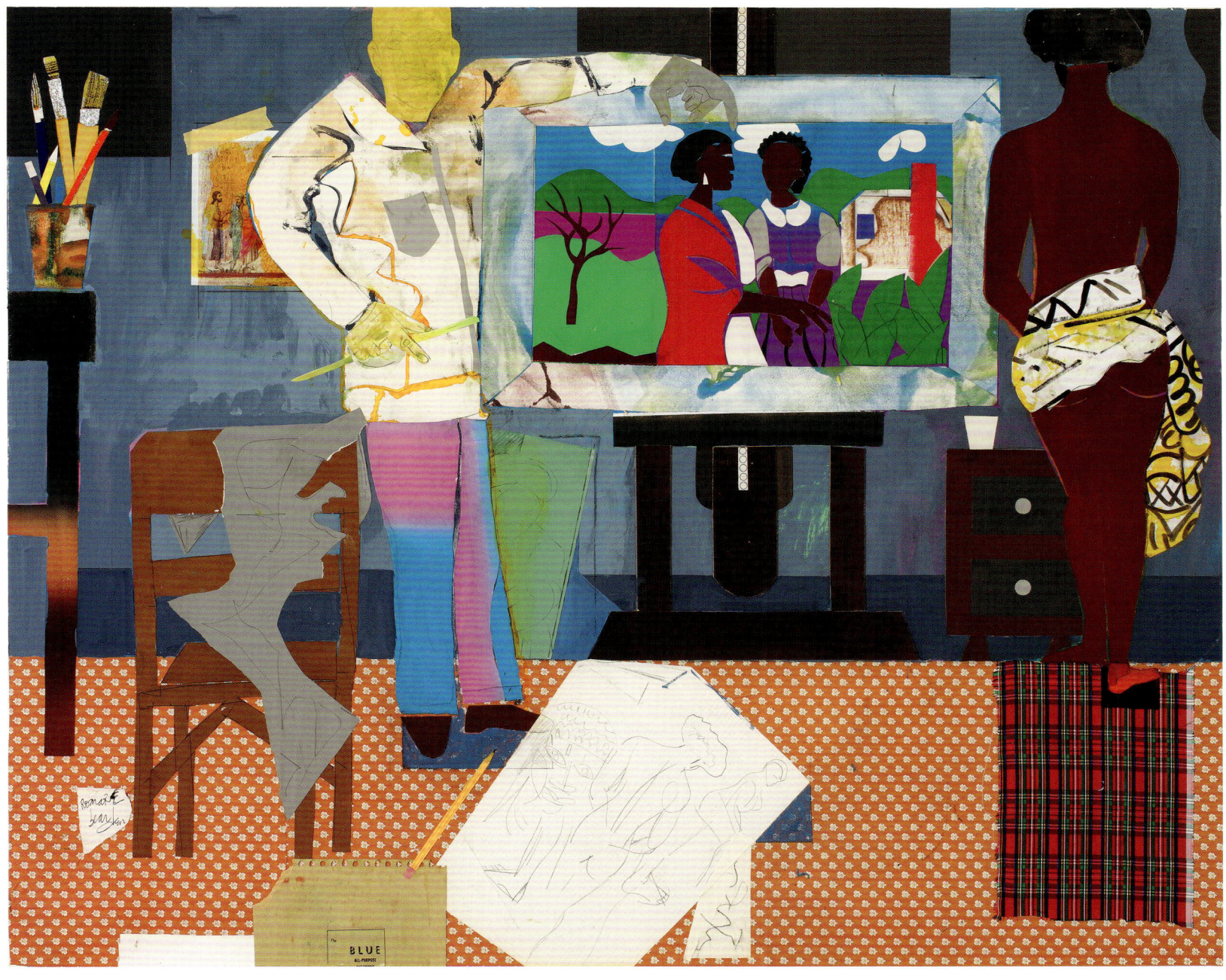

Profile/Part II, The Thirties: Artist with Painting and Model, 1981. Collage of various papers, fabric, foil, and tape with paint and graphite on fiberboard. 44 × 56 in.
High Museum of Art, Atlanta

The music also comes from the prevalence of ritual. Over and over again the subject of Bearden's *Paris Blues/Jazz* paintings is ritual confirming human continuity, beyond the rudiments of survival. In a 1977 interview, Bearden remembered attending a funeral in Spain in 1950 whose contrasting rhythms were similar to those of New Orleans: "In Málaga," he said, "there was all that mournful music, and then, after the burial, somebody began to blow on a trumpet, another kind of sound entirely, and an Englishman who was standing next to me turned and said, 'You see, now life has taken over again.'"[126] Likewise, Bearden's *New Orleans: Ragging Home* (1974) portrays a funeral as a public ritual of continuity (and of resistance, for these particular styles are unapologetically Black and cosmopolitan) in the face of death. Master New Orleans drummer Warren "Baby" Dodds recalls playing many such Crescent City homegoings: "As the family and people went to the graveyard to bury one of their loved ones, we'd play a funeral march. It was pretty sad, and it put a feeling of weeping in their hearts and minds."[127] But then "it became a tradition to play jazzy numbers going back, to make the relatives and friends cast off their sadness. And the people along the streets used to dance to the music. . . . Coming back from funerals, we'd play the same popular numbers that we used to play with dance bands."

If this painting's soaring birds are spirits fleeing home ("Flee as a Bird to a Mountain" has been a favorite funeral hymn for over a century in New Orleans), and if the person on the balcony with a white handkerchief waves a last goodbye to the departed, the rhythm of the bandsmen's legs signifies a will to dance the funereal blues away: to get-on-the-good-foot home (to paraphrase James Brown) as *life takes over again*.[128]

Bearden often said that, although he departed the Deep South of Mecklenburg County as a youngster, its impact was forever; and that, furthermore, in Pittsburgh and Harlem he met conjure women, blues-idiom musicians, quilt makers, soul-food cooks, preachers, and storytellers along with other culture bearers recognized from down home. The *Paris Blues/Jazz* collage *Club Singer, Stage Comedian All Purpose Orisha* (1981) exemplifies this complex sense of kinship and continuity. For here in a Harlem theater, Billie Holiday and Johnny Hudgins, both from the North/South country/city of Baltimore, are named as "orishas," i.e., as bearers of the spirit of ancient West African power figures.

This complexity also reverberates through the 1981 work *Artist With Painting & Model*, where within a self-portrait set in his Harlem studio, Bearden samples/revises a version of his own early painting of the mothers of Christ and John the Baptist as Southern Black women, associating them with a Queen Mother Goddess from Benin and with female deities from traditions East and West who swim the world. As Bearden biographer Glenda Elizabeth Gilmore emphasizes, the South was "the homeland of his imagination," even if Bearden actually lived just a few childhood years there. And so look in the *Paris Blues/Jazz* project for images associated with the Deep South—quilts, birds, guitars, trains, gardens, spiritual figures—that appear all through Bearden's oeuvre; they flow from a place he accessed in Paris or Harlem or NOLA or anyplace else he went, for the rest of his life. In these collages, and then throughout the *Paris Blues/Jazz* paintings, Bearden clearly presents images of kin from the Deep South of the United States, but look also for cultural cousins from the Deeper South of the African diaspora and of the imagination.[129]

The journey of Bearden's *Paris Blues/Jazz* collaborator Albert Murray, in his novelistic essay *South to a Very Old Place* (1971), offers a telling case in point here, for Murray's turn toward the homeland of the South starts in a New York City subway car pointed north! Southern homebound Murray takes the A train from midtown's Columbus Circle toward Sugar Hill up in Harlem, and then continues farther north from the city to New Haven, Connecticut. Loving irony, Murray trips north to go south with the goal of conferring with two Deep South–born scholars (both white men specializing in Southern and Black studies) at Yale. "But then," says Murray, "going back home has probably always had as much if not more to do with people as with landmarks and place names and locations on maps and mileage charts anyway.... The way certain very special uptown Manhattan people talk and the way some of them walk, for instance, makes them homefolks. So whoever says you can't go home again, when you are for so many intents and purposes back whenever somebody or something makes you feel that way."[130]

Note that Bearden met down-home folk in New York and Paris, too: these magnificently overgrown country-in-the-city towns. Native Harlemite James Baldwin, for example, struck the artist as more Southern, culturally speaking, than some of his most born-and-bred Southern friends.[131] And Bearden, like Murray, met Baldwin and Beauford Delaney (all of them Harlemites with Southern roots) in Paris. It's the interplay of countryness and cityness that gives these city spots, North and South, much of their fresh vibrancy and mix of flavors. Such are the vibes of the *Paris Blues/Jazz* series.

And so as we watch for Bearden's collaged depictions of his famous protagonists, let's also take note of his everyday people—in the Luxembourg Garden, at the circus, at the Apollo and Lafayette theaters, in small contact sheets of house parties and clubs. The series' scenes with Romani people—those living in caravans, in both Europe and the Americas—are especially significant in this regard.[132] (These collages were never completed, so all we have are drafts of the Romani works.) They are people on the move, with as many country and city ways as Black American migrants from the country to these countrified cities: Harlem, New Orleans, and Paris. And by the way, during his years as a New York City social worker, Bearden's beat was the Romani, with whom he strongly identified.

Before we turn from this meditation on geography and jazz, and specifically on the terrain of the *Paris Blues/Jazz*

project, let us take a moment to correct those histories of the music form that draw a straight line north to Chicago up the Mississippi River from New Orleans and then East. They forget not only that the Mississippi does not flow through Chicago (it runs through St. Louis) but also that, according to significant witnesses, the music "first" appears in other cities, too—dramatically in the towns of Texas and Alabama, and according to jazz historian Rudi Blesh, all over the South—as well as in the North.[133] Stride pianist/composer Willie "The Lion" Smith (one of Ellington's mentors) said he first heard boogie-woogie in Atlantic City, New Jersey, in the early 1900s and first heard ragtime music at that time in upstate New York![134] The three vital stations on the map of jazz that Bearden chooses—Harlem, New Orleans, and Paris—make the point that jazz is North and South (country-in-the-city, as argued), American and yet not only American. Maybe he was aware that some French historians have claimed jazz as essentially French (born in French New Orleans but raised on the Left and Right Banks)! The music's development, Bearden surely knew, was a matter of multiple cities, and also of *circuits*: this book's thesis is that jazz wants running space. The music moves.

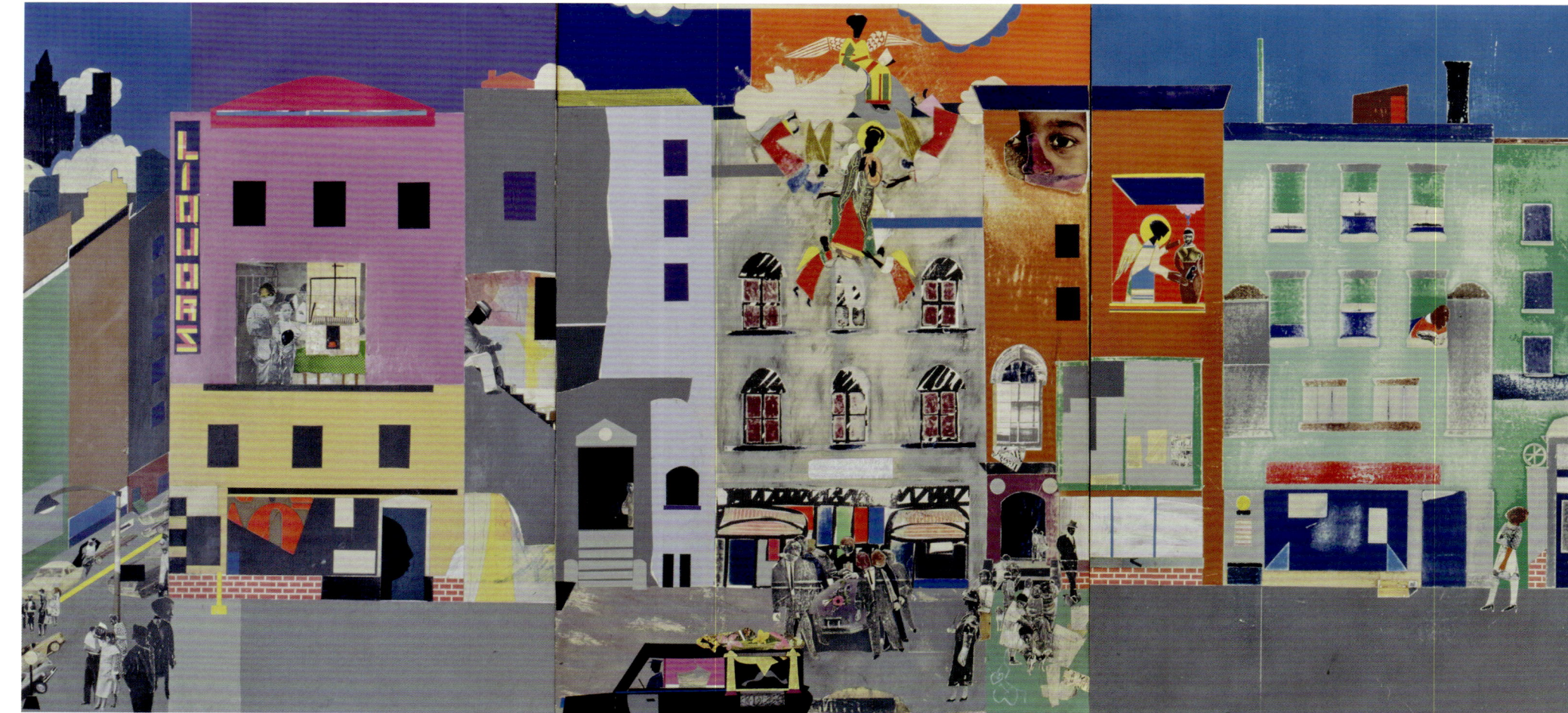

The Block, 1971. Collage of various papers, mixed media on fiberboard. 48 x 216 in. Metropolitan Museum of Art, NY, Gift of Mr. and Mrs. Samuel Shore, 1978

THE BLOCK AS TOUCHSTONE

A friend of mine had a house off Lenox Avenue. Whenever I visited him, I was intrigued by the series of houses I could see from his windows. Their colors, their forms and lives they contained within their walls fascinated me. When I sketched this block, I was looking at a particular street, but as I translated it into visual form it became something else. I lost the literalness and moved into where my imagination took me. I x-rayed the façades with my imagination.[135]

—Romare Bearden

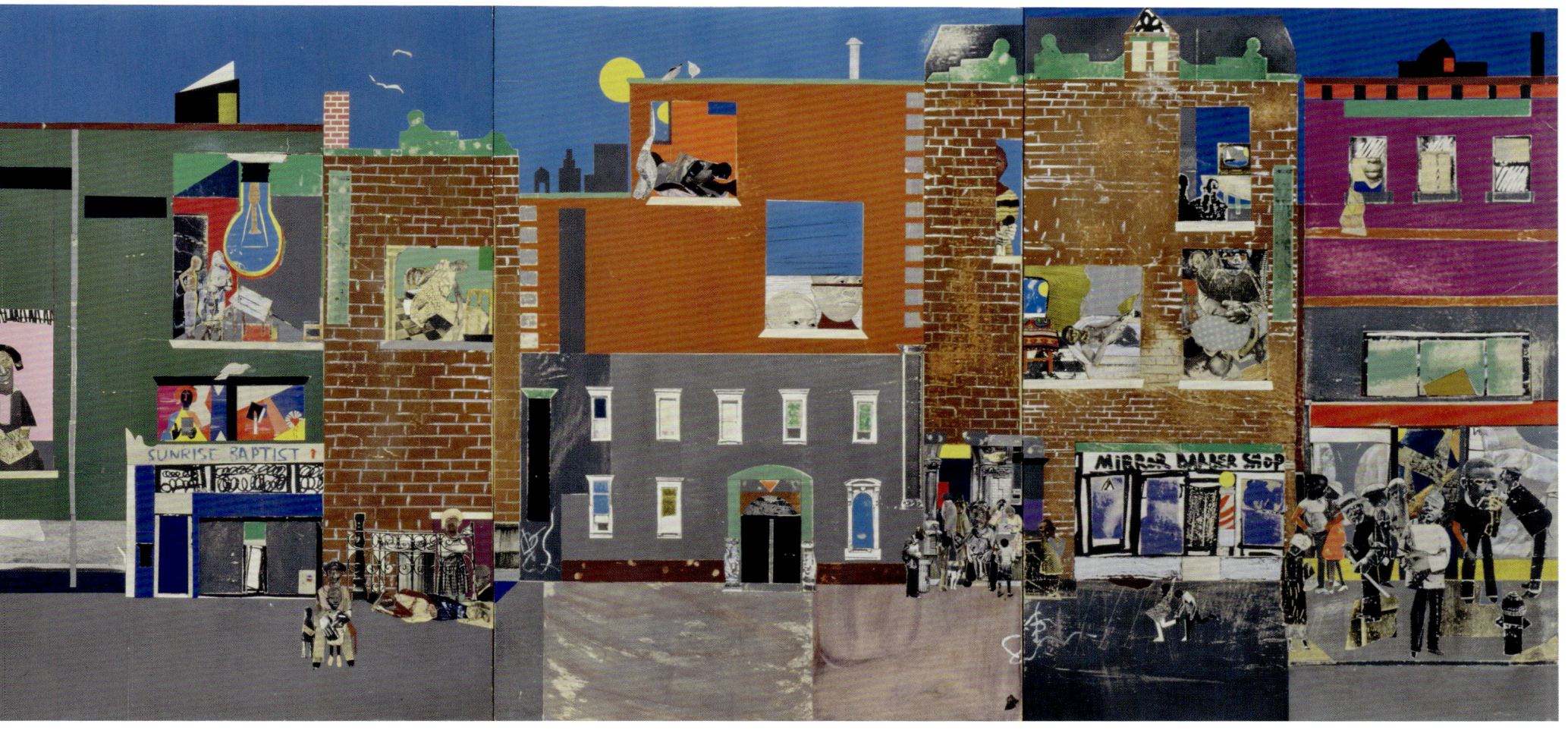

Before engaging with Shaw and Murray in response to the movie *Paris Blues*, Bearden already had created what is without doubt his best-known collage, *The Block* (1971). I explore it at some length here for the light it sheds on the *Paris Blues/ Jazz* pages he made for the collaborative book project. This multipanel *tour de force* is the artist's most comprehensive effort to represent the beauty and liveliness of Harlem as well as its bluesy hauntedness. Revealing both the singularity and representativeness of a particular street in Harlem (Lenox Avenue/Malcolm X Boulevard between 132nd and 133rd Streets), *The Block* radiates what Ellison called "the harlemness of the national predicament"—that is, the precarity and stubborn vitality of life on the Black-hand side of America's color line.[136] While music is not *The Block*'s overt theme, the work is highly musical in form—especially as we recall Bearden's assertion that he regarded the row houses here as piano keys. Like music, *The Block* moves! And it signals that jazz emerges from cityscapes like this—from the unselfconscious voices of Black people in conversation and at play, from traffic sounds and sirens.

As we approach Bearden's *Block*, let's invite Duke Ellington to speak of the role of Harlem's soundscape (and sensorial flavors) in his music:

Take "Harlem Air Shaft." So much goes on in a Harlem air shaft. You get the full essence of Harlem in an air shaft. You hear fights, you smell dinner, you hear people making love. You hear intimate gossip floating down. You hear the radio. An air shaft is one great big loudspeaker. You see your neighbors' laundry. You hear the janitor's dogs. The man upstairs' aerial falls down and breaks your window. You smell coffee. A wonderful thing is that smell. An air shaft has got every contrast. One guy is cooking dried fish and rice and another guy's got a great big turkey. Guy-with-fish's wife is a terrific cooker but the guy's wife with the turkey is doing a sad job. . . . You hear people praying, fighting, snoring. Jitterbugs are jumping up and down always over you, never below you. . . . I tried to put all that in "Harlem Air Shaft."[137]

As if to confirm Duke's point, when *The Block* was first presented at the Museum of Modern Art, curator Carroll Greene (one of very few African American curators operating at that level at the time) commissioned a soundtrack to accompany the exhibition, a mixtape called, in internal correspondence, a "pre-recorded tape collage."[138] Once installed along with the multipanel collage, this nearly eight-minute recording surrounded visitors with Charlie Parker–inspired bebop music.

Like a Parker solo—which could, as his biographer Stanley Crouch put it, be executed at the tempo of an emergency[139]—*The Block* is full of asides and quotations. Its cutaway view of the interiors of houses on Lenox Avenue, that quintessential Harlem street (now renamed Malcolm X Boulevard), has clear precedents, some quite personal to Bearden. The technique was introduced to him, as we've seen, by Eugene Bailey, the childhood friend from Bearden's Pittsburgh years, who taught twelve-year-old Romare how to create on paper the scenes Eugene secretly observed through the floorboards of the bordello where his mother worked. This cutaway technique reappears in Bearden's use of Sam Shaw's photographic contact sheets in the *Paris Blues/Jazz* collage *Ellington, Auric, Hodeir* (1981). The gridded sheets suggest window views of parties—within the work's skylined Paris buildings?—where Ellington and others are having fun. They suggest the complex interiority that is one of the themes of *Paris Blues/Jazz*. And the markings on the contact sheets make clear that Bearden wanted this entire work to have the feel of ongoing improvisation, experimentation in rehearsal—beauty that refuses completion.

Another likely source for *The Block* (and for the whole *Paris Blues/Jazz* series) could be the cityscapes of George Grosz, the German refugee artist with whom Bearden studied in New York in the 1930s. The Bearden scholar Glenda Gilmore compares *The Block* to Grosz's *The Suburb* (1922–23), with the key difference that while the Grosz work foregrounds the stark menace of post–World War I Berlin, Bearden's collage celebrates Harlem life in spite of the inevitable blue notes.[140] Bearden's block is a relaxation and play space, mostly: a neighborhood street where children frolic and, even if there's trouble in the air (a blazing fire, a funeral), there's a prevailing sense of block-party conviviality. Here's a space where the way people stand and move is music, the overriding theme, *freedom*.

Bearden was a lifelong student of art history, and so his influences radiate in many directions and stretch back in time. He knew Bruegel's jam-packed city scenes of the mid-sixteenth century. He knew Piet Mondrian's fantastically spare New York City paintings, created to capture in square "blocks" the dance-beat rhythms of the boogie-woogie dance

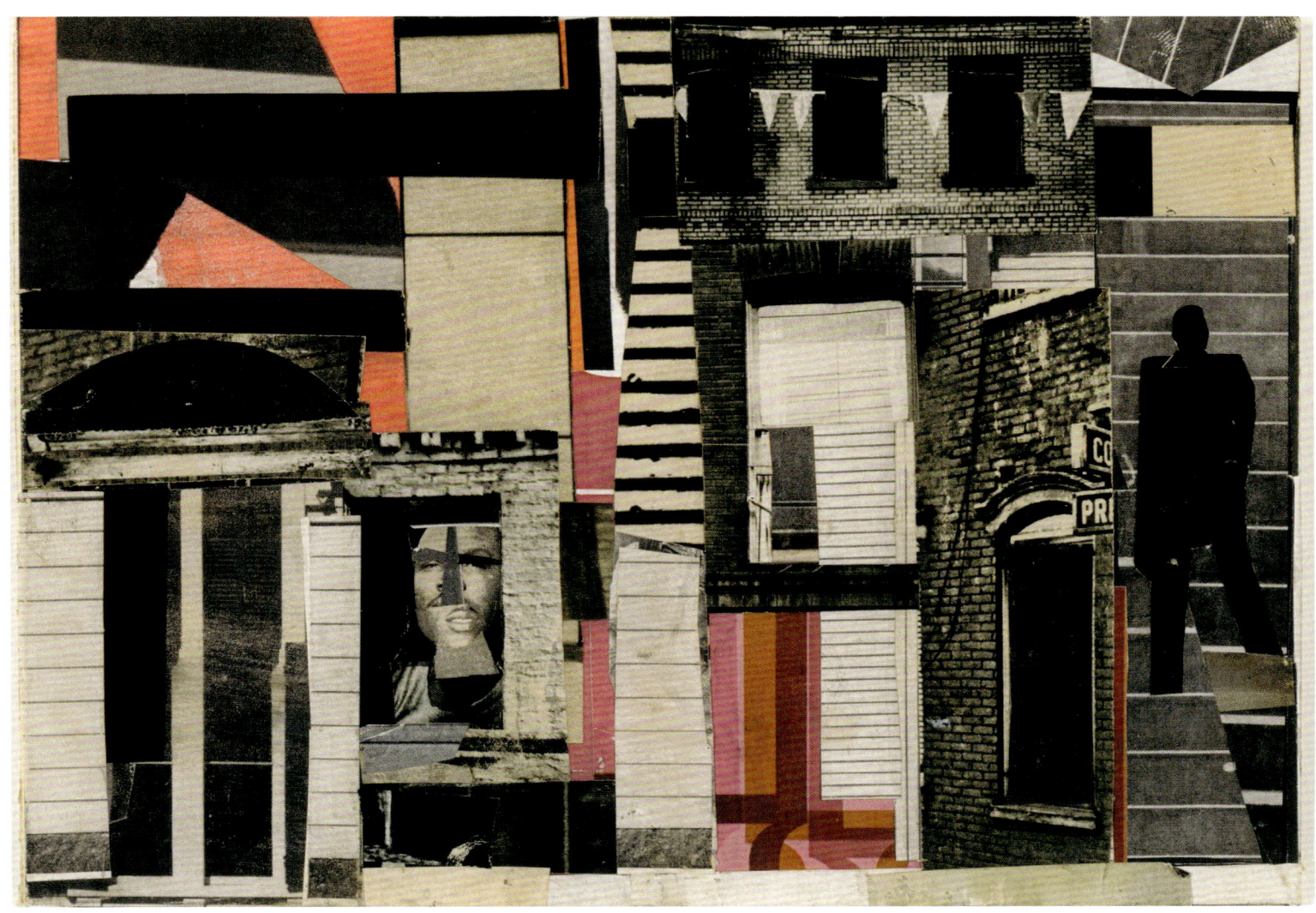

Spring Way, 1964. Collage of various papers on board. 6 ⅝ × 9 ⅜ in. Smithsonian American Art Museum, Bequest of Henry Ward Ranger through the National Academy of Design, 1999.9

music of the 1930s and 1940s, which the Dutch artist (who loved to get up and dance) adored.

This Mondrian-Bearden connection is particularly significant, as Bearden's letters and journal entries testify, and as we can see in *The Block* and in *Paris Blues/Jazz*'s Harlem works. As a modernist who was a crucial inheritor of the seventeenth-century Dutch tradition of Pieter de Hooch and Johannes Vermeer, whose doorways, windows, and geometric shapes meant so much to Bearden, Mondrian was a very present model. Mondrian's radical reduction of the world and its players to rhythmically arranged lines and boxes represented for Bearden a thrilling new take on Cubism, a mode of abstraction by subtraction that had both spiritual force and this-worldly grounding. Once in New York City, where he spent the war years 1940–44, Mondrian was drawn to jazz venues ranging from Café Society downtown to Harlem's landmark Minton's Playhouse. How, Mondrian wondered, to rearrange the straight lines and boxes of Cubism to reflect contemporary New York's heavily rhythmical boogie-woogie and bebop musical paces and energies? How to paint jazz? (Again: What is the piano lesson?)

I see Bearden's *The Block* as a radical updating of *Broadway Boogie Woogie* (1942–43) and *Victory Boogie Woogie* (1942–44), this time with buildings, sidewalks, and a full cast of New York figures in place.[141] Mondrian aspects are also strongly in play in Bearden's *Paris Blues/Jazz* series, where most book pages, single and double rectangles, contain tilted boxes (and boxes inside boxes), reflecting boogie-woogie as a "rolling bass" piano style with solo right-hand action that can be dazzling. For both artists, jazz is a dance, full of movement that is rhythmic but never dully redundant. Concerning the label "boogie-woogie," by the way, I believe that when Mondrian used that term to title his works, he meant not only the rolling bass style of Meade Lux Lewis, Albert Ammons, and Pete Johnson (and the few other masters of the form who show up in Mondrian's record

collection), but other forms of jazz he encountered at Café Society and in clubs like Harlem's Minton's, where bebop was taking shape. By "boogie-woogie" I think he meant throbbing dance-beat jazz rhythms soundtracking New York City. It's much more interesting to think of the roots of boogie-woogie, back into the nineteenth century, and its fresh young shoots, tended by the likes of Billie Holiday, Charlie Parker, and Thelonious Monk.

While other sources came into play in Bearden's *The Block*—from Jacob Lawrence's *Rooftops* (1942) and Aaron Douglas's cityscapes to Abstract Expressionism and photomontage—Bearden's own words about creating the collage help us see clearly the city-as-jazz idea it so beautifully unfolds. In the documentary film *Bearden Plays Bearden* (1980), the artist stands on the balcony of Albert Murray's apartment in the landmark Harlem residence Lenox Terrace, the two of them overlooking the very block that Bearden had recreated in his masterwork.[142] Speaking to Murray and to the camera, Bearden invokes the city/jazz connection: "Looking at those buildings now, Al . . . See that one; those two red ones; and this one a little longer; this one coming back to here. Actually, what I'm doing here is making a keyboard."[143]

Continuing to speak of visual rhythms during the terrace interview, Bearden refers to the avenue's musiclike interplay of geometric shapes: long and short houses, rooftop details, and so forth. "Now the thing that we have to think about here," says Bearden, "is interval." Looking at the sequence of row houses, he goes on: "See this one's dark, see, and this [is a] big light area. . . . And we're already defining this as a musical composition . . . moving from one point to another. And this is the basis of it. And then you have to look for things that repeat themselves, like those chimneys, you see, going along, and you move. Repetition. And then you see those triangular movements? And you get these here. And the first thing you know, you've got a sonata."[144]

So we must watch, throughout the *Paris Blues/Jazz* series, for patterns of images—heads, horns, masks, light fixtures, other circles and rectangles—rhythmically arranged. Rhythm is not only the basis of all music; according to Toni Morrison, it's one of the artistic features, along with color and structure, that all artists seek. Rhythm is indispensable; creating anticipation, *rhythm is a promise*.[145]

And interval is the building block of rhythm. As we've seen elsewhere in this book, Bearden's friend Stuart Davis first pointed out to him Earl "Fatha" Hines's use of spaces in both chord and note sequences—the great Pittsburgh-born pianist's deployment of sonic interval. "I listened and listened and listened to Earl Hines," said Bearden, "until I couldn't hear the music, only the silences—in order to pick up the intervals of his playing."[146] The term *interval* became one of Bearden's key ways of zeroing in on jazz's influence on his art. On some level Bearden's efforts to paint the music were all about vibrant images rhythmically spaced and the spaces themselves: an interval also is a promise.

In Bearden's on-camera exegesis of *The Block*, the artist agrees with Murray that, as compelling as the work's specific images of the street scene may be, he is not functioning as a photojournalist, reporting "objective" reality. Nor is he reproducing the techniques of prior art. While part of his mission (and part of his fun) as an artist involves embracing allusions to, and rhymes with, prior art, Bearden says he's also spurred by what the tradition *lacks*. "An artist," he says, "is an art lover who finds that in all the art he sees, something is missing. To touch at the core of what he feels is missing, to put there what needs to be there, becomes the center of his life's work."[147] Clearly, what Bearden felt was missing in prior renderings of the cities he loved was "the Black thing," or a certain down-home/uptown soulfulness that Bearden termed "the innerness of the Negro experience."[148] In this vein, he also wanted to add

a contemporary American sense of speed and movement, and an Armstrong/Ellington improvisatory attitude. (Cubism, he said, was too static for him, too *square*). You get started on a work, he says, and then begin to see images emerging. "You actually fill the painting by taking the options as they open up, as you play with them, as you improvise," says Murray. Bearden: "Exactly."

And so, I recommend seeing *The Block* as a touchstone or a lens through which to regard Bearden's *Paris Blues/Jazz* series. *The Block* tells us what to watch for: cityscape keyboards where the intervals also have stories to tell, where space is the place; the overall visual rhythm of the compositions; the effort to capture Black culture in moments soulful and free. The way these city works unfold across the pages is jazz.

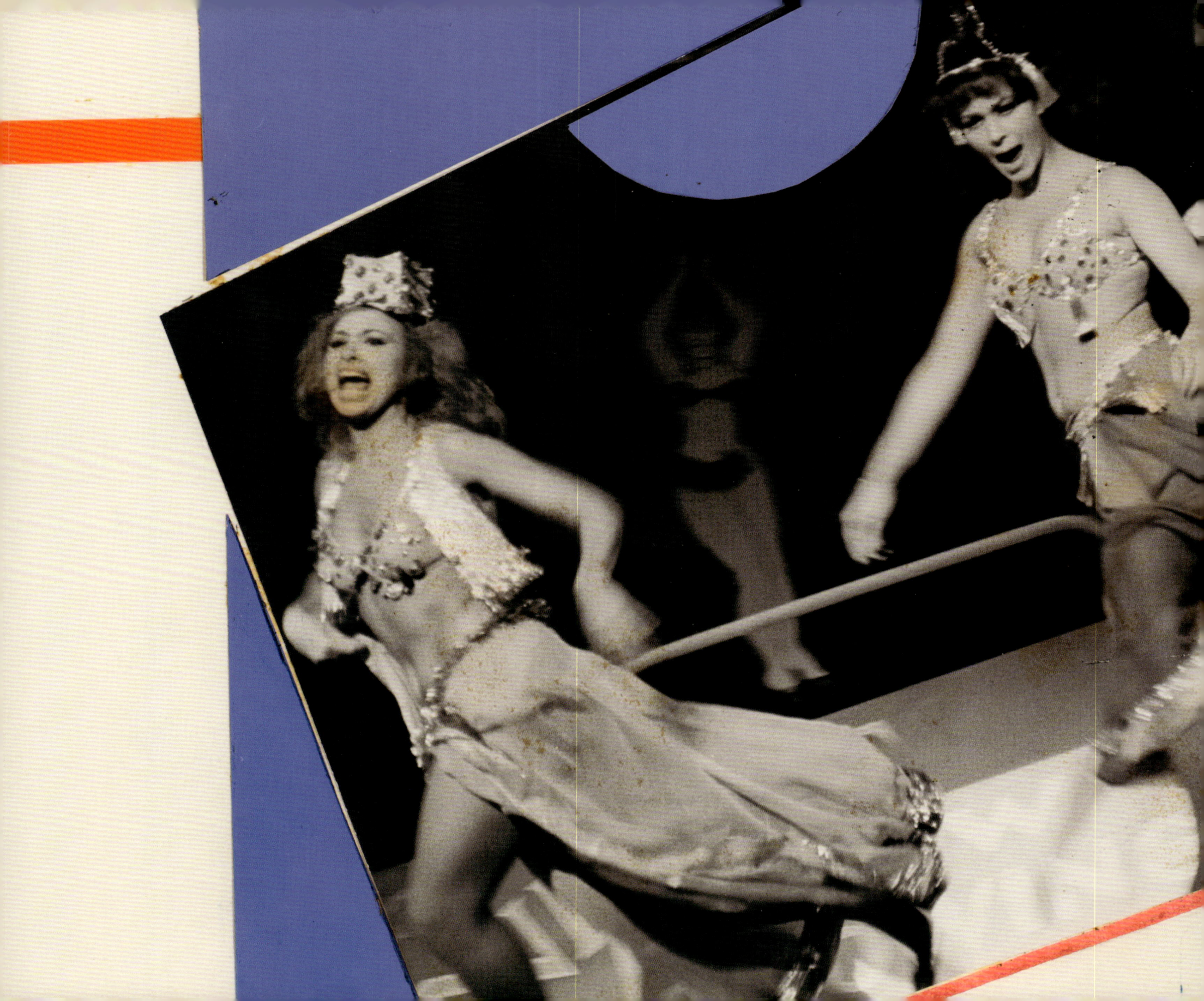

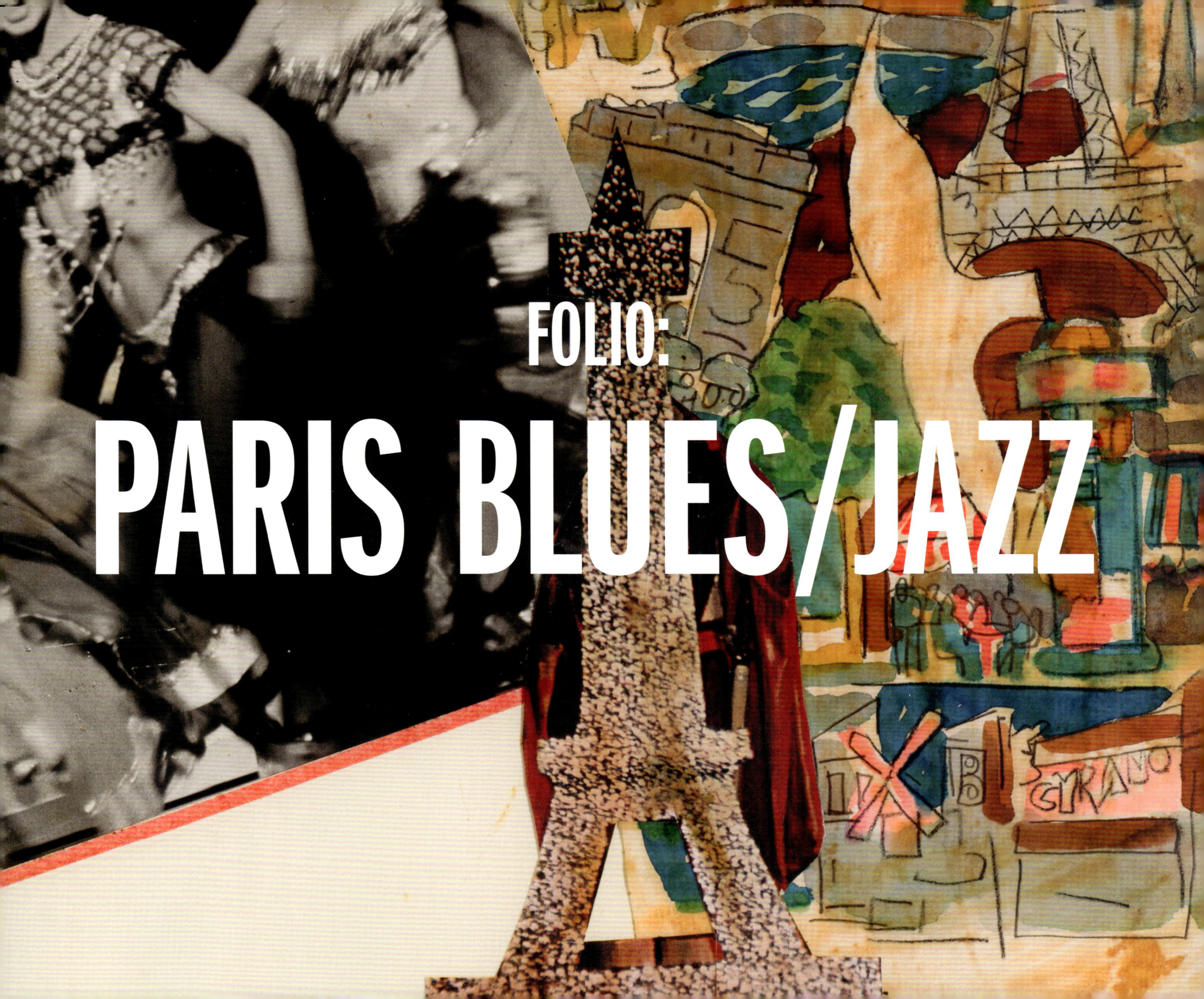

FOLIO:
PARIS BLUES/JAZZ

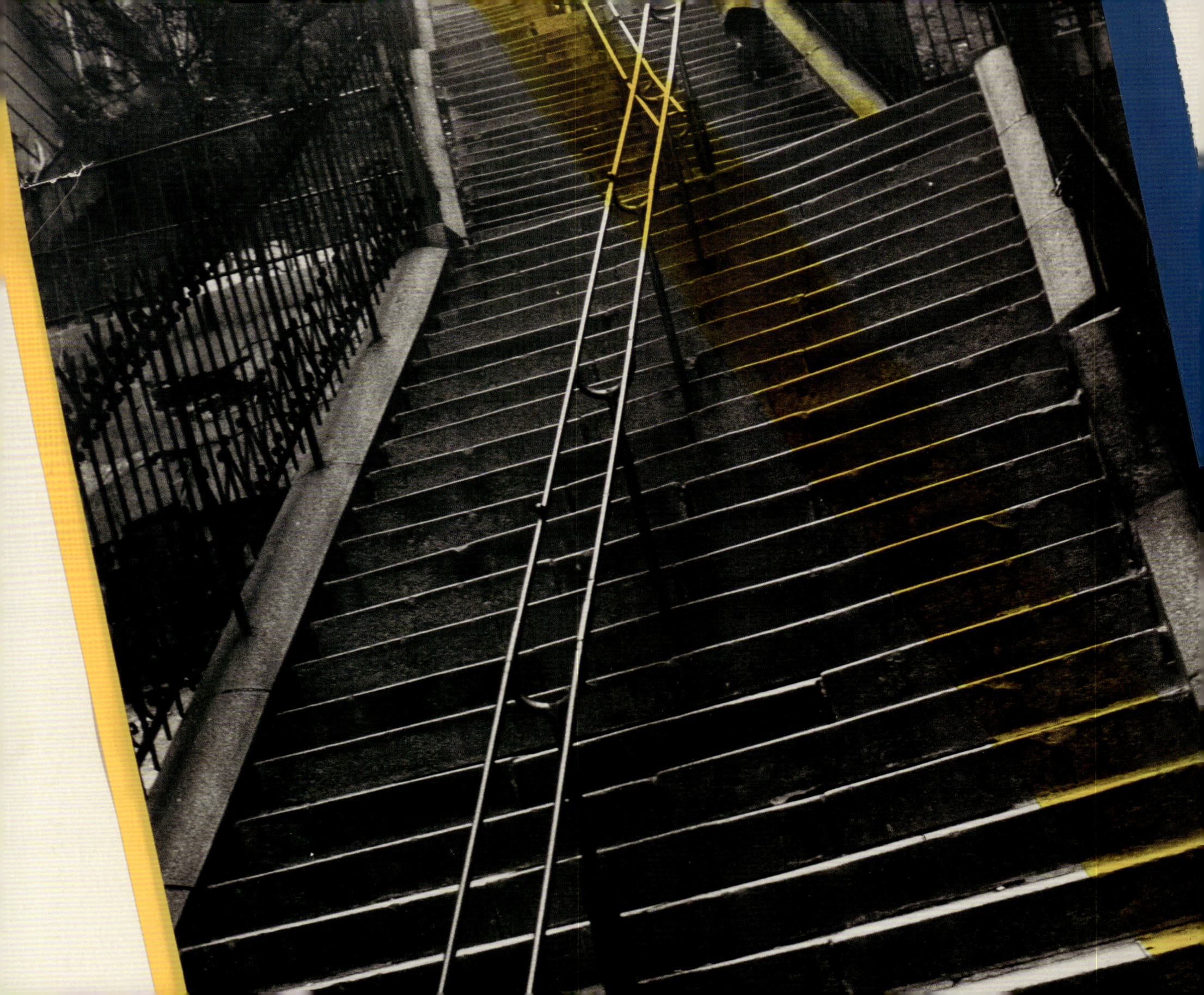

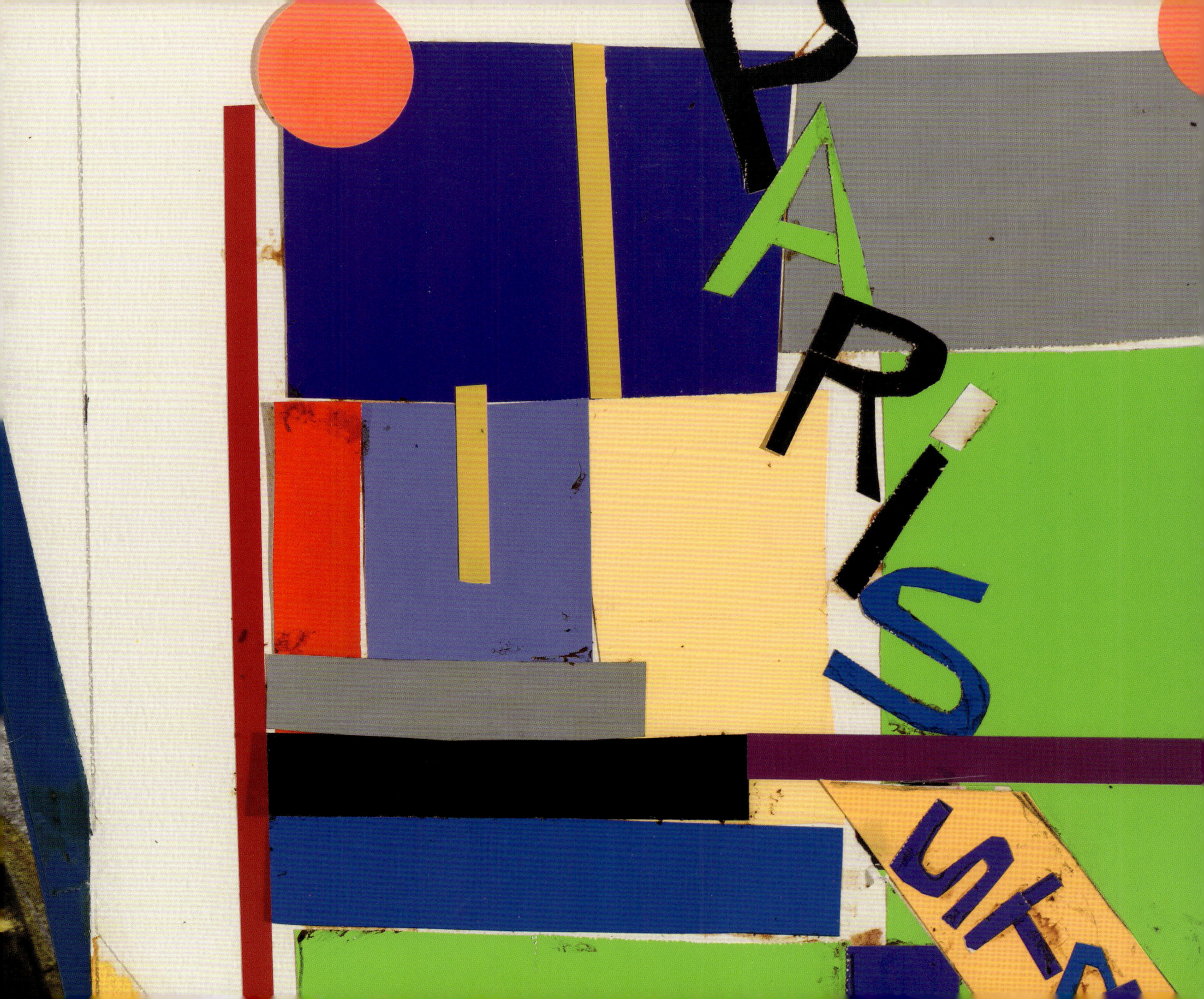

PARIS

Given the collage book's origins in the movie *Paris Blues*, we must start our tour of its three cities in Paris. In doing so, we'll also challenge the up-the-river-from-New Orleans jazz narrative, as well as the America-only map of the music's geography. Perhaps most importantly, we'll acknowledge the City of Light as an *ur*-source for art making in general, especially in the West. There's a quality of that city that can't easily be captured in words: the soft but brilliant light from its skies (Sam Shaw saw it as "a beautiful tone of silver gray"),[1] the spring in one's step while meandering its streets, the long history of artistic production there, the welcome that artists feel. "There *is* no square block in Paris, that's the beauty of it," said Gordon Heath, the expat Black American actor-singer who in the 1950s owned a Left Bank club where Bearden liked to hang. "I think maybe that's why I'm here. What's wrong with the States is, the streets are too straight!"[2] Bearden's longest stretch there was for seven months in 1950 following his military service. He returned home to New York with a plan to do whatever it took to get back; while the plan was never realized, the love of Paris endured. Perhaps he shared with Richard Wright, whom he met in Paris, something of the sentiments the author of *Native Son* expressed in his 1950 essay "I Choose Exile." Said Wright:

> I live in exile because I love freedom, and I've found more freedom in one . . . block of Paris than there is in the entire United States! . . . Some people need more freedom than others, and I'm one of them. Unless I'm uninhibited in letting my instincts range, unhampered in my comings and goings, free to question and probe my environment, I languish, I wither. . . . I want the right to hold, without fear of punitive measures, an opinion with which my neighbor does not agree; the right to travel wherever and whenever I please even though my ideas might not

coincide with those of whatever Federal Administration might be in power in Washington; the right to express publicly my distrust of the "collective wisdom" of the people; the right to exercise my conscience and intelligence to the extent of refusing to "inform" and "spy" on my neighbor because he holds political convictions differing from mine; the right to express, without fear of reprisal, my rejection of religion.[3]

Paris certainly was a favorite "home" for the circuit-riding heroes of the *Paris Blues/Jazz* series, Armstrong and Ellington. Its traces are everywhere in their work. Check out Armstrong's superb version of "La Vie en Rose" (1950)—a loving serenade scented with the special atmosphere of the walkways along Paris's River Seine. The magical name *Paris* appears in more Ellington and Strayhorn song titles than the name of any other place, aside from Harlem. Three Ellington albums—*Midnight in Paris*, *The Great Paris Album*, and *Paris Blues*—offer extended songs of praise to the city. The protagonist of one of Strayhorn's first masterworks, "Lush Life," suffering from world-weariness and love gone wrong, muses that "a week in Paris would ease the bite of it." According to Ellington, his first trips to Paris, in 1933 and 1939, made him aware of the international appeal of his own music. Like Bearden's, Ellington's Paris—which, by the 1950s, he and Strays knew much more intimately than the former GI—was a place for Black men and women to live and breathe in more freely, where they could party without regard to race or sexual preference, and where they could dream of joining that city's tradition of creating new forms of art. Where they could get their work done.

Bearden loved Paris as much as anyone. His *Lovers in Luxembourg Garden* (1981) is a visual love poem to match "La Vie en Rose." His primary theme, however, is the diversity of sites in the City of Light where music flourished—the circuses,

Romani encampments, and recording studios with musicians at the controls. His *Cirque du Soleil* (1981) depicts what was and is an important venue for jazz players, a vital stop on the circuit of the music. And the collage simply called *Ellington, Auric, Hodeir* (1981) is a paean to artistic sites, sources, and kinship. The work places Ellington alongside French composer George Auric and French jazz historian-producer Hugues Panassié, the threesome arrayed like statues of saints or Rushmore heads.

DUKE AND STRAYHORN

Seen here are composer-pianists Duke Ellington and Billy Strayhorn, who co-wrote the soundtrack for the film *Paris Blues* (1961). Trimming and pasting down photos by Sam Shaw (*collage* comes from a French verb *coller* meaning "to paste"), Bearden makes them monumental figures riding through a bright garden of Paris landmarks, missing nothing. A dove sails through the blues, proclaiming the collagist's kinship with Picasso and the main theme of the entire *Paris Blues/Jazz* series (and of jazz itself): freedom! Mona Lisa is part of the city's welcome committee!

Paris Blues/Jazz
Ellington, Billy Strayhorn (Sacré-Cœur), 1981
Collage on paper
14 × 11 in.

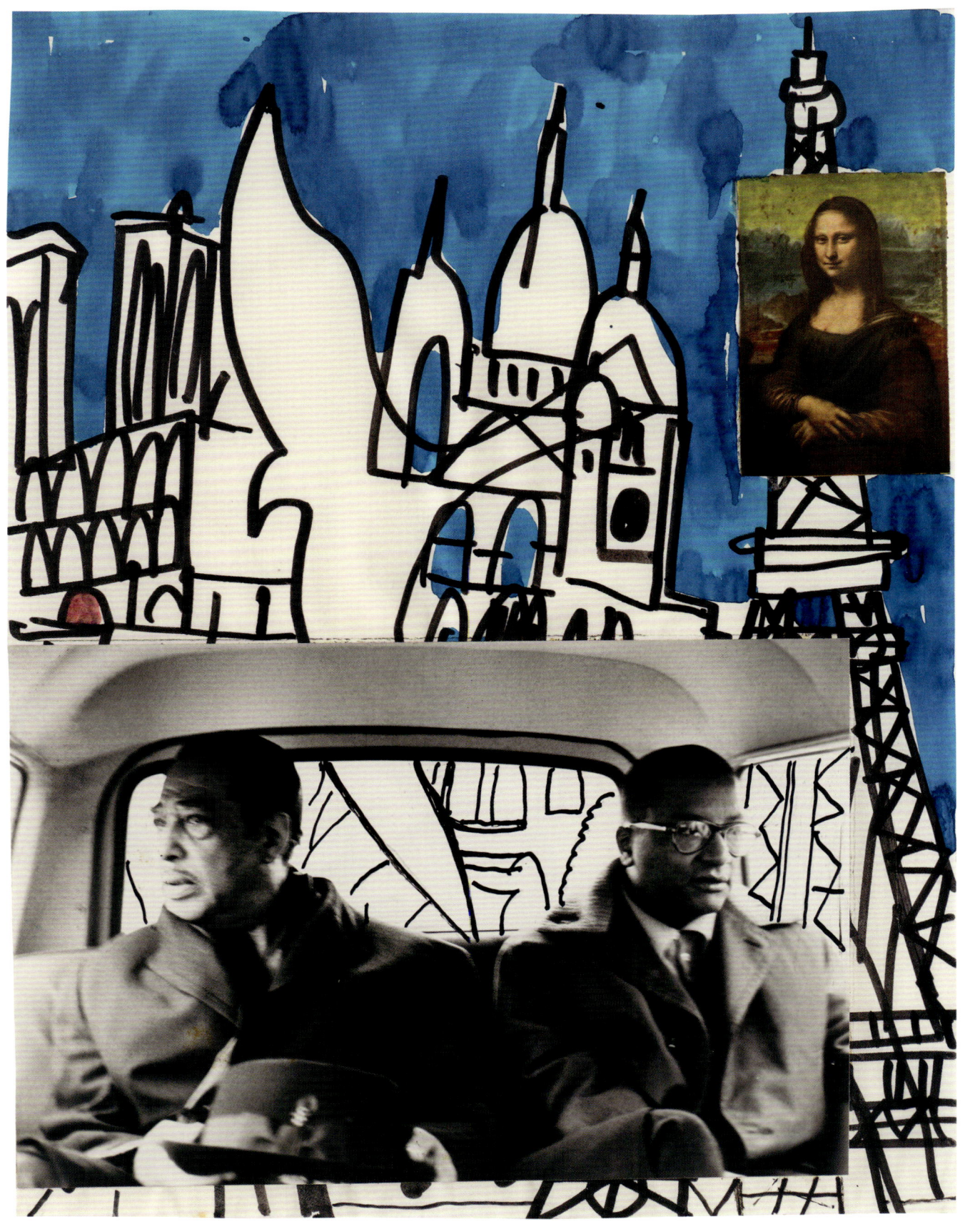

ELLINGTON, RAINBOW

The cluster of Bearden works from the 1960s to the 1980s that refer to his friend Duke Ellington could make a show unto themselves. Among these, the collage *Ellington, Rainbow* (1981) stands out for its emphasis on Duke the colorist broadcasting luminescence from his fingertips whether as conductor, composer, or pianist. This work reminds us that the maestro, who once turned down a scholarship to study visual art at Pratt Institute in Brooklyn, was extraordinarily mindful of color, texture, and other aspects of visual art. With his song titles and program notes he announced that in certain instances he created "tone parallels" to people, scenes, and scenarios. "Black, Brown and Beige," "Mood Indigo," "Blue Light," and "Magenta Haze" are among his color titles. Another is "Transblucency" (aka "A Blue Fog That You Can Almost See Through"). Such word pictures, and his persistent uses of blues harmonies, call out the mixes of sound color throughout the Ellington canon.

Part of what's been called the Ellington Effect is created by his sometimes very surprising combinations of instruments, and by the way his handpicked musicians play them—the horn men at times employing "fake fingerings" to create the kaleidoscope of harmonies and textures on command. In one filmed version of Ellington's "David Danced before the Lord with All His Might/Come Sunday" (1968), a solo singer's raspy-cool voice (Jon Hendricks's), call-and-response choral sections, and the quicksilver beats of a tap dancer's feet (Bunny Briggs)[6]

interweave with solo, and then shouting, ensemble horns—all with a rhythmical play of colors, textures, and layers corresponding with the elements of this special portrait. Here, too, Ellington's raised hand welcomes viewers into the *Paris Blues/Jazz* series' full tapestry of pieces where colors arc and glow. In this Sam Shaw photo, could Ellington be conducting the *Paris Blues* soundtrack?

Paris Blues/Jazz
Ellington, Rainbow, 1981
Collage on paperboard
13 ¾ × 22 in.

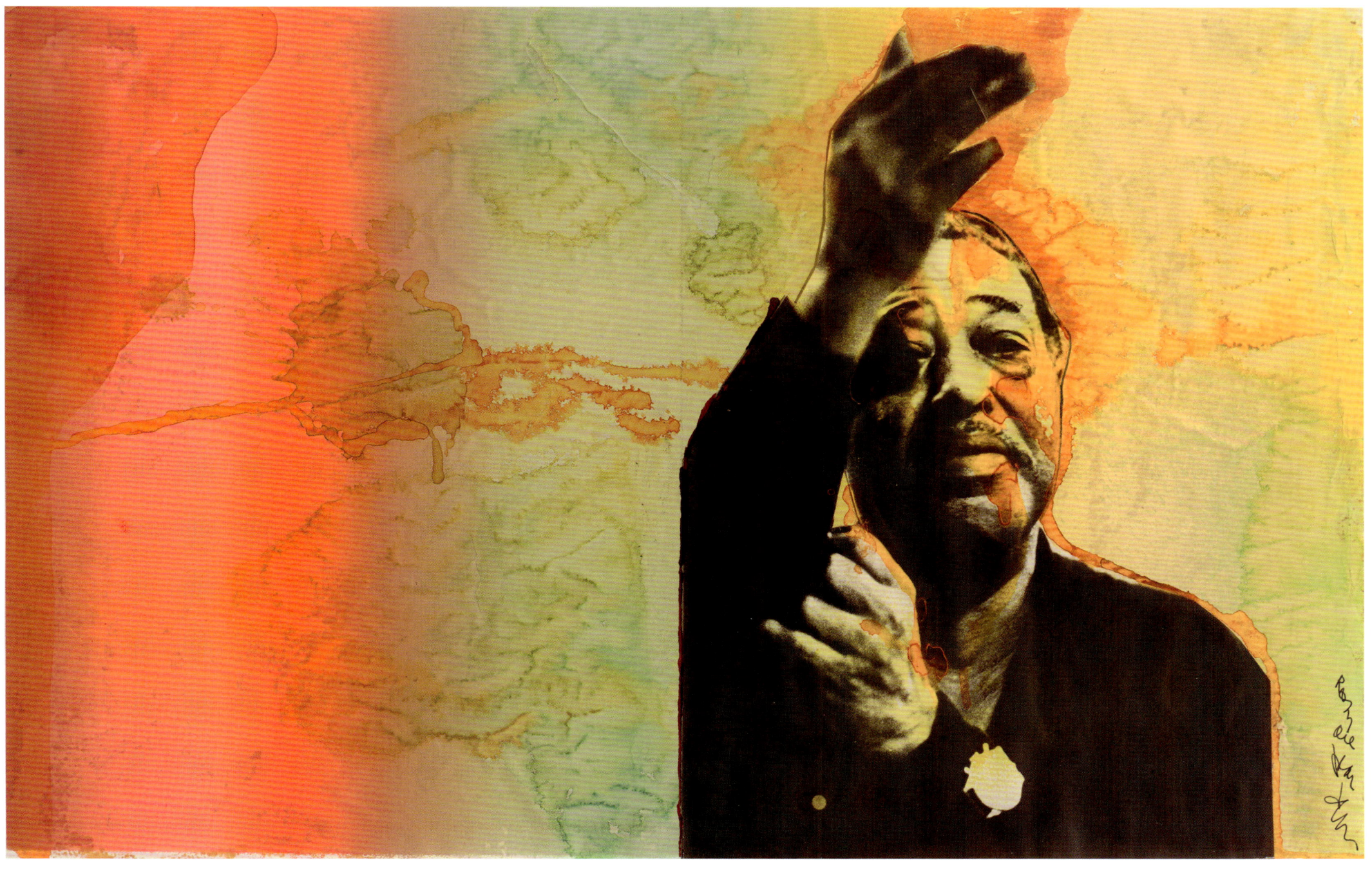

PARIS MAP

Bearden's collage map *Being in Paris* shows Paris romantically dappled in the soft-lit colors of a citywide flower garden. This Paris is furnished with unmistakable landmarks (two of them so tall they exceed the collage's top edge), so those navigating the city never feel lost there—a quality one urban studies scholar associates with the visitor's overall sense of well-being.[4] Above all, the collage emphasizes this town's possibilities for movement: boats meander the curvy river, multiple bridges rhythmically connect its banks. One landmark is a Metro station standing alongside *Guide Bleu* pages and three Metro tickets, glued (collaged) into place. Another is a café, which recalls the time when Bearden saw Henri Matisse in just such a place in 1950. When the waiters spotted Matisse (by then an old man) walking past, they began to applaud him with white-gloved hands. "Where," Bearden frequently said to interviewers when recounting this story, "would this happen in the United States?"[5]

Framing it all are the French colors—city map as national flag. The sun seems to roll between the hills: the source of orange light across the city's reds and blues. *Oh*, as the church song says, *what a beautiful city!*

Paris Blues/Jazz
Being in Paris, 1981
Collage on paper
16 ¼ × 25 in.

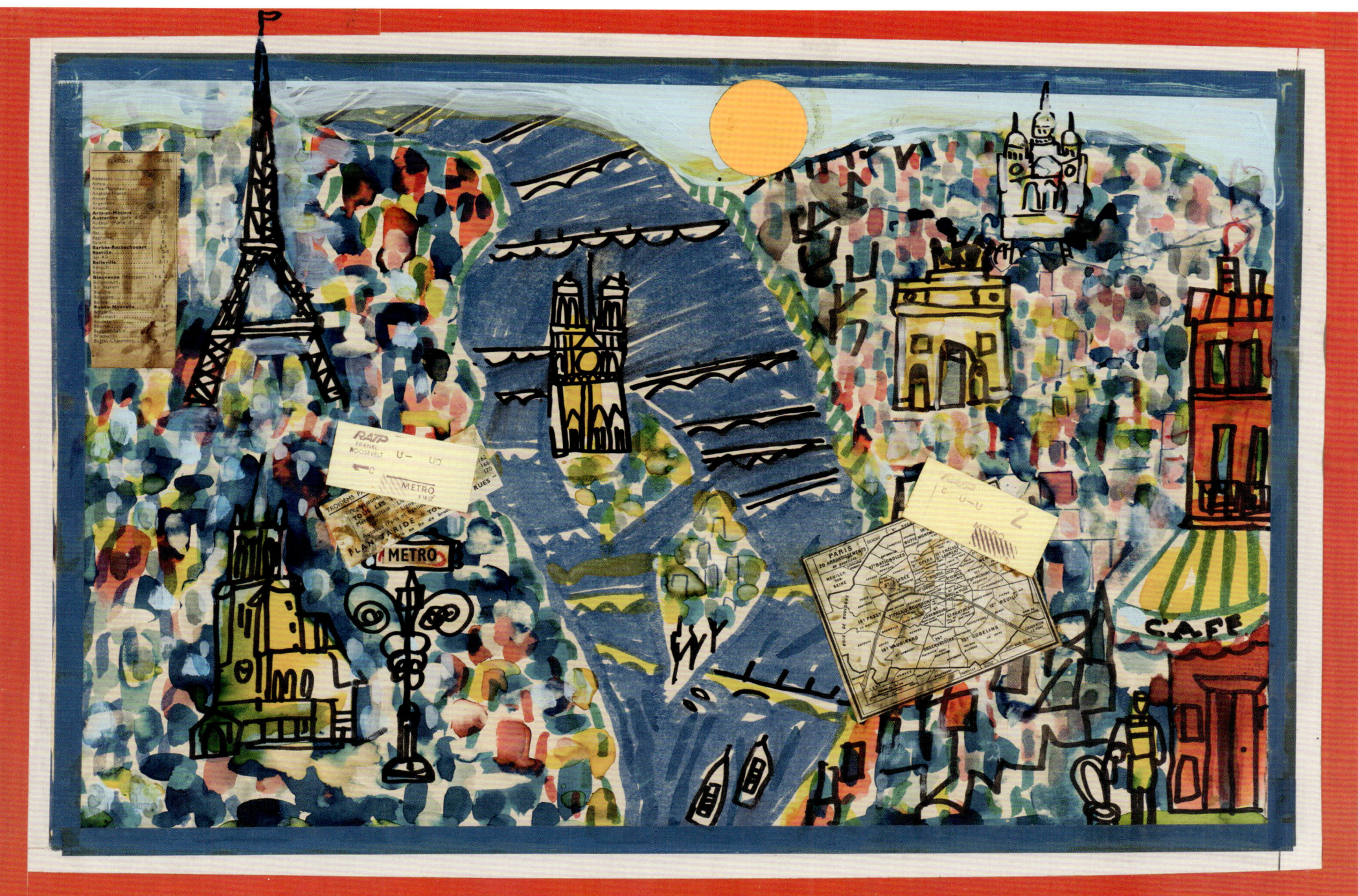

PARIS STAIRS

One idea from the film *Paris Blues* retained in this series of collages is that of the up-and-downness of travels through the City of Light. The film's characters fall in love while joyously strolling Paris. Up flight after flight to Montmartre they go, across bridges great and small, through the winding streets of Bastille and Saint-Michel, down the steps to the riverfront, moving to the rhythm of the city. In Harold Flender's novel *Paris Blues* (but not in the film), the Sidney Poitier character Eddie surprises Connie (Diahann Carroll on screen) with a casual reference to Henry James, who declares that the inspiration to write certain novels "proceeded quite directly from the habit and the interest of walking the streets." James is speaking of London, but the same is true of Paris. In interviews Bearden said that after a certain point in his artistic development he was basically a Cubist who wanted to add more movement to his rectangles. Like the Sam Shaw photo that appears in the left panel, Bearden's collage is angled to create a sense of movement. Bearden's cutout words "P-A-R-I-S" and "S-T-A-I-R-S" themselves make staircases that are well lit by the collage's three red suns and by a yellow source of light at the city's center: City of Light, City of Flights!

Paris Blues/Jazz
Paris Stairs, 1981
Collage on paperboard
14 × 22 in.

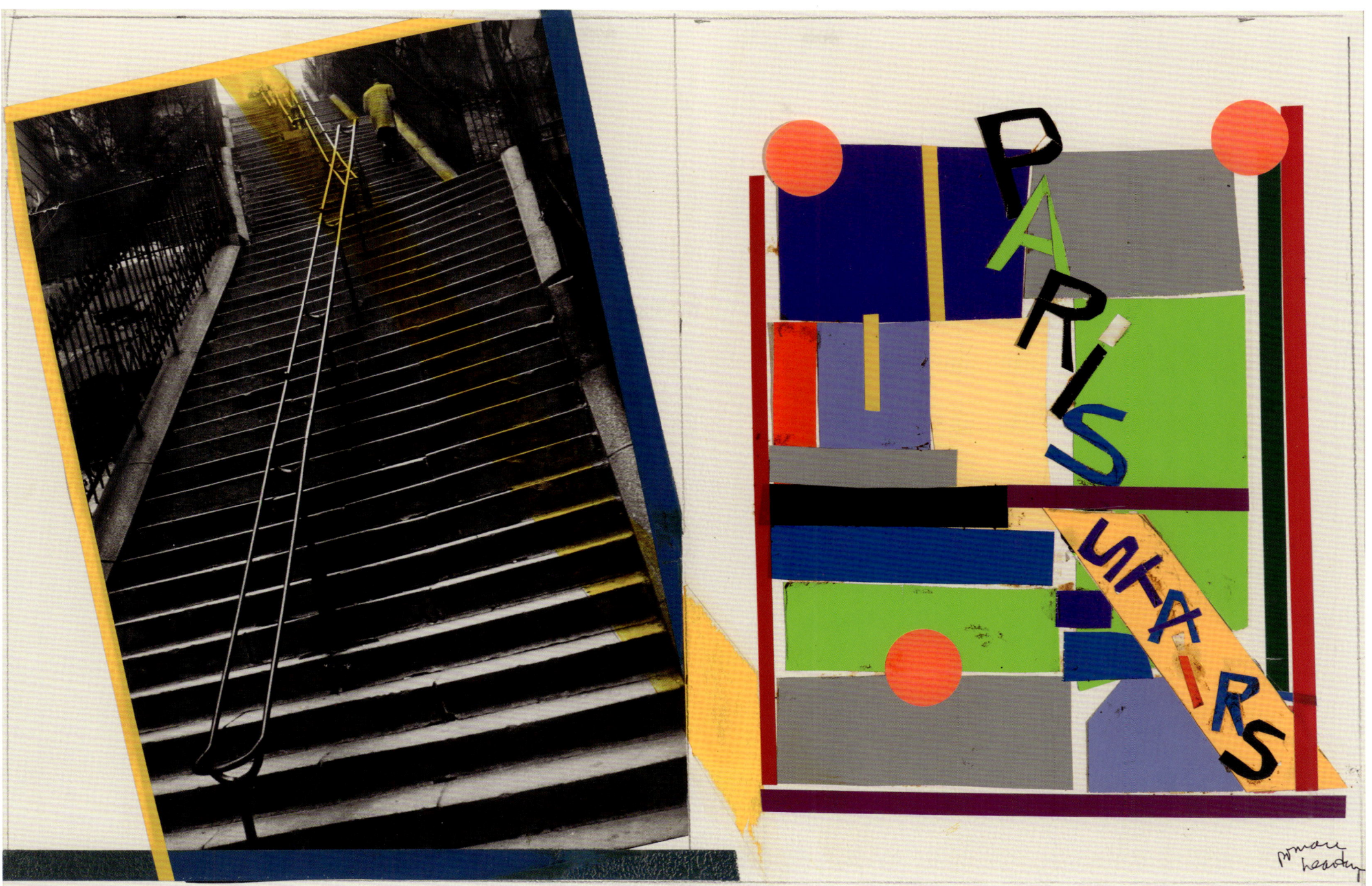

IN PARIS

Ellington, Auric, Hodeir is one of this project's luminous double-page collages whose subject is artistic sites, sources, and kinship. Marked on the work's left panel with a green sticky note reading "Page 41/42"—not visible behind the exhibition frame—*Ellington, Auric, Hodeir* has the fresh air of work for the *Paris Blues/Jazz* book in progress. This and other handwritten marginal notes attached to the work's edges, and the marked-out and circled images on the contact sheets affixed here, all suggest the artist's ongoing process of improvisation by addition and subtraction, revision and redaction. (Certainly Bearden would have revisited this piece to correct the misidentification of the French music historian Hugues Panassié as André Hodeir, the French composer/music theorist.)

Capping the monumental headshots of the three music men is the city's rooftop skyline—itself a gorgeous Parisian signature, in this instance outlining the famously independent and multi-ethnic neighborhood Belleville (not the Montparnasse famously associated with many of Bearden's artistic contemporaries). These rooftop details recall Bearden's comment that the building tops in *The Block* (1971), his portrait of Harlem, comprise "a musical composition."[7] The work's three huge heads compose a sort of skyline, too—a Mount Rushmore evidently nominating the musicians as set-in-stone founders and sustainers, not of a single-state nation but of the Transnational Realm of Music.

Bearden's play with form in *Ellington, Auric, Hodeir* is highlighted by the rhythmical juxtaposition of rectangular shapes in the cityscape with those same shapes on the contact-sheet strips—that is, a play between architectural windows and photographic framing. Mirroring aspects of *Ellington with Paris Graffiti* (1981), each of this work's small contact-sheet photos has a windowlike aspect, offering sightlines into social gatherings. This is Paris as a place of serious work and business, but also of flirtation and big fun. The music of Ellington, said Amiri Baraka, is "where you go if you are good."[8] Ellington's music and Paris? Who could ask for any place more?

Paris Blues/Jazz
Ellington, Auric, Hodeir, 1981
Collage on paper
14 × 22 in.

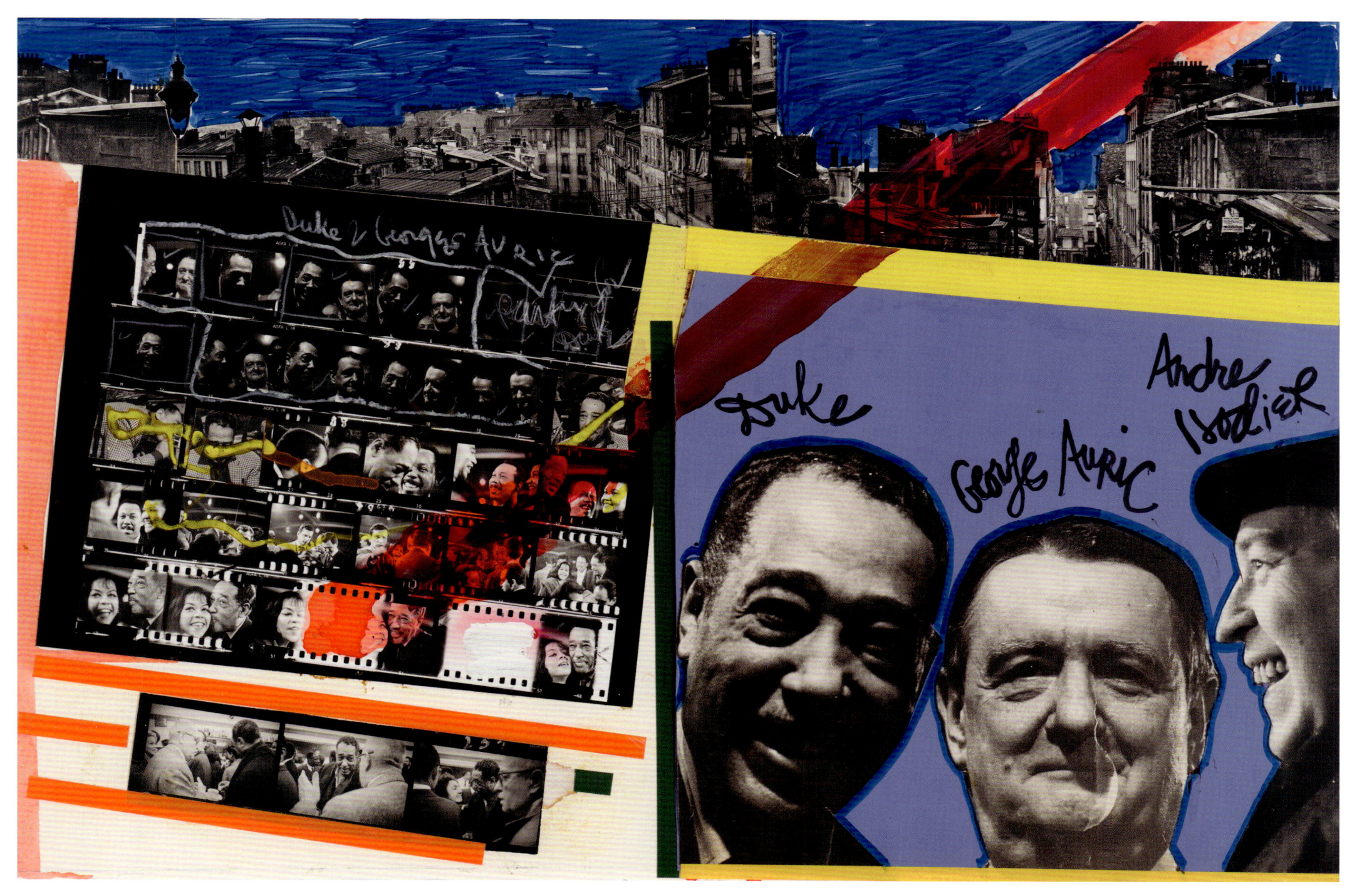

ELLINGTON WITH PARIS GRAFFITI

Like several other collages in the series, *Ellington with Paris Graffiti* stretches across the drafted open book's two-page spread. With one tilted rectangle per page, it projects the "American" sense of dynamic movement that Bearden said he found lacking in the European Cubist tradition. Here a light spring-green predominates, with fresh new growth overflowing the borders like flowers. On the left-hand page (marked "1A"), the *Paris Blues/Jazz* series' two protagonists, Duke Ellington and Louis Armstrong, are pictured on the set of the film *Paris Blues*—perhaps announcing that the score by Ellington and Billy Strayhorn and the cameos by Armstrong are by far the best things about that Hollywood project. But Bearden's statement about these Black American artists' sense of artistic affiliation and purpose goes far beyond the movie set. Writers and painters are shouted out here, all French except for the vigorous American transplant Gertrude Stein, along with iconic Parisian sites of artistic activity—not only explicitly musical spaces but also favorite visual artists' party spaces, haunts, and 'hoods.

The work's right page (marked "2A") features a light-table view of Sam Shaw's contact sheets: here one finds Yoruba metalwork (left column), prints by Picasso (left center), and unattributed contemporary works. The juxtapositions make the point that modern European masters like Picasso or Matisse (both named in the work) drew on African art, and that as-yet-unknown artists and those with roots outside Europe are part of the American musicians' circle of influences. The gesture of including Shaw's photos takes us eons beyond the movie's narrow scope of cultural inheritance and geography. Indeed, *Ellington with Paris Graffiti* answers *Paris Blues* the film with a sweeping statement about Black artists' prospects for choosing artistic ancestors, and for choosing the artistic world in which they'll operate.

Paris Blues/Jazz
Ellington with Paris Graffiti, 1981
Collage on paper
13 ¾ × 22 in.

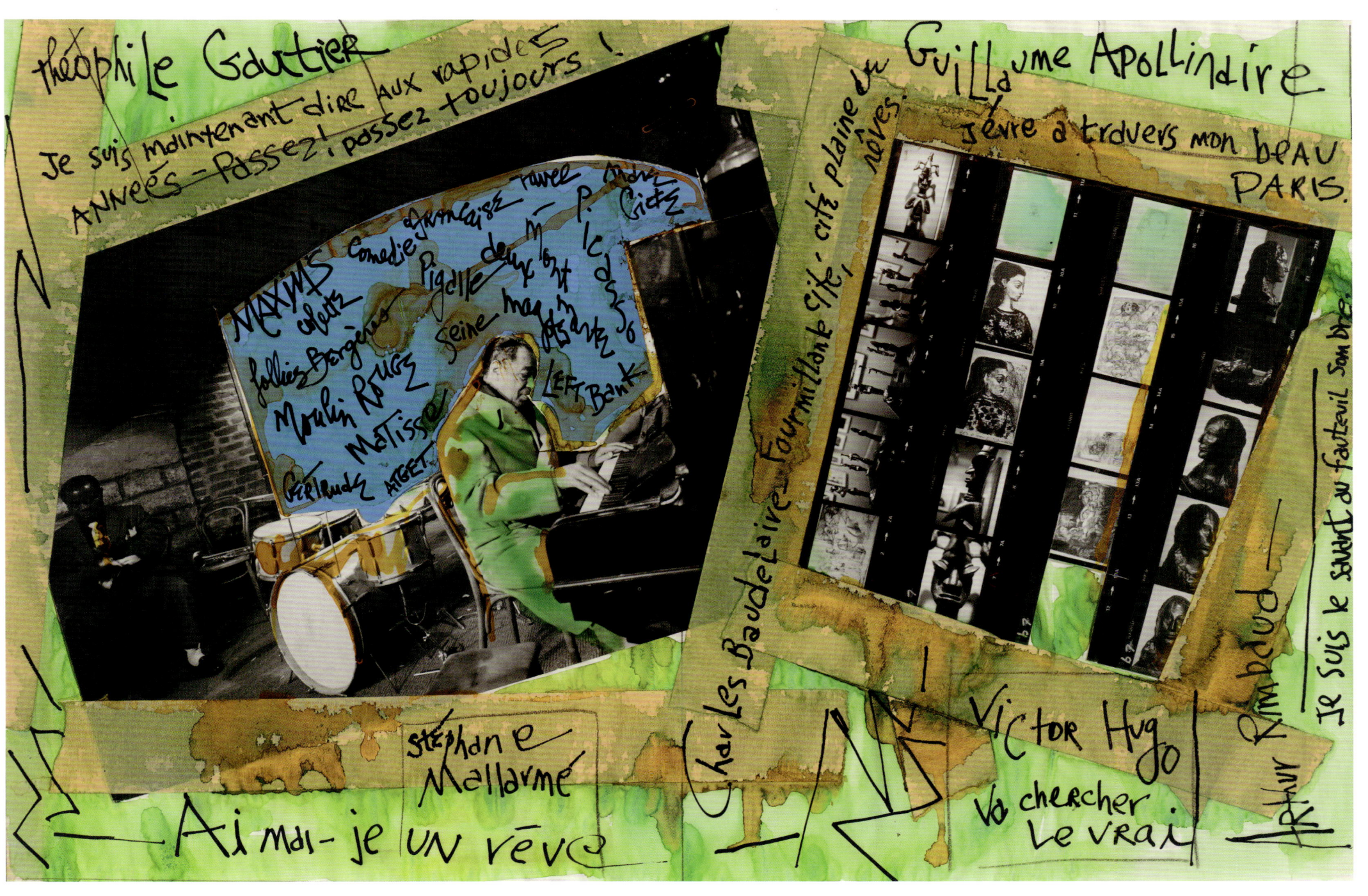

CIRQUE D'HIVER and CASINO DE PARIS

More than any other pieces in the *Paris Blues/Jazz* series, these two collages pay homage to Henri Matisse. On the long shelf of books about Matisse in his Canal Street home library, Bearden had two copies of the French modernist's 1947 book of collages called *Jazz*, where circuses abound. What does the circus have to do with jazz? To begin with, there's plenty of live and recorded music in circuses and carnivals worldwide, some of it jazz or jazz-related. And the Cirque d'Hiver and Cirque du Soleil in Paris were (and remain) important jazz venues—vibrant stops on the international circuit. But what's most significant here, aside from the Matisse reference (see his wonderful *Le Cirque*, in particular), is the effort to offer a visual equivalent of jazz without referring directly to the music or its players as such. "If the music is acrobatic enough," Ellington told an interviewer, "people will respond."[9] Bearden's acrobatic collages in this series seem to say the same thing. Circus acrobatics are like jazz performers: they're all about highly disciplined high-wire work, alone and as part of a team, safety nets not always in place. Here the soundtrack could be Ellington's 1956 Newport Jazz Festival recording of "Diminuendo in Blue" and "Crescendo in Blue" (two Bearden pieces from the period of the *Paris Blues/Jazz* series bear these Duke titles).[10] Surely that record's famously extended, surging solo by tenor saxophonist Paul Gonsalves has a trapezistic aspect. The soundtrack also could be Armstrong's "Chantez-les Bas," where, despite the title ("Sing 'em Low"), Armstrong the high-wire trumpet man plays high as the sky, and then higher.

Paris Blues/Jazz
***Cirque d'Hiver**, 1981*
Collage on paperboard
14 × 22 in.

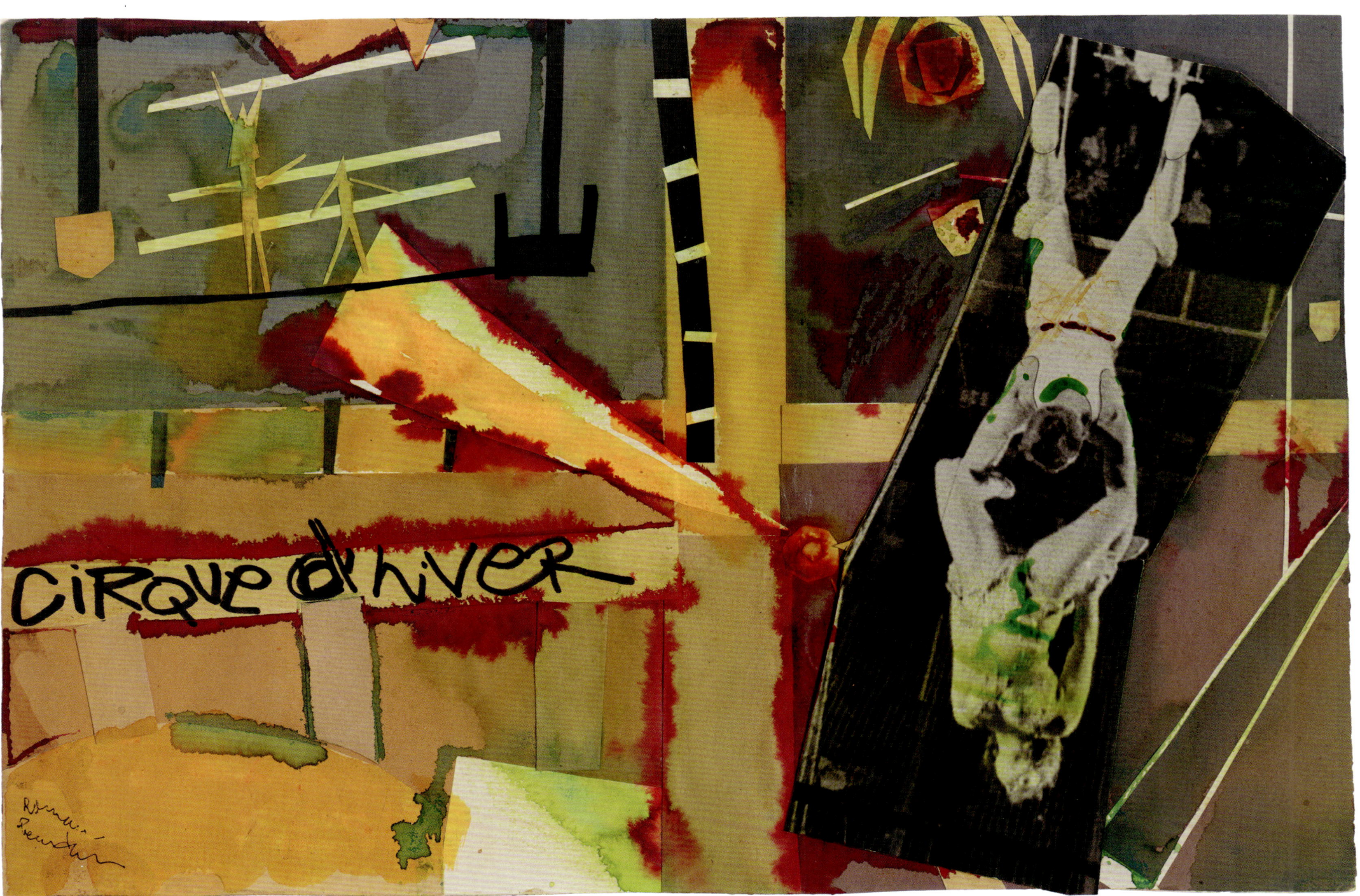

Paris Blues/Jazz
Casino de Paris, 1981
Collage on paper
14 ¼ × 22 ¼ in.

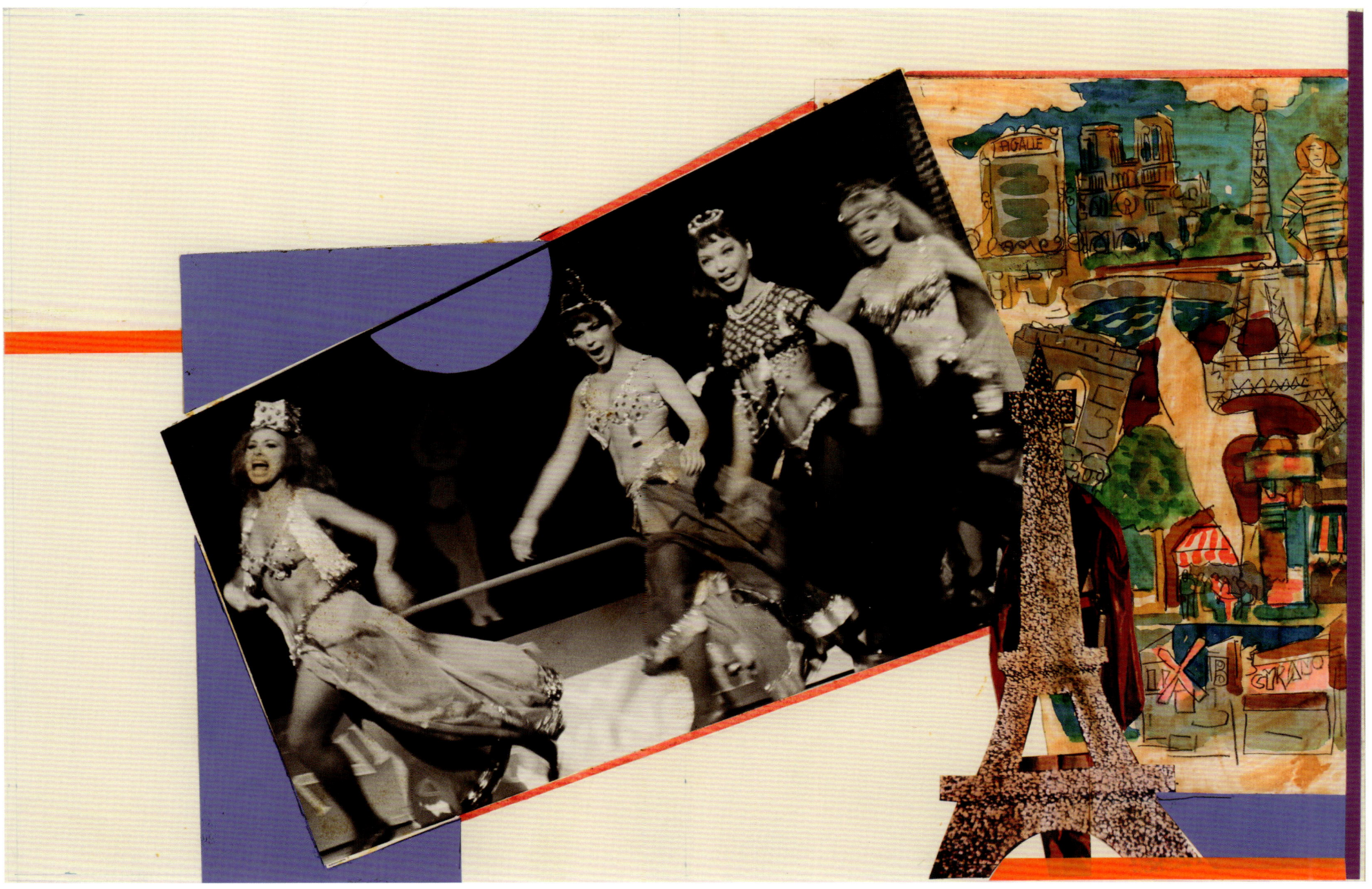

LOVERS IN LUXEMBOURG GARDEN

This collage features a Sam Shaw photograph of lovers and another of a statue of the Rhône as river god (attended by Cupid?) that's not actually in the Luxembourg Garden: it adorns one of the fountains at Versailles.[11] Here again Bearden invokes Matisse—this time with water-plant shapes. The lovers seem to stroll through a blue-green watery space presided over by the reclining river deity, whose staff offers a blessing and an invitation to love that is physical as well as metaphysical. The lovers' race (and gender?) goes unspecified: this is Paris, an ocean apart from American fictions of race and gender.

Paris Blues/Jazz
Lovers in Luxembourg Garden, 1981
Collage on paper
14 ¼ × 22 in.

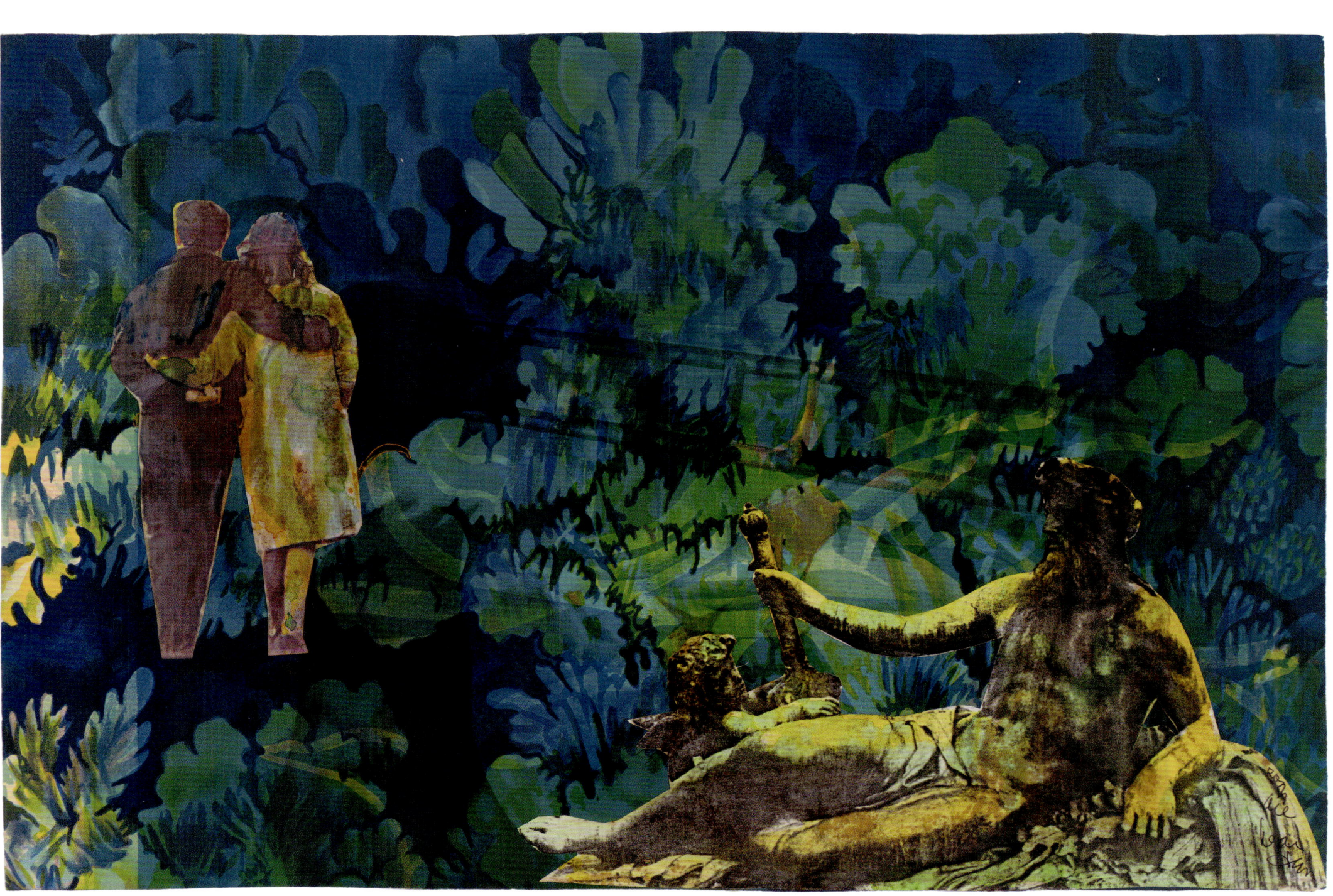

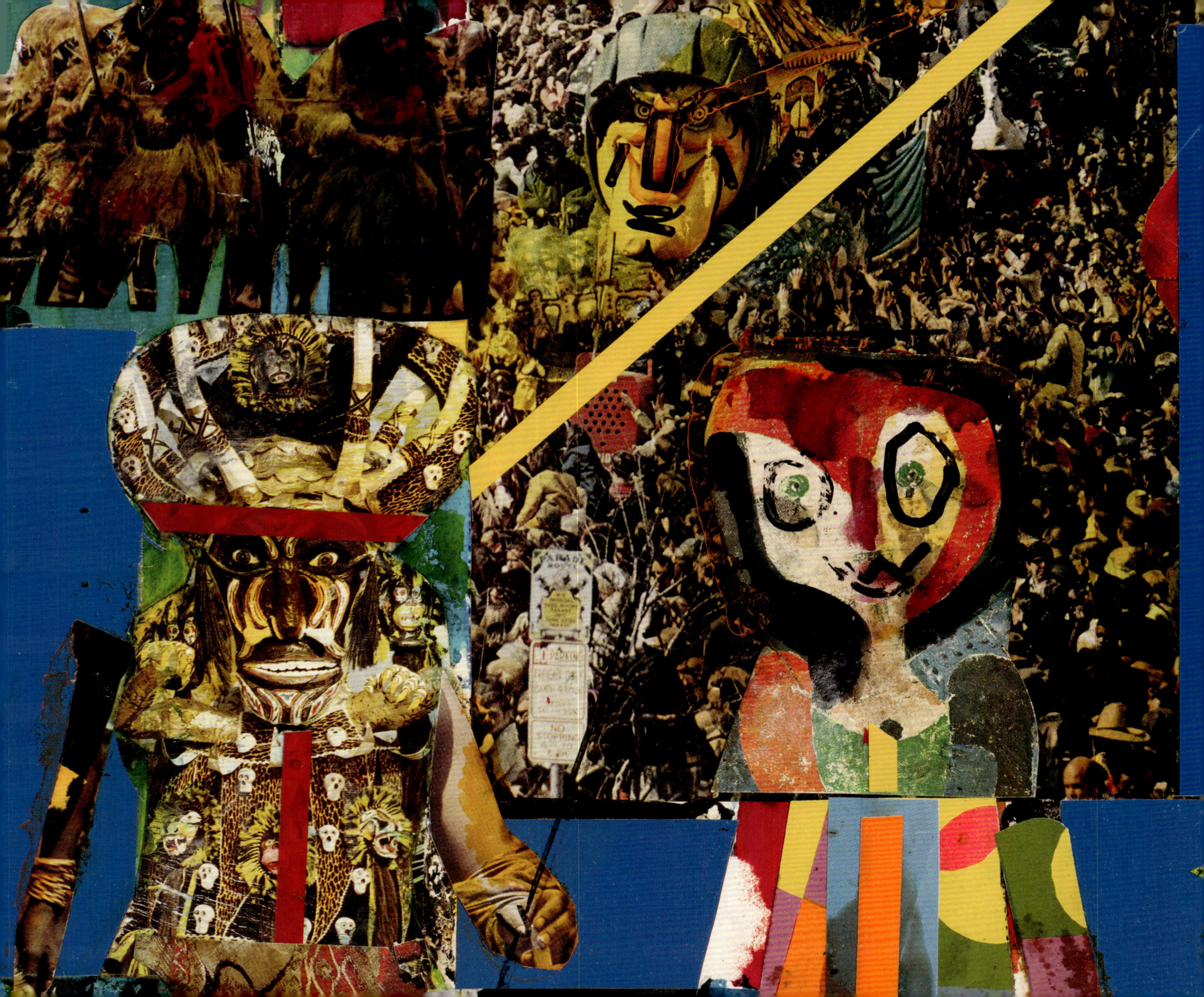

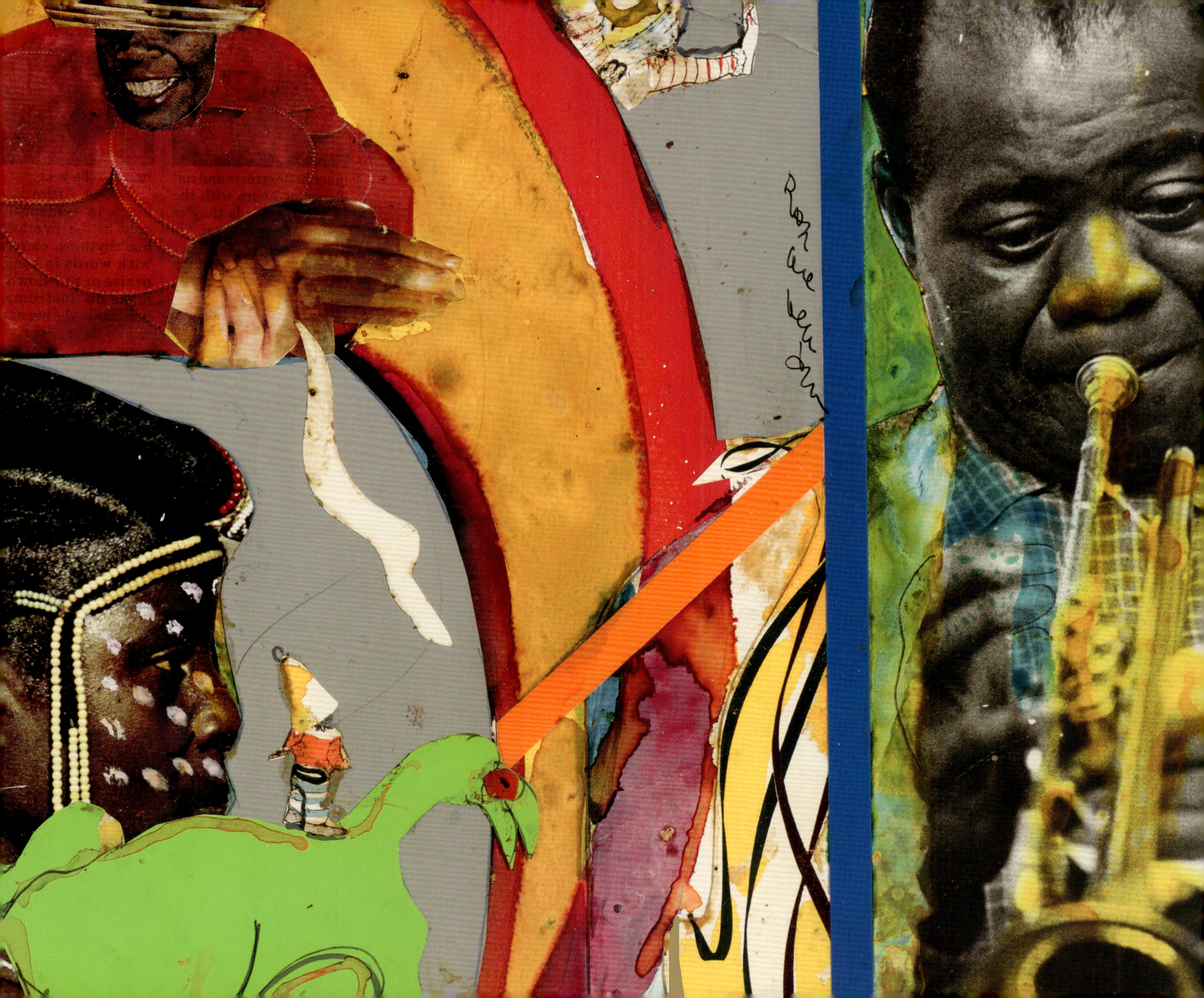

NEW ORLEANS

Although limited to a couple of cameos, Louis Armstrong is arguably the epicenter of the film *Paris Blues*. Playing approximately himself—a world-famous American jazz musician, passing through Paris with his band—he's the jazz authority whom disciples Paul Newman and Sidney Poitier look to for approval. The scene when Armstrong's band visits the bohemian nightclub where they work, entering in a New Orleans–style procession, anchors the film musically and, in a sense, ethically. For, after a lot of fake trombone and sax playing by the actors (to the soundtrack Ellington's musicians recorded in studio)[12]—we finally see a real musician on screen. But Armstrong is not allowed to be really, fully himself: he's freighted with the moniker "Wild Man" Moore and put in competition with European classical music, which the Newman character is drawn to. Maybe, the viewer begins to suspect, Paris is not the land of the free. Maybe Bearden, Shaw, and Murray had work to do, to restore Louis to his rightful place—and with him, jazz itself, requiring no approval from the French academy.

Louis Armstrong left New Orleans in 1922, but as Bearden said of his hometown, Charlotte, North Carolina, the Crescent City never left *him*. To the end of his life, Armstrong played and sang elaborations and variations on the relaxed-beat music of his native town—the sparkling blue-black sounds he was instrumental in codifying as jazz. (Albert Murray referred to Armstrong as the music's Chaucer, Ellington as its Shakespeare.) Ellington reported that after the early 1920s, when he first heard New Orleans–style blues, with its fat tones, street-strut bodaciousness, and will to dance—when he felt the full force of the gospel according to Louis A. and his Crescent City sisteren and bretheren—he could never play the "sweet music" of his native Washington, DC, again. Having failed to convince master New Orleans clarinetist/soprano saxophonist Sidney Bechet to join his band (unshy Bechet wondered why Ellington did not want to sign on as the pianist in *his* band), Ellington always had at least one New Orleans–style reed player in his orchestra and several trumpet graduates of the school of Louis Armstrong. In fact, Ellington reportedly often told all his horns, as well as the rhythm players, that to stay on track they should think of themselves as Louis Armstrongs: as rough and smooth-tone Afro-hip talk-on-horn players and street steppers in the key of New Orleans. Ellington's album *New Orleans Suite* (1970), featuring outstanding "Portraits" of both Armstrong and Bechet (as well as New Orleans musicians Mahalia Jackson and Wellman Braud and the pirate Jean Lafitte), is a multicolored love letter to that city.

So too are Bearden's New Orleans works in the *Paris Blues/Jazz* series, where he pays homage to the source of the music that had so charmed the French capital. For in these collages one sees the shapes and colors of the Crescent City's people and places while witnessing the ritual functions of jazz at Mardi Gras, in funeral processionals, and in settings like side-street jukes and brothels, always with pianos in the party rooms. (See *New Orleans* [1981] and *New Orleans Bordello and Pianist* [1981].) The music for such spaces and occasions connects to Bearden's overall theme of bluesy bawdy revelry as part of the vigorous will to continuity in the face of the world's inevitable ills. Somehow, these New Orleans ritual pieces tell us, life goes on. As an apt soundtrack to these paintings, I recommend Ellington's soulful "Blues for New Orleans" or "Portrait of Wellman Braud" from *New Orleans Suite*. Or his *Deep South Suite* (1946) with its rockin' train section called "Happy-Go-Lucky Local."

In his many paintings of New Orleans bordellos, Bearden reminds us that such were the frequent settings for the experimentation and creativity of 1910s and 1920s jazz, North and South, and of 1930s and 1940s jazz, nationwide. New Orleans–born Jelly Roll Morton and many early jazz musicians were sought-after pianists on bordello circuits. Billie Holiday (whom,

as discussed above, Bearden knew in Harlem before she made any records) learned to serenade customers in Baltimore's East Side "good time houses." And it certainly is significant that in several other "red light" works, whether through titles, captions, or pictures on back walls, Bearden reminds us of the humanity of the sex workers he depicts. His *Profile*-series collage *Railroad Shack Sporting House* (ca. 1978), for example, is captioned, "When I was old enough I found out what [Bearden's girlfriend] Liza's mother did for a living."

NEW ORLEANS

These two halves of a horizontal page continue the tilted box-iness of the entire *Paris Blues/Jazz* series, suggesting again the sense of movement Bearden wanted for his updated, Americanized Cubism. The two images are framed within a NOLA-style shotgun house—which we now know to be a West African creation.[13] (See Bearden's *Spring Fever* [1978], where this kind of house is also featured.) On the "porch" of the house is a New Orleans processional, an *ur*-source of Black American music, including, of course, jazz. Inside the "house" is a bordello, where along with the shapely women that Bearden so often featured as muses in his work, the artist places a piano player.

In connection with the violence of such places, note Bearden's comment regarding the sex-worker in *Railroad Shack Sporting House* (ca. 1978), who was also a neighbor. "She was still quite a lady," he said. "And I tried to give her some dignity here, which she deserved—as we all deserve."[14] The strips of color—blue, yellow, green—connect this work with others in the series.

Paris Blues/Jazz
New Orleans, 1981
Collage on paper
14 × 22 in.

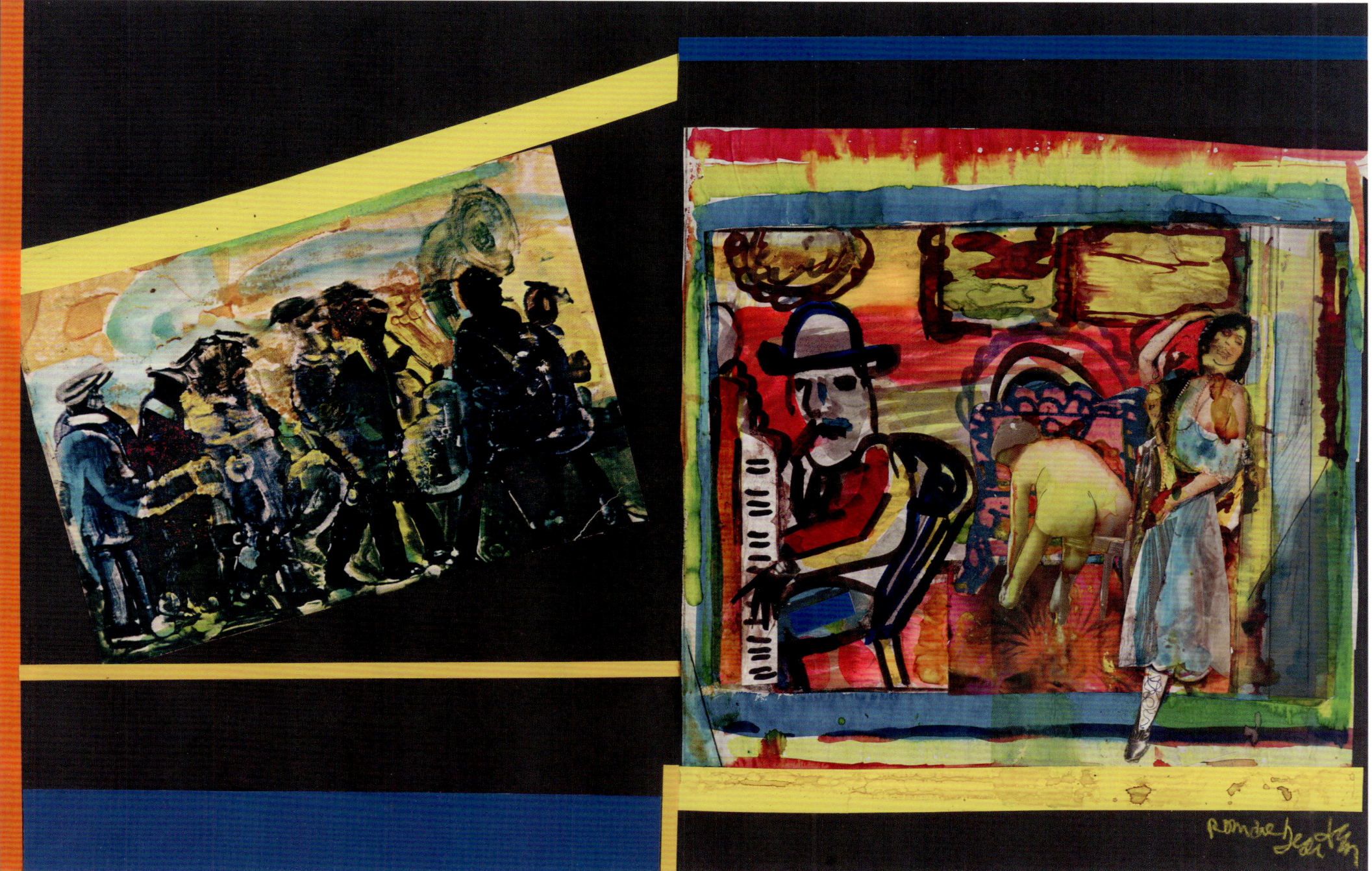

NEW ORLEANS BORDELLO AND PIANIST (STORYVILLE SOUNDTRACK), 1981

The bordello scene of this collage evokes the Storyville photographs of E. J. Bellocq (ca. 1912). But instead of Bellocq's figures, some posed enticingly, others as if dressed for church, the working women here grasp and tuck away their wages while others relax. As in *New Orleans*, the pianist and instrument are prominently featured. Bearden is as interested in the bordello as a place of music as anything else. Most fascinating here is the right-hand panel, where, from within a window with parted curtains, evidently lit in Storyville reds, a woman poses for potential street customers. Her face is indistinct, recalling that several of Bellocq's prostitutes' faces were masked or, unaccountably, marked out. If Bearden's lady of the evening bears an African mask, what might it signify? I should add that there's a further jazz connection here. The Bellocq photos were initially published by the outstanding jazz photographer Lee Friedlander, who first saw them at a gallery on St. Peter Street that was known for its presentation of fine New Orleans music.[15]

Paris Blues/Jazz
New Orleans Bordello and Pianist (Storyville Soundtrack), 1981
Collage on paperboard
13 ¾ × 22 in.

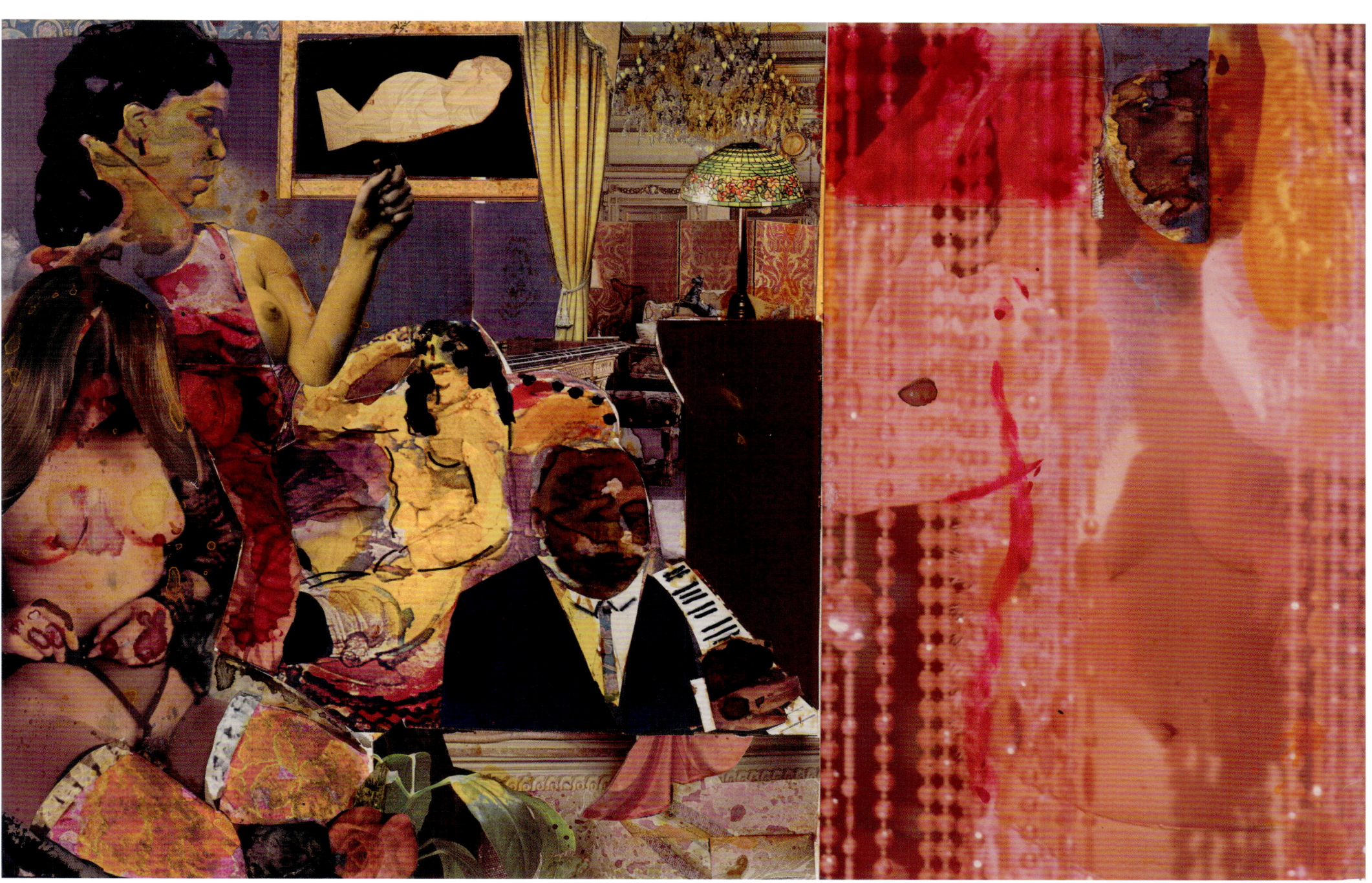

JAZZ WITH ARMSTRONG

Like other works in the *Paris Blues/Jazz* series, *Jazz with Armstrong* (1981) is laid out as a two-page spread, divided this time by a vertical blue line at the work's center. Each side retains its own integrity, as does the double-image spread as a whole, while additional yellow and blue central lines seem to mark off yet another book page, one storyline opening another. This work proclaims the multisensory, multilayered turbulence of that Franco-American—that Black cosmopolitan *omni*-American—city's Mardi Gras. To catch some of the flavor of that NOLA festival, Bearden fills the entire frame, every inch of it, and then lets the paint and other materials spill into and over the margins—literally off the charts, *offa da hook*. "Although I am increasingly fascinated by the possibilities of empty space on a canvas," said the master of what he called the "open corner" in art, "in [certain cases,] I was working for maximum multiplicity."[16]

Bearden's *Jazz with Armstrong* uses this approach to pay tribute to the layeredness of a great city whose traditional ensemble music, sacred and secular, makes room for every voice improvising at the same time—a feast of *gumbo ya-ya* (Louisianan for "everybody talks at once") mixed with soliloquies and mucho side-talk. The idea of public and private lives is underscored, too, by the many masked figures here—the African masks used not for lines and structures alone, but for their multiple meanings within NOLA's Black community and its Afro-diasporic extensions. Does this image of Mardi Gras owe something to the block party–style carnival celebrations Bearden had been observing on the Caribbean island of Saint Martin, his wife Nanette's ancestral home, where by the late 1970s the Beardens had been spending extended stretches of time every year?

The rhythmical play of rectangular and triangular structures confirms Bearden's inheritance as a Cubist and a lifelong student of certain Dutch masters: windows everywhere, again suggesting exterior and interior storylines and characters as well as mysteries just beyond our view. Note the presence of Louis Armstrong here–at center and right. Is he somewhere in the crowd on the left? The man himself was a man of many parts: the instrumentalist, singer, actor, autobiographer, Sunday collage maker, philanthropist, and artist who told the world that because of his hometown's violently enforced lines of segregation, he did not want to return to it after his death. In this spirit, along with his playfully raucous side, Bearden's *Jazz with Armstrong* captures Satchmo's sober, contemplative aspect—the artist on whom none of these complexities were lost.

Paris Blues/Jazz
Jazz with Armstrong, 1981
Collage on paperboard
14 ¼ × 22 ½ in.

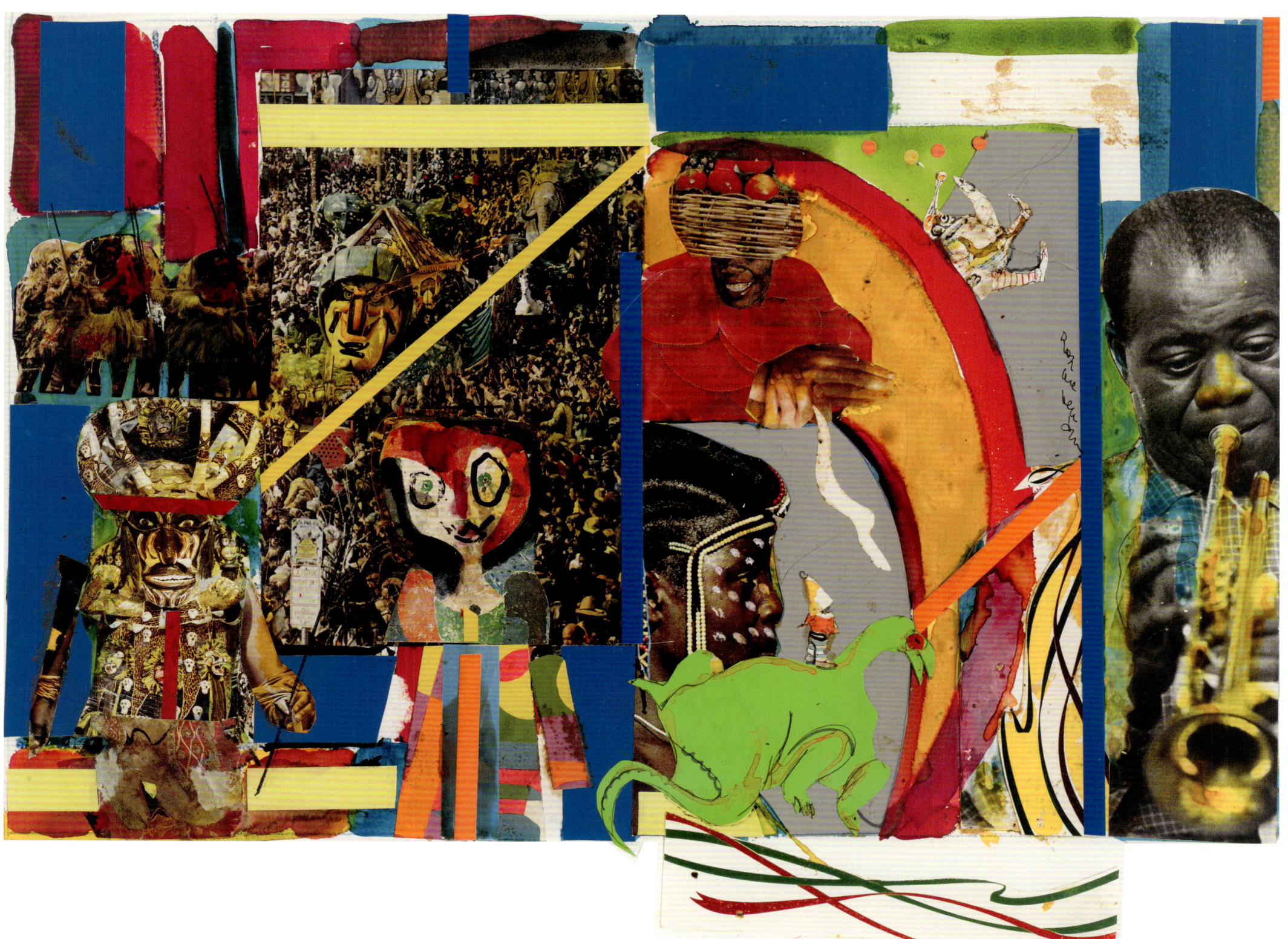

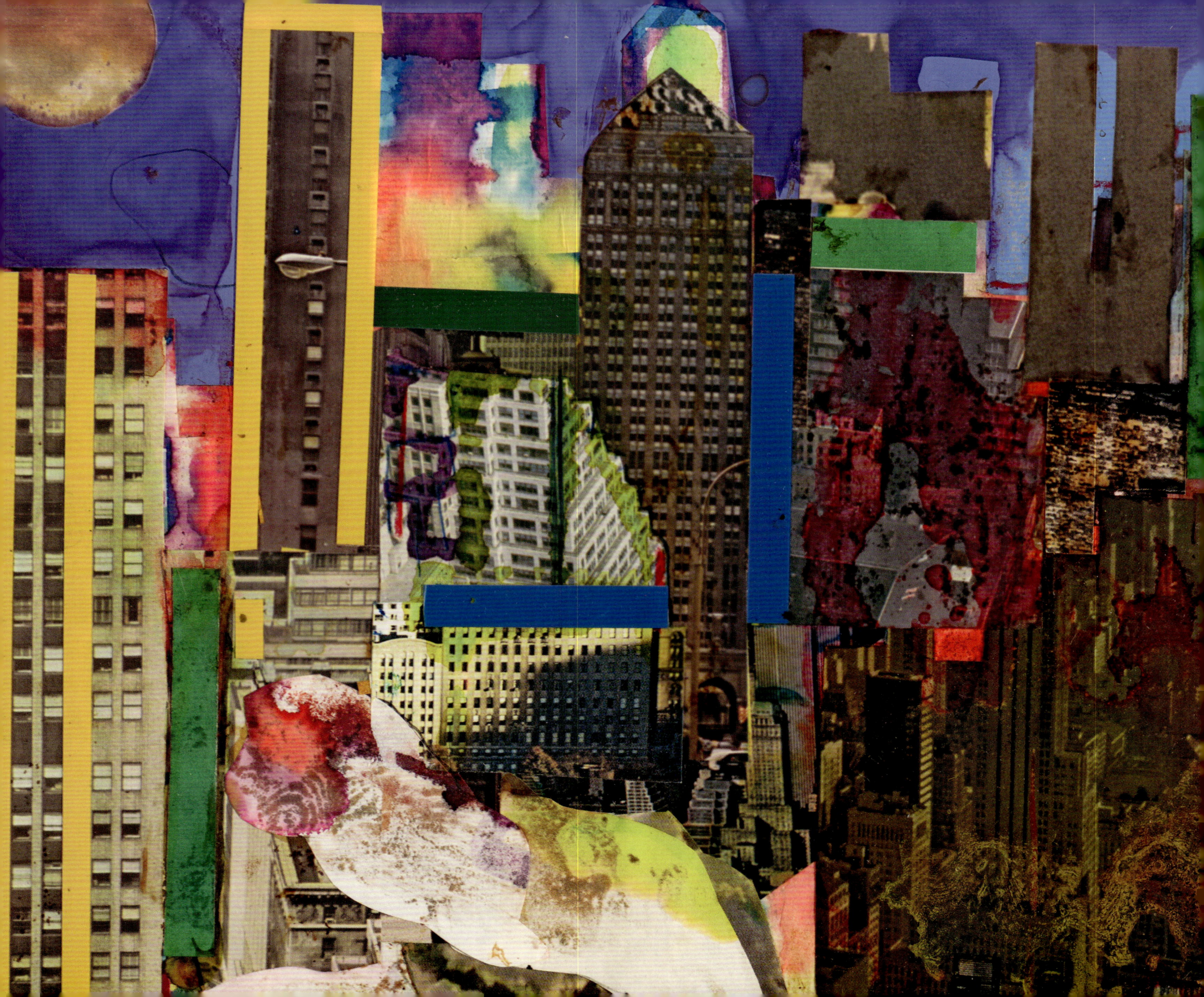

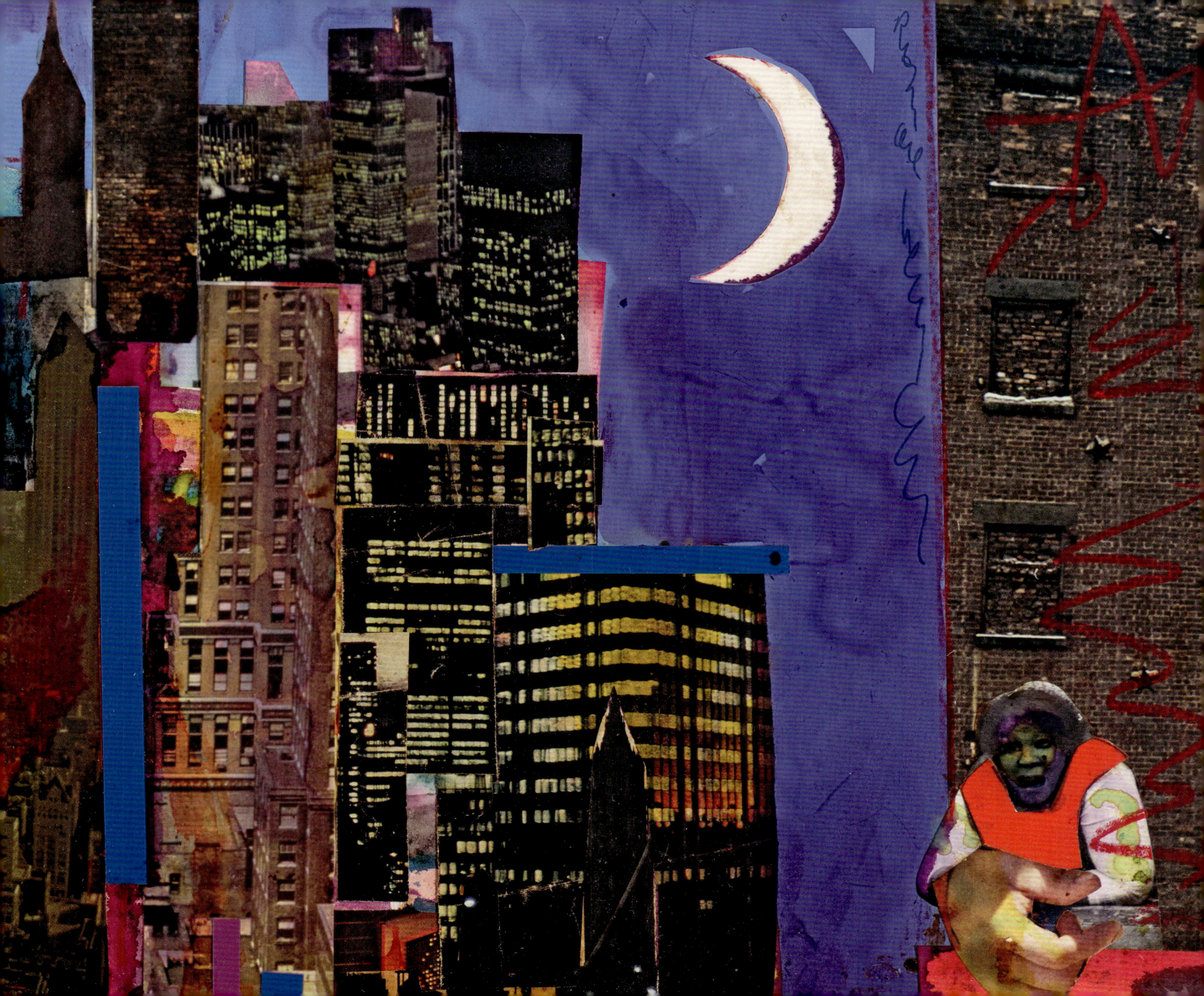

NEW YORK

If the *Paris Blues/Jazz* series celebrates its jazz heroes as members of an international Afro-diasporic community, New York, arguably the most worldly of U.S. cities, was the place that confirmed their cosmopolitan citizenship. It was also a "homeland" they needed to return to periodically, to refresh certain connections. Particularly after the mid-1950s, Louis Armstrong and Duke Ellington were constant world travelers, but their annual performance schedules invariably included swings back to New York, to the music venues along 52nd Street in San Juan Hill (an important Black neighborhood, where jazz flourished, before it was razed to make way for Lincoln Center) and in Harlem. Above all, they needed to connect with Harlem. "This single section of a great metropolis," wrote their friend Ralph Ellison, "was able to endow New York City (and thus the entire nation) with so much of its hope, its style, its dash." Harlem was "site and symbol of America's freewheeling sense of possibility," Ellison went on. "It was our own homegrown version of Paris."[17] Coming of age in the late 1920s, Bearden said that for him Harlem was what Paris had been for Henri de Toulouse-Lautrec. "It's the rhythm of Harlem, the characters, the colors," Bearden said. "These give tremendous inspiration to the artist, creative energy. Harlem is my Paris."[18]

For Bearden, Harlem's streets were a place he had called home, first as a young man, still living with his family, and then as a working artist whose studio was above the Apollo Theater. It was there that he had gotten to know Sam Shaw, who became studio mate and friend, and he regaled Shaw with stories of Paris freedom. In Harlem of the 1960s and 1970s he often visited Albert Murray in his apartment on Lenox at 132nd. Along with Paris, Harlem was a vital origin point, the source, of the film *Paris Blues*, and now Bearden would build a visual jazz portrait of it.

In the Harlem of the *Paris Blues/Jazz* series, as in the New Orleans works, continuity is the theme. This is the Harlem not of slick touristic entertainment or economic/social problems but of the community's own ritual music sounding through ritual spaces—the theaters, clubs, ballrooms—and sometimes along the streets, as in *The Block*. As Bearden knew well, Ellington and Armstrong regularly played Harlem's Smalls Paradise, Savoy, and Alhambra ballrooms, and Apollo and Lafayette theaters—the latter just a block from his childhood family home on 131st Street—and many uptown private party gigs, too.

"Harlem has long been an obsession with Duke," writes Barry Ulanov, who makes the case by citing musical compositions with an uptown theme:

> Starting in 1927 with *Harlem River Quiver*, the Negro quarter of New York has made its way, street by street, atmosphere by atmosphere, through his music. There is *Harlem Twist* and *Harlem Flat Blues, Jungle Nights in Harlem* and *Blue Harlem, Drop Me Off at Harlem* and *Harlem Speaks, Echoes of Harlem* and *It Was a Sad Night in Harlem, Uptown Downbeat* and *Harmony in Harlem, I'm Slappin' Seventh Avenue* and *Harlem Air Shaft*, the Sugar Hill section of *Black, Brown, and Beige* and *A Tone Parallel to Harlem*. These are not simply a songwriter's grab bag of titles, felicitous or not as the case may be. They are names for moods and customs, people and places and events in Duke's life and his musicians.' This is what it meant to come north from Washington in 1923, to move not many miles but social leagues, to establish oneself on the Hill, to earn the title of royalty in a . . . faded neighbourhood in which the air-shafts carry a little air, more sound, and the distant odour of tenement life, even into the palace. Duke is Harlem's poet.

And so in these *Paris Blues/Jazz* works, Bearden's dancers, singers, and instrumentalists come together to stomp the blues—to purify the community—and to flirt, in rites of courtship and fertility that Albert Murray says are part and parcel of the music. Of course dreams deferred appear in Bearden's depictions of life in Harlem; but these are upstaged by freedom dreams-in-progress and dreams realized, dreams *musick'd* (quoting Amiri Baraka) and danced!

AT THE SAVOY

This collage shows Duke Ellington as the master of the Rites of Saturday Night, stomping the blues away and binding couples (and the whole community) together. Bearden's photo cutouts include Duke's band members, and in the background, members of other famous bands that played Harlem's Savoy, headed by Chick Webb and Lionel Hampton. At center right is the Ellington saxophone section of the 1930s and 1940s—Otto Hardwick, Harry Carney, Barney Bigard, and Johnny Hodges—perhaps the most brilliant reed section in the history of jazz. Along with the prevalence of rituals, what's suggested in this collage is the strong experimental impulse at the Savoy, and at the many Savoy Ballrooms across America, named for this epicenter. There were jam-session bouts of antagonistic cooperation—battles of bands and individual players that created such excitement as they pressed music and musicians into new dimensions.

The left two-thirds of the work belongs mainly to dancers—specifically to the Whitey's Lindy Hoppers and the Trinidadian anthropologist and choreographer Pearl Primus, who introduced dance forms she had studied in West Africa to the Savoy crowd and many other audiences. Whitey's Lindy Hoppers also jump the blues here. Concerning such aerial floor-show dancers Bearden said, "The greatest poem written on Charles Lindbergh's flight was done at the Savoy: the Lindy hop—the dancers throwing the girls, their skirts billowing . . . the essence of flight."[19] As noted above, Ellington said that all of his music had a "terpsichorean urge." Maybe the same is true of Bearden's artworks—in this work, obviously so. Music and dance combine here to reflect the Afro-diaspora and its American cultural flowerings, while Bearden illustrates a Harlem community ritual in full swing. We are *still here*, says the music (and now these *Paris Blues/Jazz* collages), and partying! Offered an opportunity to give up Harlem gigs and play only the Carnegie Halls and La Scalas of the world, Ellington said, "*Nooo, baby!* You're trying to cut me off from my source!"[20]

Located on Lenox Avenue (now Malcolm X Boulevard) between 140th and 141st Streets, about ten blocks north of the location in Bearden's *The Block*, the Savoy was the first ballroom in Harlem built specifically for Black musicians and dancers,[21] and was, in its heyday of the 1930s through mid-1950s, nothing less than a major American cultural institution. In Bearden lingo, it was an "open corner" (space of continuing creative labor and *co-llaboration*), with a flexible wooden heaven of a dance floor for Harlemites and friends. "Charles Buchanan was the manager there," recalled Bearden, "and he would let young artists in free. We'd be up there three or four times a week, and we heard all the great bands. The [scenes and characters] there were as great as the models Toulouse-Lautrec used. But how do you find a form to encompass them, *that was the question*."[22]

In 1966, Ralph Ellison eulogized, "In the effort to build much needed public housing, [the Savoy] has been destroyed. . . . But then it was thriving and people were coming to Harlem from all over the world. The great European and American composers were coming there to listen to jazz—Stravinsky, Poulenc. The great jazz bands were coming there. Great dancers were being created there."[23] Great painters too!

Paris Blues/Jazz
At the Savoy, 1981
Collage on paperboard
14 × 22 in.

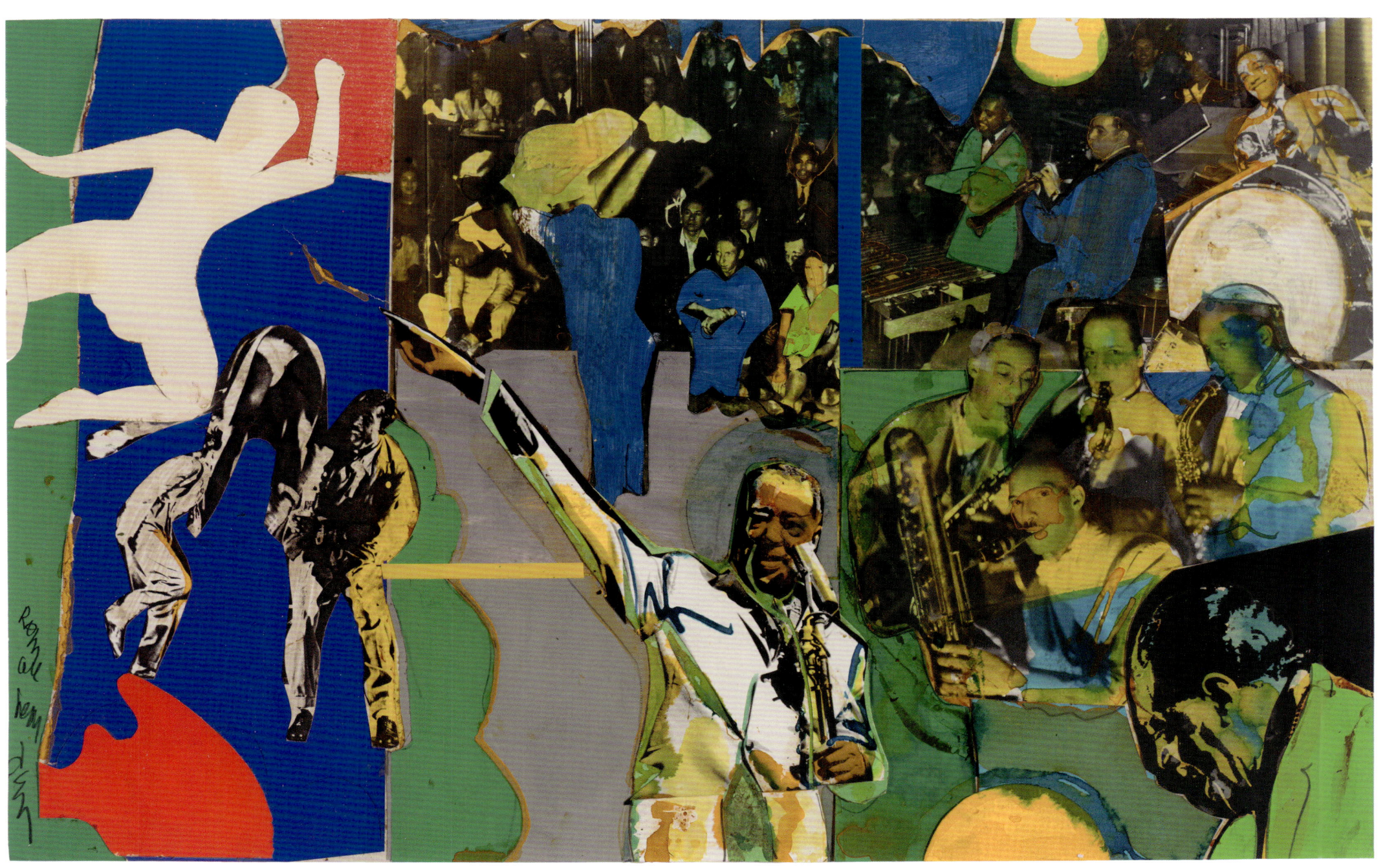

CLUB SINGER, STAGE COMEDIAN ALL PURPOSE ORISHA

At Harlem's Savoy and in such spaces all over Harlem at mid-century (and in the Savoys of the Afro-diaspora, American and beyond), Afro-songs and dances confirmed the being and belonging of Black American culture and community, their wholeness and vitality. This collage names three other Harlem venues where the music flourished: the Cotton Club, the Apollo Theater, and Smalls Paradise. We again see the Duke Ellington Band, whose long-term gig at the CC gave the maestro the time and the wide variety of acts to accompany—including dancers, singers, and comedians—to spur his career as a major composer. (This in spite of the club's whites-only policy at the time of Duke's residency there.)

While Ellington and his orchestra of the late 1920s hold down the lower right corner of this collage, two more major artists take front-center stage. On the right, with signature white-gloved hands, is dancer-pantomimist Johnny Hudgins, once very famous in Harlem and on international tours: this Baltimorean was in Paris before either Josephine Baker or Sidney Bechet, but by the 1970s almost completely unknown. Bearden credited him with helping him to see "how worlds were created on an empty canvas."[24] Another longtime Bearden friend, Billie Holiday, is also here, not as a sad lady in trouble (the tired cliché) but as the joyous lady of jewels and flowers, a shining goddess. Look closely: there are at least two more Billies in this work. For Bearden all three of these—Ellington, Hudgins, and Lady Day—were particularly vital muses and direction-givers for the artist in formation.

In this light, let us linger with Bearden's title for the collage, *Club Singer, Stage Comedian All Purpose Orisha*. Note in particular the figure at left, peeping in on the show. Evidently the title and figure confirm that the most emphatically impactful artists, in Bearden's view, were not just popular entertainers but leaders of community-wide rites—and, as such, heirs to the ancient West African power figures called orishas, who play a central role in many Afro-diasporic religions of the Caribbean and Brazil, and throughout the Americas. In most accounts, orishas may take the form of women or men as teachers of humans, guides toward their success or fulfillment in the world. They may also be waymakers, openers of doors. Could Bearden's figure at the edge be the orisha Legba, opening the door for the collagist (and the other artists), or for any audience member or viewer of this work searching for a rejuvenated sense of life or direction? Could this be a self-portrait, too, with the artist training to take his place in something more than a transactional show—a complex ritual drama? Of course all of the artists depicted here (and the one making the picture) should also be considered orishas.

Paris Blues/Jazz
Club Singer, Stage Comedian All Purpose Orisha, 1981
Collage on paper
14¼ × 22¼ in.

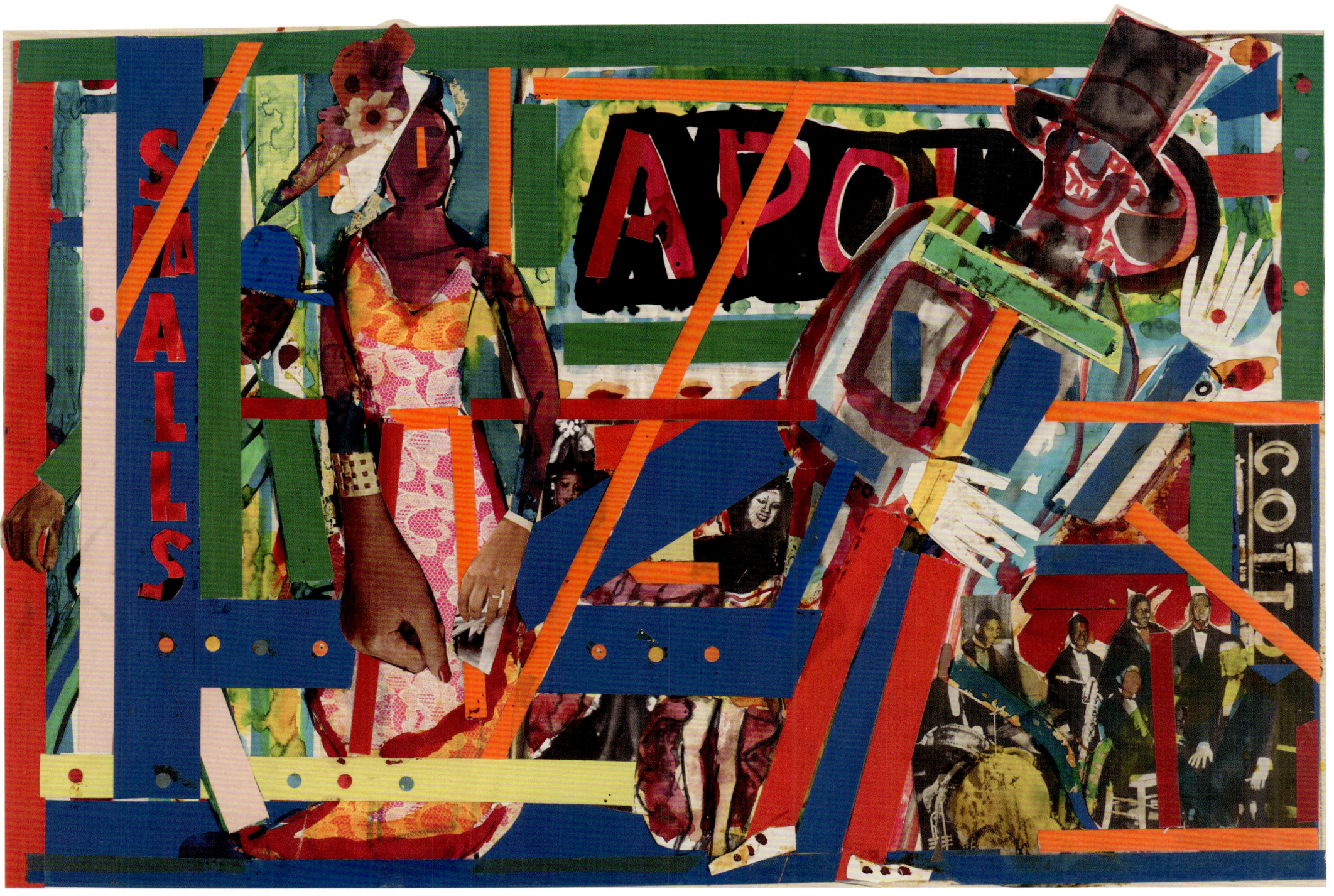

COTTON CLUB, CONNIE'S INN

Continuing the tour of Harlem music venues, this collage adds Connie's Inn, a 1920s/1930s basement cabaret on the corner of 131st and Lenox (now Malcolm X Boulevard). The only identifiable figure is the master band leader/singer/dancer Cab Calloway, known for his zoot suits and wide-brim fedoras. "Perhaps the Negro zoot suit conceals profound political meaning, or clues to political power," wrote Ralph Ellison in 1937, "if only Negro leaders would solve its mystery."[25] The crisscrossing lines of musical notation are in conversation with lines created by the figures, musical instruments, and the Connie's Inn awning. Where did Bearden learn to create visual jazz? From scenes and artists like these!

Paris Blues/Jazz
Cotton Club, Connie's Inn, 1981
Collage on paper
14 × 22 in.

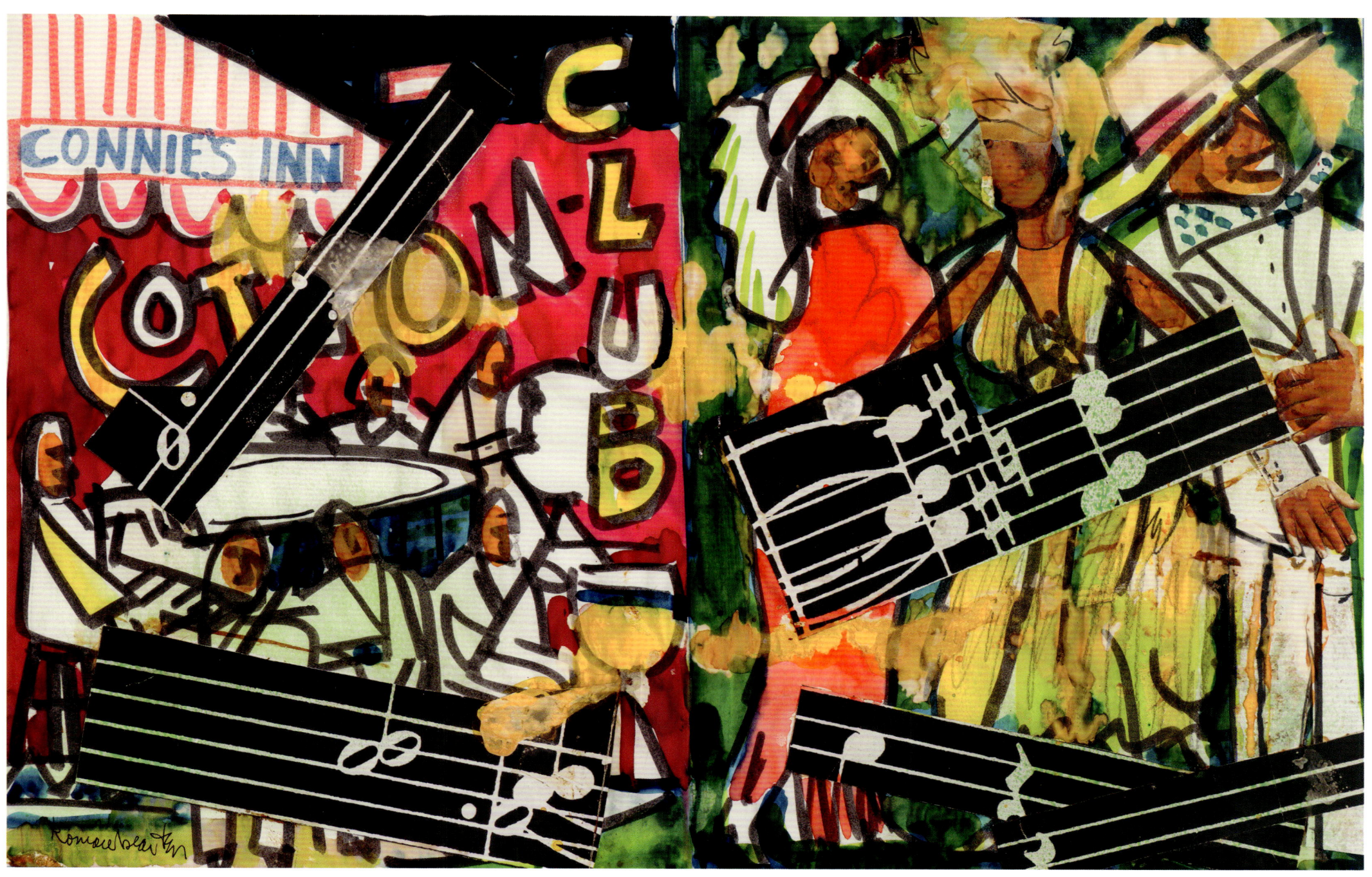

MOON OVER MANHATTAN

This tribute to the city is lit by two moons, or perhaps moon and sun. At its base (at center) is a strip of music venues where the word "PALACE"—a favorite name for clubs all over town—is discernible. Above the engine room of these nighttime play spaces, the buildings soar upward. What Bearden said about his New York skylines becomes especially pertinent here: "Actually, what I'm doing here is making a keyboard." Using this idea of the skyline as instrument of musical rhythm and melody, we can appreciate the play of colors in this work, key by key, and the way the windows, boxes within boxes, suggest microtones or polyrhythms. In defiance of any easy sense of perspective, the woman leaning from a window at the right edge becomes part of the skyline's/keyboard's play. And, flying from left to right: is that a bird sailing through? If so, perhaps it's a cousin to the Parisian doves elsewhere in this series: flyers toward freedom and peace.

Paris Blues/Jazz
Moon over Manhattan, 1981
Collage on paperboard
14 ¼ × 22 ½ in.

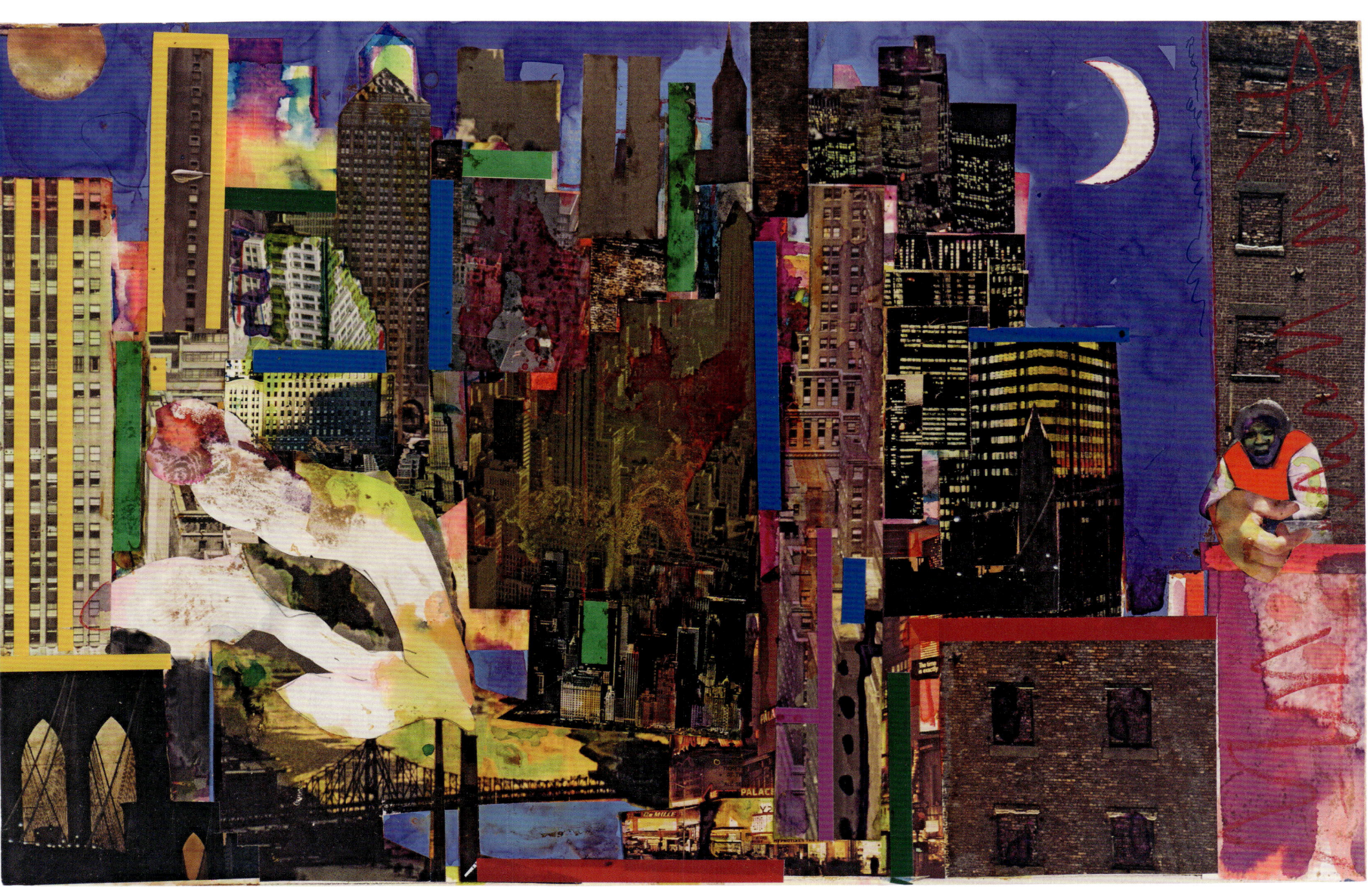

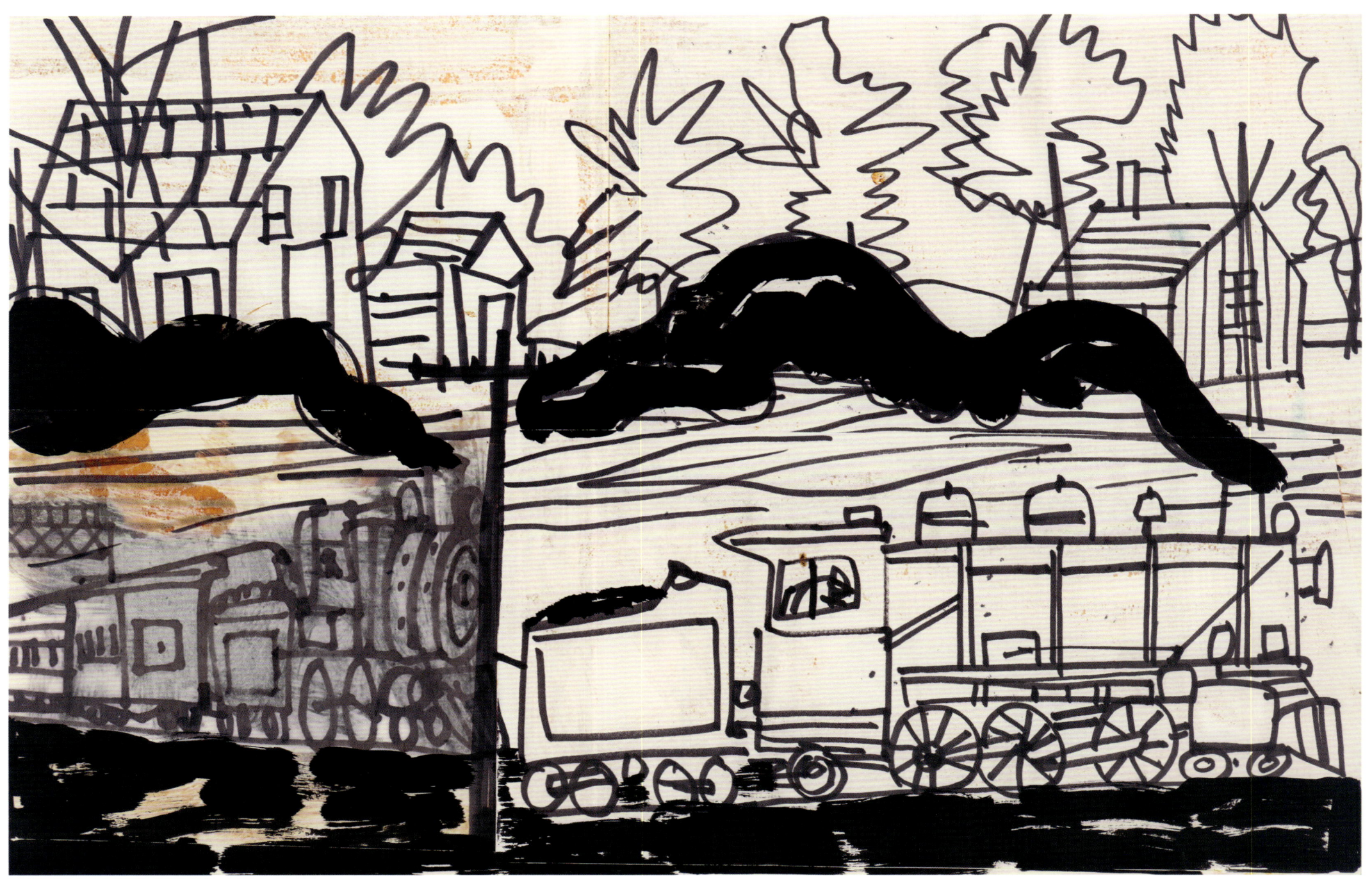

TRAINS B & W

The evident unfinishedness of this work makes it emblematic of the entire *Paris Blues/Jazz* series, most of whose pages are incomplete and remain in archives. There is a sense of a two-page spread here, the beginnings of a color scheme, and rhythmical play with foliage and house shapes. Most prominent, obviously, are the two trains and the lines of black smoke dividing the image vertically. Throughout Bearden's oeuvre, from the early 1960s onward, trains are everywhere and supercharged with meaning. In the context of this series, they recall the declaration of Bearden's friend and frequent collaborator Albert Murray that what he playfully calls "locomotive onomatopoeia" is a prime definitive element in Black American music, sacred and secular.

Through *Stomping the Blues* and other books on the music, Murray made the case that the sound of jazz depends on instrumentalists and singers who evoke big and small trains' whistles, bells, and conductor calls; the hisses and sighs of their brakes; the track-click pulses as train cars ride the rails. Bearden's jazz-themed works confirm this connection in pictures. His gospel train runs beneath the scene of a rural church house (*Spring Revival Baptism* [1978]) and thus is associated with the Underground Railroad, the fugitive's freedom train (long delayed).

Paris Blues/Jazz
Trains B & W, 1981
Collage and marker on paper
14 × 22 in.

GRAFFITI (DUKE ELLINGTON)

As if to make unmistakably clear who would co-star in the emerging picture-and-word book of Paris Blues/Jazz collages, Bearden created two works—intended as endpapers?—which consist entirely of looping, autographlike letters, spelling over and over again "L-o-u-i-s-A-r-m-s-t-r-o-n-g" on one page, and "D-u-k-e-E-l-l-i-n-g-t-o-n" on the other. These word pictures remind us of Bearden's debt to Chinese calligraphy, announced in numerous interviews, and to the urban graffiti art of the 1970s, associated with hip-hop culture and with public art from as far back as ancient Europe and the Middle East. Bearden's hand-drawn letters also send us back through the entire Paris Blues/Jazz series, where words (often complementing the works' titles) abound. And they remind us of the Bearden who collaborated with writers—with Albert Murray, especially, but also Derek Walcott and the ancient poet called Homer, among others—and of Bearden's own career as a writer: of songs, poems, children's books, journals, letters, and several books on art, notably Black American art.

Paris Blues/Jazz
Graffiti (Duke Ellington), 1981
Ink on paper
14 × 22 in.

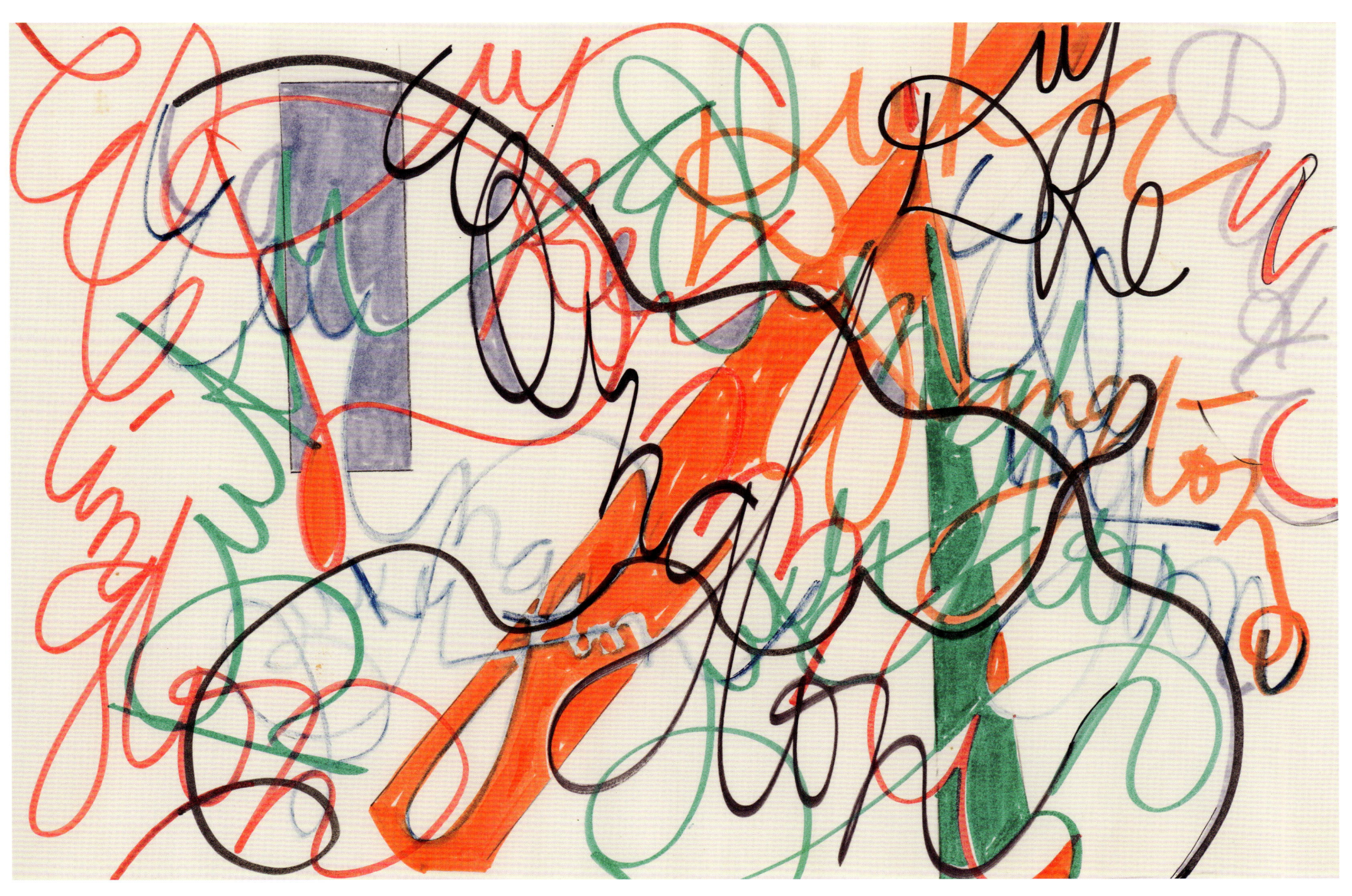

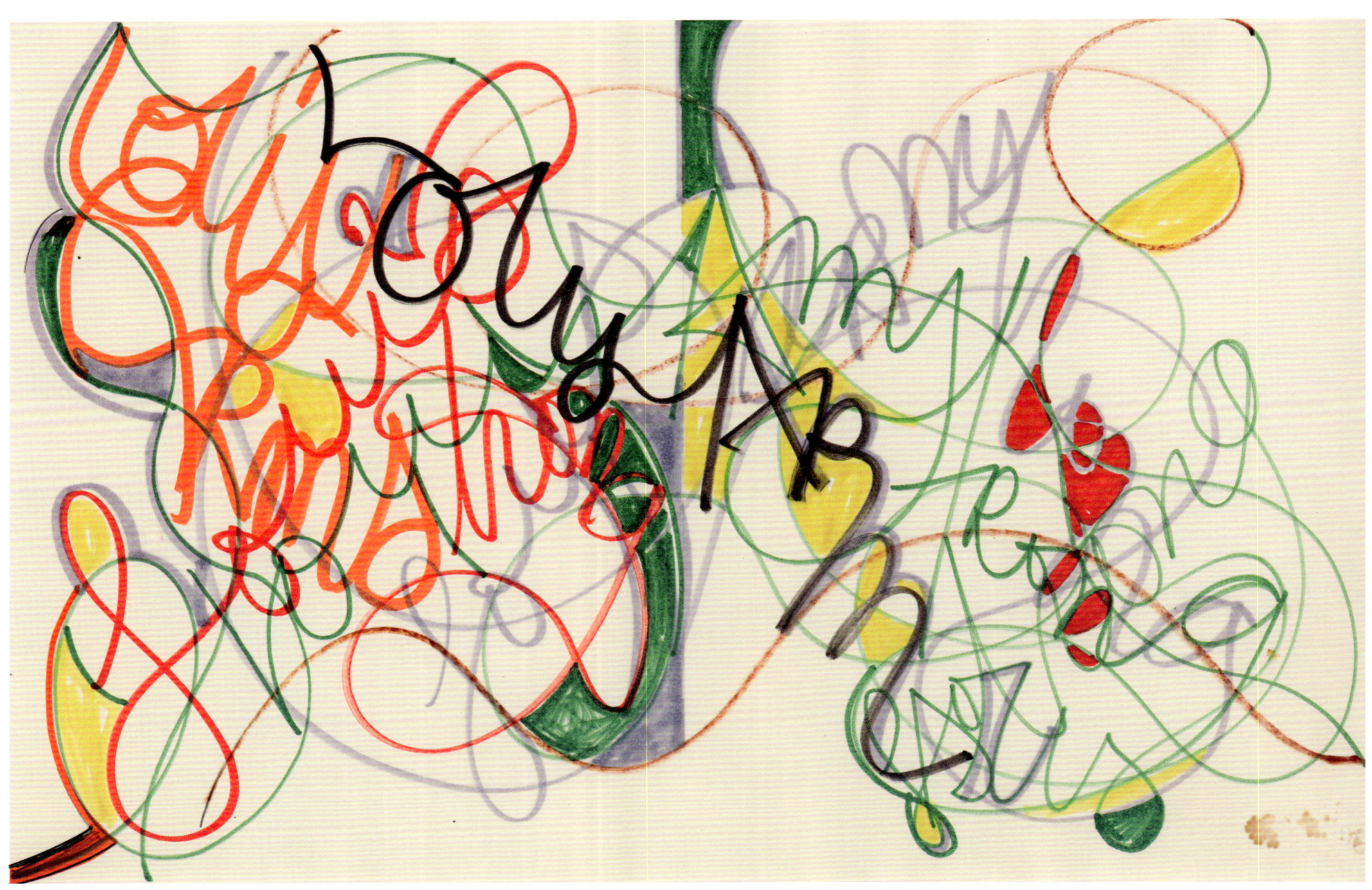

GRAFFITI (LOUIS ARMSTRONG)

Here's where Bearden and Co. evidently concluded this ambitious project, using the bright letters of Louis Armstrong's name as footlights. This was a name which, like Ellington's, echoed back, musically, to the beginnings of Black music as well as Black into the music's future. Where does this leave us, as viewers of this series? Perhaps above all it leaves us with an urgently articulated will to see the rhythms and tunes of music itself. It leaves us with an equally urgent will to look and listen again to Black Americans and their art, musical and visual, philosophical and political; with a will to see ourselves, as the poet Glissant says, *in relation*. For here is a collaborative artist's ringing statement of what it means to be human in our time—a joyous assertion of multicitification and planet-wide kinship with responsibility. These walls/these pages offer fresh and brilliant visualizations of the words Ellington routinely used to bid farewell to applauding global audiences: *"Ladies and gentlemen,"* he liked to say, *"WE DO LOVE YOU MADLY!"*

Paris Blues/Jazz
Graffiti (Louis Armstrong), 1981
Ink on paper
14 × 22 in.

FINAL COURSE: GUMBO

As a postscript, I'll add that the fact that this book was never fully finished may be regarded, ironically, as part of its good news. Many great works of art have remained incomplete—perhaps most famously, in our time, Piet Mondrian's *Victory Boogie Woogie*, Ralph Ellison's last novel, pieced together posthumously as *Juneteenth* and then as *Three Days Before the Shooting*, and Edward Said's final book, *On Late Style: Music and Literature against the Grain*, completed from lecture and manuscript notes by a colleague. That these works will never be finished by their original creators has led, in the cases of Mondrian and Ellison, to sometimes wonderful speculation about pieces and parts cut out of "final" versions, and efforts by others to complete the undone works after all. These unfinished masterpieces (for that is what they are) remind us that the engine rooms of artistic creation are dynamic play spaces where improvisation, revision, jettisoning, re-improvisation, and re-revision are the order (sometimes the creative *dis*order) of the day. Most books purporting to show Mondrian's *Victory Boogie Woogie* use photos of the work from a distance as a clean-line geometric wonder; but close-ups display the beauty of incompletion I'm talking about—yards and swatches of scissor-cut and torn tape glued alongside heavy daubs of unevenly colored gouache and oil paint. How wonderful to feel, on this big tilted square of a work, the touch of this jazz lover's fingertips!

The *Paris Blues/Jazz* project's drafts, some only a few lines, some more than half-finished, are safely archived. They could be presented in a show of their own on work-in-progress and the beauty of incompletion, *just sayin.*' But for now let us consider the quite finished *Paris Blues/Jazz* collages, showcased here, as jazzlike in their participation in this unfinished project as a whole, and also, finished as they are, as exemplary of an ongoing aesthetic of the unfinished. In a letter of 1948, Bearden quotes Henri Matisse's statement that "he just

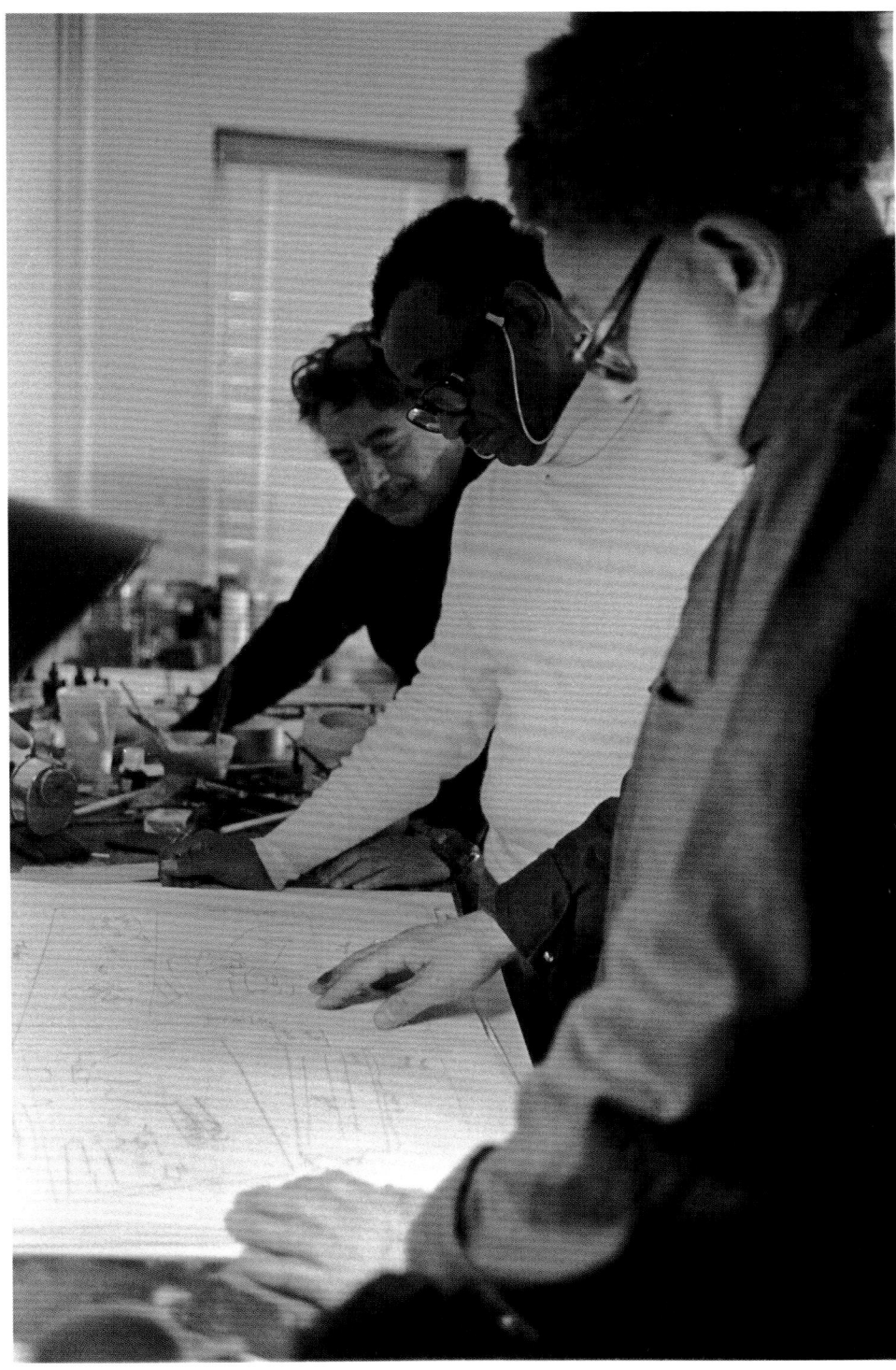

Frank Stewart. Sam Shaw, Albert Murray, and Romare Bearden, ca. 1979

finally relinquishes a painting, maybe never finishes one. . . . That gave me courage." And elsewhere: "In great art," said Bearden, "some part of it must be left for the imagination of the onlooker to complete."[26] Along with this jazzlike aesthetic of the "open corner"—the music's emphasis on process over final product, its open-ended will to call-recall/say-Amen-somebody! dialogue with the audience—this *Paris Blues/Jazz* project is Ellingtonian in its collaborative conception. It literally started with the convening of a band of three, bouncing ideas off one another as they worked to build a beautiful book together. "If I get a solo spot, what should I do there?" the drummer Leroy Williams asked Thelonious Monk when first sitting in in Monk's band. "Do whatever you want," said Monk. "You can get up and do a dance if you feel like it. You could tell a joke. It's up to you. Create something."[27]

What would you do in the open corner/solo spots of these collages?

Look for such invitations throughout Bearden's *Paris Blues/Jazz* collages. Bearden offers them as expressions of unruly Black cosmopolitanism, as lived in Paris, New Orleans, and New York: an unruly Black cosmopolitanism that includes you, that wants you in its band! Try this as a very last image, from the kitchen: without the roux from Black New Orleans and the hot sauces from the Savoy Ballroom of Harlem, the *Paris Blues/Jazz* series could never be the international gumbo of a book that Bearden intended it to be. Here is Bearden's own *Paris Blues* story, told this time as a work ever in progress by himself in collaboration with trusted friends: a jazz trio–style series served not as a tale of one city but instead, deliciously, of three.

NOTES

"More Than Oneself": Bearden's Jazz and Paris Blues

1.   From an unpublished text message from John Szwed, July 9, 2025.

2.   Albert Murray, "Bearden Plays Bearden," in *The Romare Bearden Reader*, ed. Robert G. O'Mealy (Durham, NC: Duke University Press, 2019), 238.

3.   *Bearden Plays Bearden*, directed by Nelson Breen (1980; DVD, Third World Cinema Production, 2012).

4.   "Complete" in the sense that all the known completed *Paris Blues/Jazz* works by Bearden are reproduced in this publication. There are unfinished works in archives, and the book project of which all these are a part was never completed.

5.   Bearden's aim echoes that of Toni Morrison in her novel *Jazz* (New York: Knopf, 1992), xviii: "Rather than be about those characteristics [of jazz music], the novel would seek to become them." "Bearden's meaning," wrote Ralph Ellison in 1970, "is identical with his method." See Ralph Ellison, "The Art of Romare Bearden," in *The Collected Essays of Ralph Ellison*, ed. John F. Callahan (New York: Modern Library, 1995), 697.

6.   Materials relating to Shaw's work on the film are held by the Sam Shaw Family Archives; New York, NY.

7.   The plotlines mentioned here were first developed in the novel *Paris Blues* (1957) by Harold Flender. On Flender and the novel, see Robert G. O'Mealy, "The White Trombone and the Black Cosmopolitan Trumpet, or How Paris Blues Came to Be Unfinished," in *Antagonistic Cooperation: Jazz, Collage, Fiction, and the Shaping of African American Culture* (New York: Columbia University Press, 2022), 167–218.

8.   See Stanley Dance, "More Paris Blues," *Jazz Journal International* (July 1961), 18–19, 30.

9.   Murray was a master of captioning. His *Stomping the Blues* (New York: McGraw-Hill, 1976) is as valuable for its captions as for its chapter paragraphs. Murray also collaborated with Bearden on captions for the artist's Profile exhibitions of 1979 and 1981. See Stephanie Mayer Heydt et al., "Something over Something Else": *Romare Bearden's Profile Series* (Atlanta and Seattle: High Museum of Art and University of Washington Press, 2019).

10.   See Ann Douglas, "Feel the City's Pulse? It's Be-bop, Man!" *New York Times*, August 28, 1998, E-1. See also Robin D.G. Kelley, *Thelonious Monk: The Life and Times of an American Original* (New York: Free Press, 2009), Chapter 2.

11.   See Albert Murray, *Stomping the Blues*, 432.

12.   Ralph Ellison, "Living with Music," *The Collected Essays of Ralph Ellison*, ed. John Callahan (New York: Random House, 1995), 835.

13.   Consider the Peter Wheatstraw scene in Ellison's 1952 novel *Invisible Man*, reissued, ed. John Callahan (London: Penguin Books, 2016), where (in Chapter 9), the singer of a blues associated with Count Basie (The "Boogie Woogie/I May Be Wrong," 1936) pushes a wheelbarrow of discarded blueprints through the NYC streets. Wheatstraw's explanation that the city's plans are always changing has prompted the cultural critic Stanley Crouch to surmise that Ellison is meditating here on the US Constitution as a bedrock blues document whose subsequent amendments—improvised changes as the nation moves through time—reflect the fundamentally improvised nature of the American project. Conversation with the author, June 8, 1989.

14.   The line is from "The Danger Zone" by Percy Mayfield, recorded by Ray Charles. (ABC-Paramount record 10244, 1961).

15.   Romare Bearden, "Encounters with African Art," in Robert G. O'Mealy, ed., *The Romare Bearden Reader* (Durham, NC: Duke University Press, 2019) 165.

16.   It's very likely that the photos sampled in *Rehearsal Hall* were taken by Sam Shaw. Other Shaw photos of Ellington scores from that recording date have turned up in the Sam Shaw Family Archives.

17.   Other Bearden titles present more oblique jazz references—often with an insider's sense of the jazz world's turns of phrase: *The Woodshed* (1969), *New Orleans Raggin' Home* (1974), *Vampin'* (1976), *Out Chorus* (1979). The titles of several exhibitions of Bearden's work held during the artist's lifetime (and many more after his death) have highlighted this musical intersection: *Romare Bearden: Of the Blues* (1975), *Of the Blues (Second Chorus)* (1976), *Jazz Collages* (1980), *The Portrayal of the Black American Musician in American Art* (1980), among others.

18.   See "Still Here" by Langston Hughes, *The Panther and the Lash* (New York: Alfred Knopf, 1967), 32.

19.   By "jazz photography," I mean not just photographs of jazz scenes and subjects but distinct approaches and processes (formal and technical) to photography. As examples, I particularly have in mind the work of Roy DeCarava, Herman Leonard, Gerald Cyrus, Frank Stewart, and Petra Richterova.

20.   See Fred Moten, *In the Break: The Aesthetics of the Black Radical Tradition* (Minneapolis: University of Minnesota Press, 2003), 162; Robert G. O'Mealy, Brent Hayes Edwards, and Farah Jasmine Griffin, eds., *Uptown Conversation: The New Jazz Studies* (New York: Columbia University Press, 2004); and George E. Lewis and Benjamin Piekut, eds., *The Oxford Handbook of Critical Improvisation Studies*, vols. 1 and 2 (New York: Oxford University Press, 2016).

21.   Ellison, "Living with Music," *The Collected Essays of Ralph Ellison*, ed. John Callahan (New York: Random House, 1995), 227.

22.   James Weldon Johnson, *God's Trombones: Seven Negro Sermons in Verse*, ed. Henry Louis Gates (New York: Penguin Books, 2008).

23.   Heydt et al., "Something over Something Else": *Romare Bearden's Profile Series* (Atlanta and Seattle: High Museum of Art and University of Washington Press, 2019), 92.

24.   Myron Schwartzman, *Romare Bearden: His Life and Art* (New York: Abrams, 1990), 26.

25.   Myron Schwartzman, *Romare Bearden: Celebrating the Victory*, (New York: Grolier, 1999), 29.

26.   See Derek Walcott, *What the Twilight Says* (New York: Farrar, Strauss, 1999), 3–4.

27.   Zora Neale Hurston, "Characteristics of Negro Expression," in *The Norton Anthology of African American Literature, Vol. 1* (3rd ed.), ed. Henry Louis Gates Jr. et al. (New York: Norton, 2014), 1050–61.

28.   Romare Bearden, an unreleased outtake from the documentary film *Bearden Plays Bearden* (1980; DVD, Third World Cinema Production, 2012). Kindly provided by Nelson E. Breen, from his personal archive.

29.   See Romare Bearden and Harry Henderson, *A History of African-American Artists: From 1792 to the Present* (New York: Pantheon, 1993), 260–92, 503–4.

30.   John Hammond, Letter to Aida Winters Wishonaut (Charles Alston's half-sister), May 19, 1977. Read at a funeral service.

31.   Ibid.

32.   Calvin Tomkins "Putting Something over Something Else," a *New Yorker* profile (1977), reprinted in Robert G. O'Mealy, ed., *The Romare Bearden Reader*, 34.

33.   Part of Eugene's story is retold by the Pittsburgh-born writer August Wilson in the play "Joe Turner's Come and Gone," which in manuscript was named for a Bearden collage, "The Mill Hand's Lunch Bucket," 1978. Drafts of that play show that the young character who mourns a deceased friend, "Eugene," was originally named "Romare." When Wilson says he was directly influenced by Bearden, we need to pay special attention. In his notebooks, Wilson wrote one Bearden sentence—copied from one of his exhibition catalogues—over and over again: *I am trying to explore, in terms of the particulars of the life I know best, those things common to all cultures.* Wilson's plays—done in ten-year cycles like Bearden's *Profile* series—strongly reflect this sense of the resonances of Black American culture with all cultures: "the prevalence of ritual" as both Black and universal.

34.   Bearden, in outtakes from the documentary *Bearden Plays Bearden*, directed by Nelson E. Breen. Kindly provided by Nelson E. Breen.

35.   Nelson Breen, "'To Hear Another Language': Alvin Ailey, James Baldwin, Romare Bearden, and Albert Murray in Conversation," *Callaloo*, no. 40 (Summer 1989), 439.

36.   Of course, Bearden's collage owes a lot to Henri Matisse's many piano lessons, and doubtless also to Henry O. Tanner's "Banjo Lesson," 1893, and to the long tradition of the music lesson as an artistic genre.

37.   "What is the piano lesson?" was Wilson's private question—during its rehearsal of

"Piano Lesson" in New Haven, 1987–to the play's music consultant, Dwight Andrews. Reported in a private conversation between Andrews and the author, November 4, 2023.

38. Murray, "Bearden Plays Bearden," in *The Romare Bearden Reader*, ed. Robert G. O'Meally, 236–55.

39. Ibid.

40. Ralph Ellison, *Invisible Man*, 148.

41. This is from a conversation with the author: September 1980.

42. Langston Hughes, *The Big Sea: An Autobiography, in Collected Works of Langston Hughes*, vol. 13 (Columbia: University of Missouri Press, 2002), 178.

43. Amy Helene Kirschke, *Aaron Douglas: Art, Race and the Harlem Renaissance* (Oxford: University of Mississippi, 1995), 40.

44. See Brent Hayes Edwards, *The Practice of Diaspora: Literature, Translation, and the Rise of Black Internationalism* (Cambridge: Harvard University Press), 2003.

45. *Calvin Tomkins Papers*. Romare Bearden file, Museum of Modern Art, New York City.

46. See "The Sound of Jazz," CBS television special, Columbia/Legacy, 2000. The show, part of the "Seven Lively Arts" series, was originally broadcast live on December 8, 1957. See also Farah Jasmine Griffin, *In Search of Billie Holiday: If You Can't Be Free, Be a Mystery* (New York: Random House, 2002), 193–97.

47. Romare Bearden and Harry Henderson, *A History of African-American Artists: From 1792 to the Present*, 234.

48. Ralph Ellison, "The Art of Romare Bearden," The introduction in the catalogue *Romare Bearden: Paintings and Projections* for an exhibition held at the Art Gallery of the State University of New York at Albany, November 25–December 22, 1968. Reprinted in *The Massachusetts Review*, Winter 1977.

49. Ellison, "Living with Music," *The Collected Essays of Ralph Ellison*, 835.

50. Robert G. O'Meally and Ralph Ellison, "My Strength Comes from Louis Armstrong," in O'Meally, *Living with Music*, 286.

51. *Homage to Jazz: A Colorful Tribute in Paint to a Great American Art*," exhibition catalogue (New York: Samuel M. Kootz Gallery, December 3–21, 1946).

52. Donna M. Cassidy, *Painting the Musical City: Jazz and Cultural Identity in Modern Art, 1910–1940* (Washington: Smithsonian Institution), 15.

53. James Brown was not a jazz singer but could have been one. At times when vocalizing above his "famous flames" of singers and instrumentalists, JB operates in the tradition of big band blues shouters like Big Joe Turner and Jimmy Witherspoon, both important forerunners of rhythm and blues.

54. From an unpublished text message from John Szwed, July 9, 2025.

55. I'm paraphrasing a line from Ellison's *Invisible Man*, 6.

56. Schwartzman, *Romare Bearden: His Life and Art*, 149.

57. Holty to Bearden, May 14, 1949. Carl Holty Papers, AAA, roll 670, frames 536–39. See also Schwartzman, *Romare Bearden: His Life and Art*, 158.

58. In 1971, Bearden told the curator Carroll Greene that he was doubtful of this claim by the building's concierge; so he checked Cézanne's biographies, which confirmed it. Carroll Greene-Bearden Interviews, Museum of Modern Art, NYC.

59. Henri Ghent, "Interview with Romare Bearden" in *The Romare Bearden Reader*, ed. Robert G. O'Meally (Durham, NC: Duke University Press, 2019), 58.

60. See Tomkins "Putting Something over Something Else," reprinted in Robert G. O'Meally, ed., *The Romare Bearden Reader*, 40.

61. Ibid, 42.

62. From the headnote accompanying Murray's essay, "The Luzanna Cholly Kick," which later became Murray's debut fiction *Train Whistle Guitar*. See Albert Murray, *Train Whistle Guitar*, 1st Vintage International ed. (New York: Vintage International, 1998).

63. Mentioned in Nelson Breen, "To Hear Another Language,"432.

64. Nelson Breen, "To Hear Another Language," 437.

65. James Baldwin, "Why I Stopped Hating Shakespeare" 1964); reprinted in *The Cross of Redemption: Uncollected Writings of James Baldwin*, ed. Randall Kenan (New York: Vintage, 2011), 56.

66. "Biography." Herbert Gentry. https://www.herbertgentry.com/biography.

67. Romare Bearden, "Herbert Gentry," introduction to *An Ocean Apart: American Artists Abroad*, October 8, 1982–January 9, 1983, The Studio Museum in Harlem, 1982, https://www.herbertgentry.com/romare-bearden.

68. See Romare Bearden and Herbert Gentry in *Core of the Apple*, directed by Peter Ringgaard (Denmark: 1986), film.

69. Bearden, *Core of the Apple*.

70. Schwartzman, *Romare Bearden: His Life and Art*, 73

71. From Romare Bearden and Jackie McLean, "Sound Collages and Visual Improvisations" (Wadsworth Atheneum, May 4, 1986), in Ruth Fine Papers.

72. Tracy Fitzpatrick, *Romare Bearden: Abstraction* (Purchase, NY: Neuberger Museum of Art, 2017), 26.

73. Conversation with the author, November 1980.

74. Ghent, "Interview with Romare Bearden" in *The Romare Bearden Reader*, ed. Robert G. O'Meally, 58.

75. Schwartzman, *Romare Bearden: Celebrating the Victory*, 75.

76. Romare Bearden, interview with Charlayne Hunter-Gault, *The MacNeil/Lehrer Report*, PBS, June 26, 1987.

77. Myron Schwartzman, *Romare Bearden: Celebrating the Victory* (New York: Grolier, 1999), 76.

78. Fitzpatrick, *Romare Bearden: Abstraction*, 13.

79. Not that Mondrian's works were always pristine in their mathematical exactness, as close-ups of *Victory Boogie Woogie* (1944) reveal. As one also in love with Black American music, the Dutchman knew that capturing its spirit meant dealing in torn fragments and provisional colors—the beauty of imperfection and the unfinished, torn, or open corner.

80. Fitzpatrick, *Romare Bearden: Abstraction*, 26.

81. These lines come from Paul Laurence Dunbar's poem "We Wear the Mask" (1895), *The Complete Poems of Paul Laurence Dunbar*. (New York: Dodd, Mead and Company, 1922), 71.

82. "The Tears of a Clown" was written by Hank Cosby and Stevie Wonder, with lyrics by William "Smokey" Robinson, who released his recording of the song in 1967.

83. See Albert Murray, *The Hero and the Blues* (Columbia: University of Missouri Press, 1973), 101–2.

84. Jack D. Flan, *Matisse on Art* (New York Dutton, 1978), 99.

85. Bearden and Henderson, *A History of African-American Artists*, 400.

86. Schwartzman, *Romare Bearden: His Life and Art*, 211. For more on the Spiral Collective and Bearden's constitutive relationship between his career and his artistic community see Brent Hayes Edwards, "The Political Bearden," in Robert G. O'Meally, ed., *The Romare Bearden Reader*, 256–69.

87. Schwartzman, *Romare Bearden: Celebrating the Victory*, 217.

88. Romare Bearden and Avis Berman, "Interview with Romare Bearden, 1980 July 31." See Avis Berman research material on art and artists, 1976–1988, Archives of American Art, Smithsonian Institution.

89. Albert Murray, "Bearden Plays Bearden," in *The Romare Bearden Reader*, 238.

90. Romare Bearden, *Core of the Apple*.

91. *Calvin Tomkins Papers*. Romare Bearden file, Museum of Modern Art, New York City.

92. See Schwartzman, *Romare Bearden: Celebrating the Victory*, 97.

93. During the period roughly from 1970 to 1990, he constructed numerous covers for magazines and books related to jazz. He made collages for the covers of Albert Murray's first novel *Train Whistle Guitar (1974)*; Dizzy Gillespie's autobiography *To Be or Not to Bop (1979)* and in addition to the LP art by Billie Holiday, he made album covers for the music of Charlie Parker, Donald Byrd, Max Roach, Ricky Ford, and Wynton Marsalis.

94. Bill Caldwell, "Romare Bearden," *Essence* 6, no. 1 (May 1975), 72.

95. *Calvin Tomkins Papers*. Romare Bearden file, Museum of Modern Art, New York City.

96. This is one of the theses of Albert Murray's *The Hero and the Blues* (Columbia: University of Missouri, 1973).

97. In a conversation with Camara Holloway, June 14, 2025.

98. From the interview Billie Holiday gave for the "Sound of Jazz," a CBS television broadcast that aired on December 8, 1957.

99. Carmen McRae, interview with the author for the PBS documentary film *Lady Day: The Many Faces of Billie Holiday* (Toby Byron Multiprises: 1990).

100. *Calvin Tomkins Papers*. Romare Bearden file, Museum of Modern Art, New York City.

101. Schwartzman, *Romare Bearden: His Life and Art*, 153.

102. See Sterling Stuckey's on the "ring-shout" in Global African cultures: *Slave Culture: Nationalist Theory & the Foundations of Black America*, 1987. See too the patting-juba shout scene in August Wilson's "Joe Turner's Come and Gone," Act 1, Scene 4.

103. The Johnson material is quoted in John Szwed and Morton Marks, "The Afro-American Transformation of European Set Dances and Dance Suites," Dance Research Journal 10.1 (Summer 1988): 33. And see Sterling Stuckey, *Going Through the Storm: The Influence of African American Art in History* (New York: Oxford University Press, 1994), 54.

104. Thanks to Henry Drewal for this information.

105. Quoted in Robert Farris Thompson, *The Four Moments of the Sun: Kongo Art in Two Worlds* (Washington, DC: National Gallery of Art, 1981).

106. Frederick Douglass, *Narrative of the Life of Frederick Douglass, an American Slave*, written by himself (Boston: Anti-Slavery Office, 1845).

107. See Édouard Glissant, *Poetics of Relation*, trans. Betsy Wing (Ann Arbor: University of Michigan Press, 1997); Fred Moten, *In the Break: The Aesthetics of the Black Radical Tradition* (Minneapolis: University of Minnesota Press, 2003), 162.

108. Moten, *In the Break*, 25–31. This echoes an Ellington composition title, "The Sound of Love."

109. Duke Ellington and His Orchestra, "Something to Live For," recorded February 2, 1939, *Duke Ellington: The Blanton-Webster Band* (Bluebird, 1986), audio CD.

110. Albert Murray, "Armstrong and Ellington Stomping the Blues in Paris," *The Blue Devils of Nada: A Contemporary American Approach to Aesthetic Statement* (New York: Pantheon, 1996), 97–113.

111. Jacqui Malone, *Steppin' on the Blues: The Visual Rhythms of African American Dance* (Urbana: University of Illinois Press, 1996), 107.

112. Louis Armstrong, "Dan's Den," radio interview by Dan Serpico at Storyville Cape Cod, in Harwich, Massachusetts, 1961. Louis Armstrong House and Museum Collection, object ID 1987.3.673.

113. See Glenda Elizabeth Gilmore, *Romare Bearden in the Homeland of His Imagination: An Artist's Reckoning with the South* (Chapel Hill: University of North Carolina Press, 2022).

114. Ned Sublette, *The World That Made New Orleans* (Chicago: Lawrence Hill, 2008).

115. See Locke's *When Peoples Meet: A Study in Race and Culture Contacts* (1942). In 1945, Locke attended an early Bearden show in New York and wrote to the artist saying he was "amazed by the vivid and creative quality" of the paintings; Mary Schmidt Campbell, *An American Odyssey: The Life and Work of Romare Bearden* (New York: Oxford University Press, 2018), 151.

116. The phrase "set flowin'," from Jean Toomer's novel *Cane* (1923), titles Farah Jasmine Griffin's landmark study, *"Who set you flowin'?" The African-American Migration Narrative* (New York: Oxford University Press, 1995).

117. The Pepper Jelly Lady

118. From "Midnight Train to Georgia," written by Tom Weatherly and included on Gladys Knight anad the Pips's 1973 LP *Imagination*.

119. Jimmy Rushing, "Gulf Coast Blues" (1960); lyrics by Bessie Smith and Clarence Williams. Several songs on the Rushing album where "Gulf Coast Blues" appears, called *Jimmy Rushing and the Smith Girls: Bessie, Clara, Mamie & Trixie—The Songs They Made Famous*, are tributes to the Deep South. An earlier Rushing album, *The Jazz Odyssey of James Rushing Esq.* (1957), also has a geographical theme. It includes clusters of songs associated with New Orleans, Chicago, Kansas City, and New York.

120. Bessie Smith, "Florida Bound Blues" (1925); lyrics by Clarence Williams.

121. Bessie Smith, "Work House Blues" (1924); lyricist uncertain—very likely Smith herself. Smith's song echoes Mark Twain's *Huckleberry Finn*, (1885) whose hero says: "I reckon I got to light out for the Territory." The title of Ralph Ellison's collection of essays, *Going to the Territory* (1986), reflects both these sources. Twain, Mark. *Tom Sawyer & Huck Finn – The Great American Adventure (Illustrated): Complete 4 Novels: The Adventures of Tom Sawyer, Adventures of Huckleberry Finn, Tom . . . Detective* (Including Author's Biography) (p. 667). e-artnow. Kindle Edition.

122. See *The World That Made New Orleans*, and https://libguides.tulane.edu/latinos/news#s-lg-box-22519005.

123. John Szwed, "Mid-Century Modern Music: Philadelphia 1957–1977," unpublished essay.

124. Kidd Jordan, conversation with the author, September 8, 2000.

125. Toni Morrison, "Abrupt Stops and Unexpected Liquidity: The Aesthetics of Romare Bearden," in *The Romare Bearden Reader*, ed. Robert G. O'Meally (Durham, NC: Duke University Press, 2019), 183–84.

126. Calvin Tomkins, "Putting Something Over Something Else," *The New Yorker*, vol. 53 (1977): 53–68.

127. Baby Dodds, *The Baby Dodds Story: As Told to Larry Gara* (Los Angeles: Contemporary Press, 1959), 17.

128. James Brown, *Get on the Good Foot* (Polydor, 1972), audio recording. Note that Bearden's friend the novelist Ralph Ellison rendered such a New Orleans–style funeral in *Invisible Man*. Fascinatingly, Ellison (Harlemite who spent his first years in Oklahoma City and then, as a college boy, in Alabama) sets this funeral drama in Harlem, with its overflow of transplanted Deep Southerners. Among them, evidently, is an old man with a knife welt at his throat who walked a slow gait to the mournful sound of muffled drum and brass horn. "He sang with his whole body, phrasing each verse as naturally as he walked, his voice rising above all the others, blending with that of the lucid horn . . . I was listening to something within myself, and for a second I heard the shattering stroke of my heart. Something deep had shaken the crowd, and the old man and the man with the horn had done it. They had touched upon something deeper than protest, or religion" (Ralph Ellison, *Invisible Man*, 453).

129. Glenda Gilmore, *Romare Bearden in the Homeland of His Imagination: An Artist's Reckoning with the South* (Chapel Hill: University of North Carolina Press, 2022).

130. Albert Murray, *South to a Very Old Place* (New York: McGraw-Hill, 1971), 3.

131. Bearden says this in an outtake of the documentary film *Bearden Plays Bearden* (Third World Films, 1980, 2012), dir. Nelson E. Breen, Nelson Breen Archive.

132. For thirty years, Bearden made his living as a social worker assigned to the Romani people of New York City. See Aidan Levy, "The Quilt of Romare Bearden's Life," *Nation*, July 13, 2018.

133. Willie The Lion Smith, *Music on My Mind* (New York: Doubleday), 4.

134. Ibid.

135. This 1971 quotation of Bearden appears on the Metropolitan Museum's website: https://www.metmuseum.org/press-releases/romare-beardens-the-block-and-related-drawings-on-view-at-metropolitan-museum-beginning-january-15-2010-exhibitions.

136. Ralph Ellison, "The Art of Romare Bearden," in *Collected Essays of Ralph Ellison*, 688.

137. Richard O. Boyer, "The Hot Bach" (1944), reprinted in *The Duke Ellington Reader*, ed. Mark Tucker (New York: Oxford University Press, 1993), 231.

138. This mixtape was created by the photographer Daniel Dembrowsky, not by the curator Carroll Greene, as sometimes is reported. See the archival records of Carroll Greene at the Museum of Modern Art.

139. See Stanley Crouch, *Kansas City Lightning: The Rise and Times of Charlie Parker* (New York: HarperCollins, 2013), 19.

140. Gilmore, *Romare Bearden in the Homeland of His Imagination*, 54.

141. Bearden told his biographer Myron Schwartzman that ultimately he found Mondrian's lines and boxes too austere—"a surrender to a certain mathematics" that was untrue to the experience of everyday living, certainly in the United States, emphatically in Harlem. My sense is that he might have preferred not *Broadway*

Boogie Woogie but *Victory Boogie Woogie*, Mondrian's final (some say "unfinished") work, where the braided and torn lines of tape suggest something close to the jagged rhythmical lines and dissonances associated with post-boogie-woogie jazz—with bebop and beyond. Bearden could have seen *Victory Boogie Woogie* at many exhibitions in New York starting in 1945. See Schwartman, 249.

142.   For a current view of Bearden's block, see the photographs of John Dowell, who also lives in Lenox Terrace.

143.   From *Bearden Plays Bearden*. (Third World Films, 1980, 2012), dir. Nelson E. Breen.

144.   *Bearden Plays Bearden*, produced by Nelson E. Breen (Third World Cinema, 1981; re-released 2012), 29:40.

145.   Toni Morrison, "Abrupt Stops and Unexpected Liquidity: The Aesthetics of Romare Bearden," in *The Romare Bearden Reader*, ed. Robert G. O'Meally (Durham, NC: Duke University Press, 2019), 180–81. "Rhythm is a promise" is from Kenneth Burke, *Counter-Statement* (Berkeley: University of California, 1931, 1968), 140.

146.   See Romare Bearden, "Encounters with African Art" (1987), reprinted in Robert G. O'Meally, ed., *The Romare Bearden Reader* (Durham, NC: Duke University Press, 2019), 168.

147.   "Artist's General Remarks"(undated) Calvin Tomkins papers, Museum of Modern Art Archives.

148.   See Charles Childs, "Bearden: Identification and Identity," *Artnews* 63 (October 1964), 62.

Note for image on p. 33: Elmer Simms Campbell (1906–1971), creator of this "Night Club Map of Harlem," was primarily known for his witty, sharp cartoons on magazines such as *Esquire*, *Life*, and *Playboy*. Aside from comic artwork, he contributed to NAACP's *Crisis*, and notably encouraged Bearden to study at the Art Students League under George Grosz, known for his transcendent political satire.

The *Paris Blues/Jazz* Series

1.   Lorie Karnath, *Sam Shaw: A Personal Point of View* (Berlin: Hatje Cantz, 2010), 169.

2.   William Gardener Smith, "Black Man in Europe." In *Explorations in the City of Light: African-American Artists in Paris, 1945–1965*, ed. by Audreen Buffalo. (New York City, NY: Studio Museum in Harlem, 1996), 7.

3.   Richard Wright, "I Choose Exile," draft, corrected typescript (ca. 1950), Box 6, folder 110, Richard Wright Papers, Beinecke Rare Book and Manuscript Library, Yale University. See also Edward Said's discussion of the exile's productive unease in Reflections on Exile and Other Essays (Cambridge, MA: Harvard University Press, 2003), 185.

4.   Kevin Lynch, *The Image of the City* (Cambridge: MIT Press, 1960), 4–5.

5.   Calvin Tomkins, "Putting Something Over Something Else," reprinted in Robert G. O'Meally, ed., *The Romare Bearden Reader* (Durham, NC: Duke University Press, 2019), 42.

6.   Ellington loved colorfully inventive word-play, too, and at one of the Sacred Concerts introduced Bunny Briggs as the "most super-leviathonic rhythmaturgically syncopated tapster-matitionismist."

7.   Metropolitan Museum of Art, New York, 1978.61.1–6.

8.   Amiri Baraka, conversation with the author, February 7, 1988.

9.   Duke Ellington, in *A Duke Named Ellington*, directed by Terry Carter, *American Masters*, season 3, episode 2 (Eagle Rock Entertainment, 1988), film.

10.   The recordings were issued on the album *Ellington at Newport* (Columbia, 1957).

11.   Beyond Matisse, a complex sense of artistic lineage is embedded here. Bearden is using Shaw's photo of a sculpture also photographed in 1901 by the French photographer Eugene Atget, who did extensive documentation of great Parisian parks like Versailles and Sceaux. The bronze sculpture itself is by the seventeenth century French-Italian sculptor Jean-Baptiste Tuby. Aside from these artists, there's the history of Versailles itself to consider. Many thanks to the classical scholar Andrew Szegedy-Maszak for his insights on the backgrounds of this collage.

12.   In some cases, French and Afro-French Diasporan musicians and other visitors participated in the recordings. See O'Meally, *Antagonistic Cooperation*, 344–45, 436–37; and Klaus Stratemann, *Duke Ellington: Day by Day and Film by Film* (Copenhagen: JazzMedia, 1992), 429–35. See Brent Hayes Edwards,"Rendez-vous in Rhythm," *Connect* 1 (Fall 2000): 182–90,

13.   See John Michael Vlatch, *Back of the Big House: The Architecture of Plantation Slavery* (Chapel Hill, 1993).

14.   Romare Bearden, unreleased outtake from *Bearden Plays Bearden* (1980; DVD); Nelson E. Breen, from his personal archive.

15.   E. J. Bellocq, *Storyville Portraits: Photographs from the New Orleans Red-Light District, circa 1912*, reproduced from prints made by Lee Friedlander, ed. John Szarkowski (New York: Museum of Modern Art, 1970).

16.   Romare Bearden, "Rectangular Structure in My Montage Paintings" (1969), reprinted in *The Romare Bearden Reader*, ed. Robert G. O'Meally (Durham, NC: Duke University Press, 2019), 125.

17.   Ralph Ellison, jacket blurb for Jervis Anderson's *This Was Harlem: A Cultural Portrait, 1900–1950* (New York: Farrar, Straus & Giroux, 1982).

18.   This is from a conversation with the author: September 1980.

19.   A more full version of Bearden's statement is here: "The greatest poem written on Charles Lindbergh's flight was done at the Savoy: the Lindy hop—the dancers throwing the girls, their skirts billowing—you realize that everything it did in that way was the essence of flight. So sometimes we tend to look in the book store or the museum for our history, while neglecting other aspects of it." Myron Schwartzman, *Romare Bearden: His Life and Art* (New York: Abrams, 1990), 62.

20.   This story was told to me in June 1986 by Ellington's nephew, Michael James.

21.   See Stephanie Stein Crease, *Rhythm Man: Chick Webb and the Beat that Changed America* (New York: Oxford University Press, 2022).

22.   Romare Bearden and Albert Murray, caption for *Johnny Hudgins Comes On*, in *Profile Part II: The Thirties*, 1981.

23.   Ralph Ellison, "Harlem's America," *New Leader* 49, no. 19 (September 26, 1966), 23.

24.   The quote from Bearden is his caption, composed with Albert Murray, accompanying the collage called *Johnny Hudgins Comes On* (Profile Part II: The Thirties, 1981); collage on board, 14 × 22 inches. Full caption: "He was my favorite of all the comedians. What Johnny Hudgins could do through mime on an empty stage helped show me how worlds were created on an empty canvas."

25.   Ralph Ellison, "Editorial Comment," *Negro Quarterly* 1, no. 4 (1943): 301.

26.   Schwartzman, *Romare Bearden: His Life and Art*, 153

27.   Williams in a private conversation with the author, July 1995.

First published in the United States of America in 2026 by
Rizzoli Electa, A Division of
Rizzoli International Publications, Inc.
49 West 27th Street
New York, NY 10001
www.rizzoliusa.com

[Preface: Bridget Moore]
[Introduction: Mickalene Thomas]
[Essay: Robert G. O'Meally]

Front cover: *At the Savoy*, 1981 (detail)
Back cover: *Jazz with Armstrong*, 1981 (detail)
Front endpapers: *Graffiti (Duke Ellington)*, 1981 (detail)
Back endpapers: *Graffiti (Louis Armstrong)*, 1981 (detail)
Frontispiece: *Jazz with Armstrong*, 1981 (detail)

For Rizzoli Electa:
Publisher: Charles Miers
Associate Publisher: Margaret Rennolds Chace
Senior Editor: Ellen Cohen
Production Manager: Alyn Evans
Managing Editor: Lynn Scrabis

Design: Robin Brunelle

2026 2027 2028 2029 2030 / 10 9 8 7 6 5 4 3 2 1

ISBN: 978-0-8478-7625-9
Library of Congress Control Number: 2025947488

Printed in China

The authorized representative in the EU for product safety and compliance is
Mondadori Libri S.p.A., via Gian Battista Vico 42, Milan, Italy, 20123,
www.mondadori.it

Visit us online:
Instagram: @RizzoliBooks
Facebook.com/RizzoliNewYork
Youtube.com/user/RizzoliNY

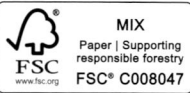

Author Biographies

Robert G. O'Meally is the Zora Neale Hurston Professor of Columbia University. His books include the *Romare Bearden Reader* (edited), and *Antagonistic Cooperation: Jazz, Collage, Fiction, and the Shaping of African American Culture*.

Mickalene Thomas is a critically acclaimed, New York–based multidisciplinary artist best known for her culture-shifting, elaborate, rhinestone-studded paintings that celebrate the beauty of Black womanhood, love, intimacy, and desire.

Bridget Moore is the president of DC Moore Gallery in New York.

Credits

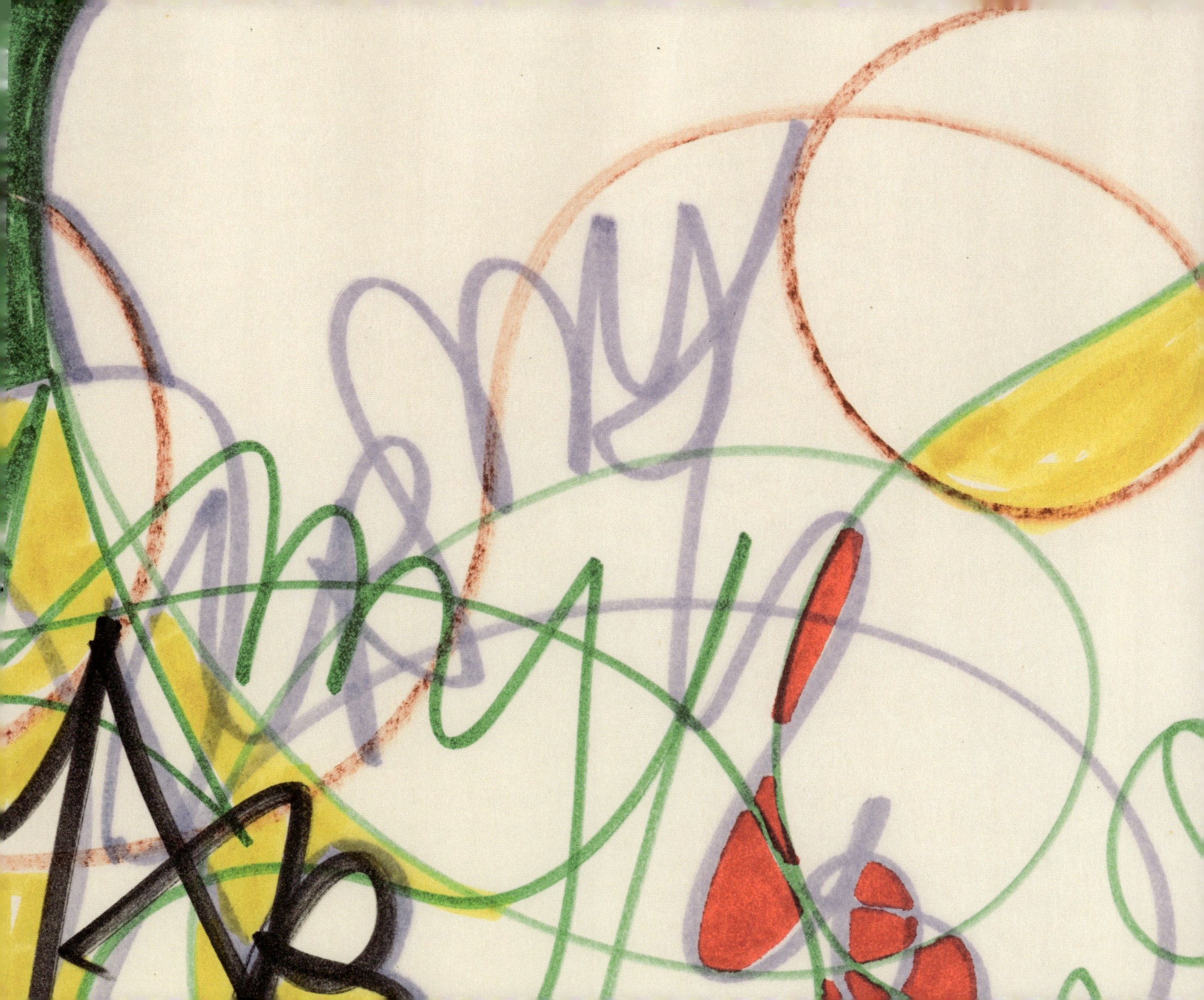

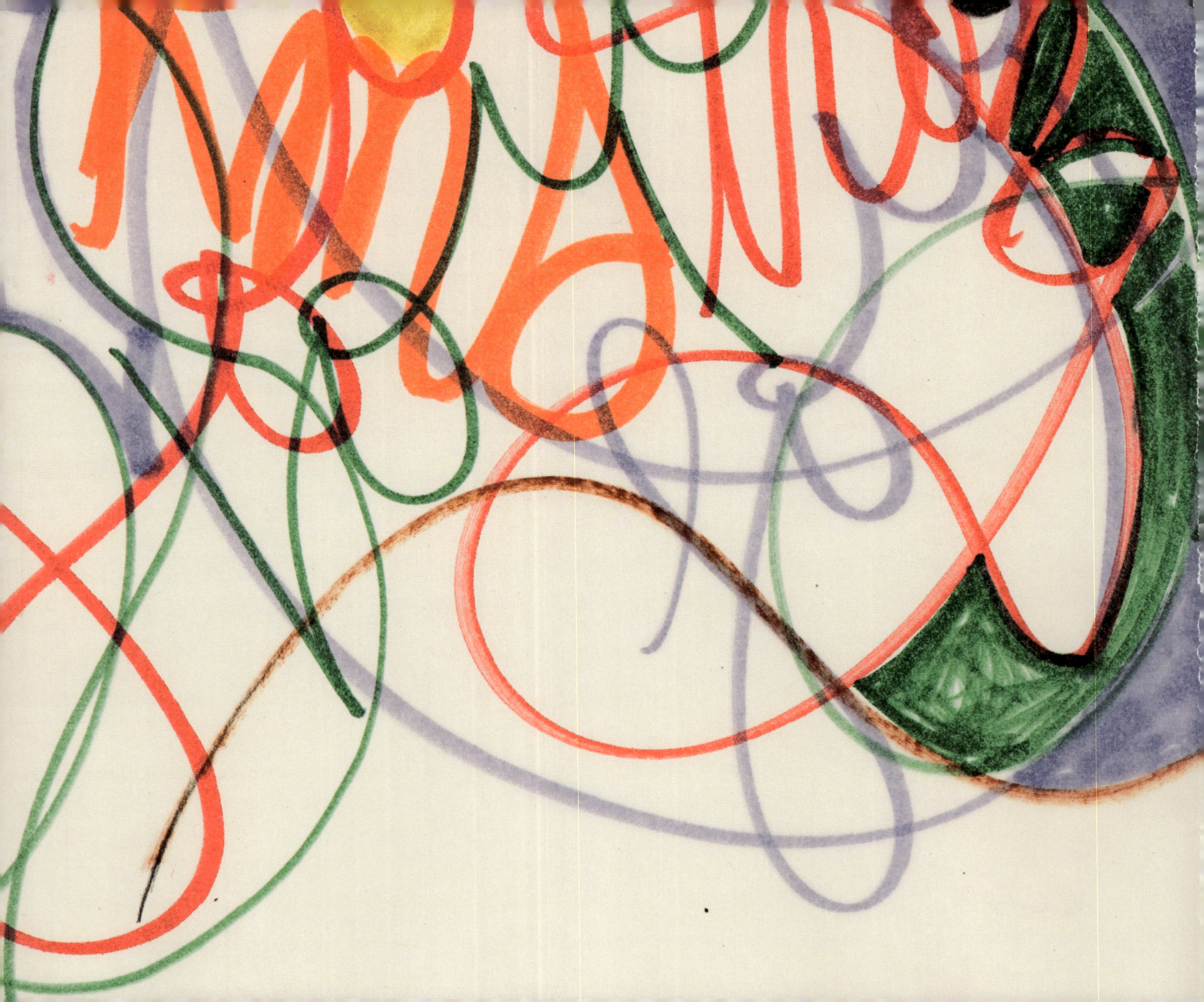